Genealogical Guide

to German Ancestors from East Germany and Eastern Europe

(AGoFF-Wegweiser — English Edition)

Edited by

Arbeitsgemeinschaft ostdeutscher Familienforscher e.V., Herne, Germany

translated by

Joachim O.R. Nuthack, Edmonton, Canada,
and Adalbert Goertz, Waynesboro, Pa., USA

Published by

Verlag Degener & Co., Inh. Gerhard Geßner
1984 · Neustadt/Aisch, Germany (West)

ISBN 3-7686-1029-2
© 1984 by Verlag Degener & Co., D–8530 Neustadt/Aisch
Printed in Germany (West)

East German Family Research Today

Awareness of family and true ties with the past are the beginning and the goal of genealogy, regardless of how we conduct it or how we record the results. Once devoted to and taken by genealogy, we cannot escape it in our lifetime. It requires effort and expenses, yet it gives us much joy and satisfaction.

We do not know whether you are an experienced family researcher or a newcomer, however we do know that here as well as in other fields team-work of likeminded people will lead to success.

For us East Germans research can only be continued with preserved material of many individuals which will bring to life the historical and cultural background of our family histories. Many a person remembers something, every newcomer adds a little more knowledge. Many have tapped sources which, after the separation from the old homeland, appeared to be dried up. Increasingly more literature is being collected by our members. This way collections, knowledge and experience are combined and can and ought to be of use for further research. Collecting and utilizing this material does not mean rummaging in the past or grieving over the lost. When the old generation remembering the homeland will be gone, then the collected material will gain in value. It will not take long until most pedigree lists (in Germany) will include East Germans. This is a natural and necessary consequence of the melting of the expelled with the natives of the Western areas of refuge. Each German land has its share of refugees.

Increasingly intermarriage between refugees and natives leads to a growing interest in East German personal and family history in local genealogical societies. Indeed, on pedigree charts of society members those places pertaining to Eastern and Southeastern ancestors are often incomplete or even totally blank because efforts for completion are considered to be hopeless; many believe that genealogical sources are not available and, therefore, research for ancestors will not be successful. This opinion is largely due to the limited knowledge about depositories of sources of Pre-World War II German provinces east of the Oder-Neisse Line as well as areas of German settlements in Central-, Eastern, and Southeastern Europe. In reality things are better. No one searching for ancestors in these regions should despair, for there still are research possibilities and opportunities.

In the following, we will show where civil and church records of these regions are located, places will be cited which deal with personal and family history research in these areas and which utilize the existing information. Listed will be hometown and village indices and regional societies which have information on the former residences of the expelled. It is important to know which cities in the Federal Republic of Germany are fosters for East German cities and counties. In these foster-cities are located information centers, resident registers, homeland houses, archives and museums from which assistance can be obtained. Sometimes, homeland newsletters are published for many counties and cities with valuable historical articles and numerous family notes.

Part "A" lists the above mentioned information pertaining to the areas cited at the beginning. Part "B" lists special information for certain regions in the same sequence.

We would appreciate your suggestions to correct and improve this guide — especially change of address information, since this will help us complete and update it.

Finally, we would like to express our sincere appreciation to all researchers and friends who have supported us, particularly to Mr. Manfred Vollack of Kiel, Germany, for permitting us to print the maps he has drawn.

Bonn, Germany, June 1978

Arbeitsgemeinschaft ostdeutscher
Familienforscher e. V.

Fritz Modler
Chairman

Preface to the 2nd and revised Editon

May this small booklet with the help and the support of all research section leaders of the AGoFF, be a reliable guide to East German family research.

Bonn, Germany, Mai 1982

Fritz Modler
Chairman

Preface to the English Edition

Even before the publication of the first edition of the "AGoFF-Wegweiser", the publishers considered publishing an English edition of that booklet. However, we wanted to wait for the echo, that book would get from family researchers in Germany and abroad. Soon the "Wegweiser" was praised. From the United States and Canada, particularly, many inquiries came and suggested an English translation. North Americans of Germany descent who no longer know the German language or who are only a little familiar with it, can use the German "Wegweiser" only with difficulty. This English publication will overcome this barrier. Among other topics, special vocabulary is mentioned and explained, vocabulary which is not found in general German-English and English-German dictionaries.

Descendants of German immigrants, who no longer read or write German, yet are still proud of their German heritage, shall be encouraged to search for their German ancestors, who emigrated from East Germany or German settlements in Eastern and Southeastern Europe.

Inquiries, however, to the listed addresses should be made in German, if at all possible. Inquiries can only be successful, when detailed information about time and locality is included. Information such as "Germany, Prussia, Pomerania etc." is not sufficient and is too general. May this English editon for its users in the United States, in Canada and in faraway Australia, be a valuable guide to important sources of East German research.

Bonn, December 1983   Arbeitsgemeinschaft ostdeutscher
                                                              Familienforscher e. V.

                                                              Fritz Modler,
                                                              Honorary-Chairman

Table of Contents

Introduction: East German Family Research Today 3
Preface to the 2nd Edition 4
Preface to the English Edition 4

Section A: Supraregional Information

1. **Research Areas** 9
   East Germany and the German settlements in Central-, Eastern-, and Southeastern Europe 9

2. **Family Research Societies** 11
   2.1 Present research societies 11
   2.2 Former research societies 12
   2.3 Research on religious exiles 12
   2.4 Nobility research 12
   2.5 Mennonite research 12
   2.6 Moravian research 12
   2.7 Emigrant research 13

3. **Vital Statistics Sources** 13
   3.1 Civil Vital Statistics Books and Records 13
   3.2 Church records 13

4. **Gazetteers** 15
   4.1 Published after 1945 15
   4.2 Published before 1945 16

5. **Bibliographies and Literature of Homeland Territories (selective)** . 17

6. **Archives and Libraries with Source Material of Homeland Territories** 17
   6.1 In West Germany – Federal Republic of Germany including West Berlin 17
   6.2 In Central-Germany – German Democratic Republic (DDR) including East Berlin .. 18
   6.3 In former homeland territories 19
   6.4 In Austria 19
   6.5 Libraries 19

7. **Other Research Aids** 21
   7.1 Homeland locality indices 21
   7.2 Local societies 22
   7.3 Other agencies 22

8. **Special Hints** 22
   8.1 Genealogical inquiries 22
   8.2 Research opportunities in Poland 22
   8.3 Difficulties with church records 25
   8.4 Compilations of research articles 25

8.5	Maps and pictorial materials	26
8.6	Rural genealogy in Prussia	27
Map 2:	Origin of German ethnic groups expelled from the East during and after World War II	28
Map 3:	Germany and former German settlements in Central-, Eastern-, and Southeastern Europe (with explanations).	29
Explanation to Map 3:		30

Section B: Regional Information

I.	**Former German Territories east of the Oder-Neisse-Line**	33
	1. East Prussia and Memel Region	35
	2. West Prussia and Danzig	44
	3. Pomerania	51
	4. Brandenburg (East)	58
	5. Silesia (Lower and Upper Silesia)	66
	6. Posen	75
II.	**German Settlements in Central-, Eastern- and Southeastern Europe**	82
	1. Poland	83
	a. Central Poland and Volhynia	83
	b. Galicia	87
	2. Baltic States – Lithuania, Latvia, Estonia	94
	3. Russia (Soviet Union)	99
	4. Sudeten-German territories, Bohemia, Moravia, Austro-Silesia	103
	5. Southeastern Europe	124
	Part I	
	a. Bukovina	128
	b. Dobrogea	129
	c. Slovakia and Carpatian Ukraine	130
	d. Western Hungary	131
	e. Slovania	132
	f. Transylvania	133
	g. Bessarabia	134
	Part II Danube-Swabian Settlements	135
	a. Southwest Hungarian Central Highlands	136
	b. Swabian Turkey	136
	c. Slavonia	136
	d. Srem	136
	e. Bácska	136
	f. Banat	136
	g. Satu Mare	136

Appendix: Objectives and Organization of the AGoFF 143

Index of Maps 150

Family name index 151

Geographical index:
a.   Countries, Regions, Provinces, Districts, Areas 152
b.   Counties 154
c.   Individual Localities 155

SECTION A

Supraregional Information

EAST GERMANY
and the German settlements in Central-, Eastern and Southeastern Europe

East Germany in political and geographical terminology, and corresponding to the boundaries of 1937, consists of German provinces situated east of the rivers Oder and Lausatian Neisse (not Glatzian Neisse). These territories include East Prussia with the governmental district of West Prussia, Pomerania, Silesia, the Grenzmark (Border territory) Poznan-West Prussia and the eastern part of the province of Brandenburg.

As a result of the Treaty of Versailles (signed on June 28, 1919, and effective on October 1, 1920) Germany ceded, partly as a result of referenda and partly without referenda, the following territories:

Large parts of West Prussia and Poznan,
Eastern Upper Silesia,
The Soldau Region and,
A small part of Lower Silesia

to Poland.

The Memelland in the north of East Prussia as a mandate of the allied and associated powers to Lithuania in 1924.

The Hultschin Region to Czechoslovakia.

The Free City of Danzig received the status of a limited independent state.

The Sudeten-German territories, as a result of the Treaty of St. Germain-en-Laye (September 10, 1919) were turned over to the newly created multi-ethnic state of Czechoslovakia. They had belonged to Austria-Hungary and from 1938 to 1945 to Germany.

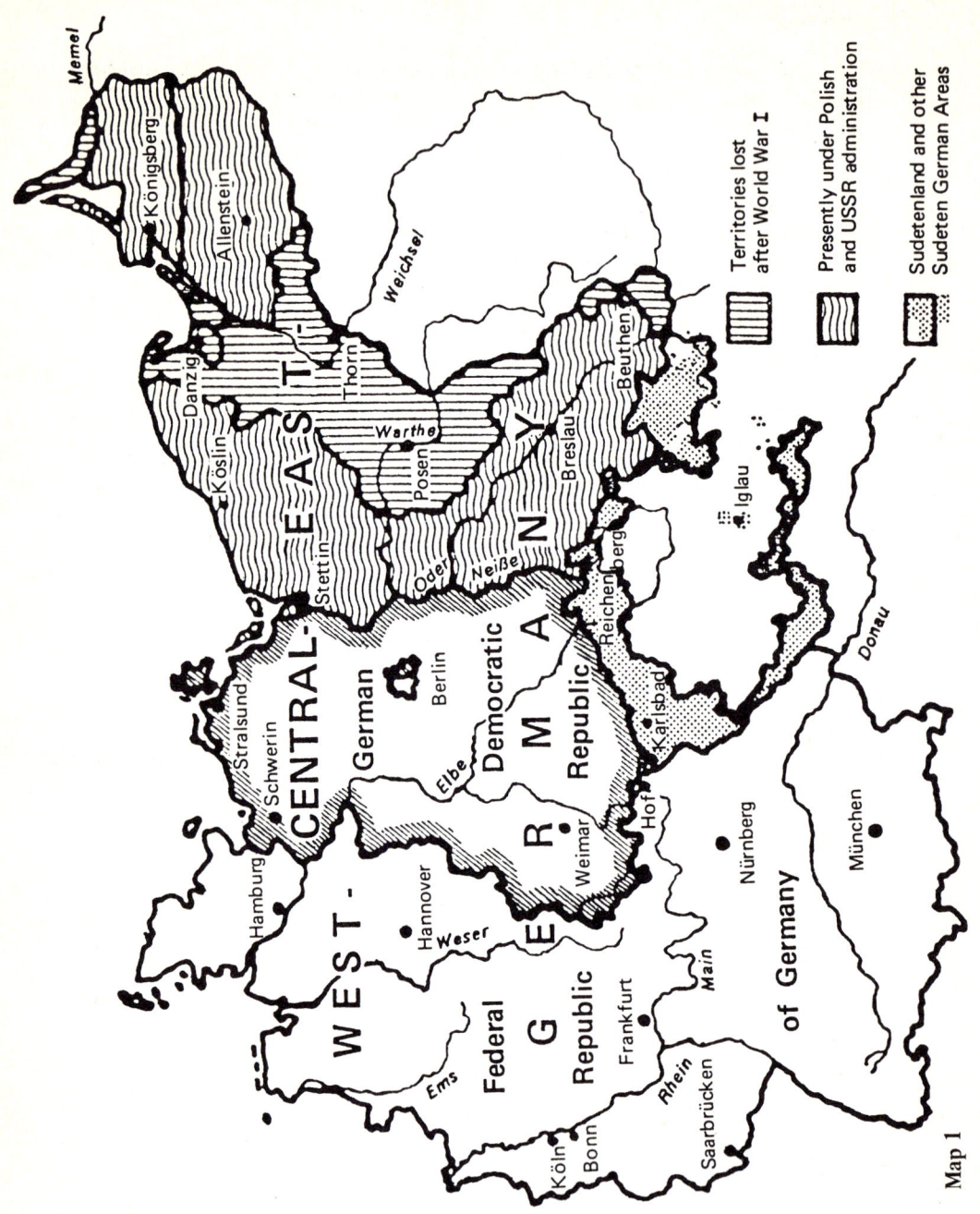

1. **Research Areas**

    East Germany within the boundaries of the former Empire (1919). Prussian Provinces east of the rivers Oder and Neisse:
    East Brandenburg, Pomerania, Poznan, West Prussia including Danzig, East Prussia including Memel Region, Lower and Upper Silesia.

    German settlements outside Germany in Eastern and Southeastern Europe:
    Sudeten German territories, Bohemia, Moravia, Austro-Silesia, Baltic States – Lithuania, Latvia, Estonia –, Soviet Union (USSR), Poland, Czechoslovakia, Yugoslavia, Bulgaria, Hungary and Rumania.

    See general map on page 29.

    Information about specific information is listed in Section B.

Note:
The former Prussian provinces of Brandenburg (West), Pomerania-West (Vorpommern) and Saxony as well as the former countries of Anhalt, Mecklenburg, Saxony and Thuringia form the German Democratic Republic today, commonly called "East Germany". Geographically it is Central Germany, which does n o t belong to the research areas of the AGoFF. The „Arbeitsgemeinschaft fuer mitteldeutsche Familienforschung e.V.", Emilienstrasse 1, D–3500 Kassel, Germany, is in charge of these research areas.

2. **Family Research Societies**

2.1 *Present research societies:*

   Arbeitsgemeinschaft ostdeutscher Familienforscher e. V. (AGoFF),
   Detlef Kuehn, Chairman, Fuhrweg 29, D–5300 Bonn 3, Germany, Ph.: 0228 – 48 28 04

   Periodicals:

   Ostdeutsche Familienkunde – OFK – (since 1953), published quarterly.

   Archiv ostdeutscher Familienforscher – AOFF – (since 1952)

   Arbeitsberichte (since 1957)

   Special Departments:

   Library
   Bibliothek der Stiftung Haus des deutschen Ostens,
   Bismarckstrasse 90, D–4000 Duesseldorf, Germany, Ph.: 0211 – 35 95 81

   For details about information see Section "A", 8.1

   Objectives and organization of the AGoFF see appendix.

2.2 *Former research societies*

See listings in Section "B".

2.3 *Research on religious exiles*

with regard to research areas:

a. Deutscher Hugenotten-Verein e. V.,
Schoeneberger Strasse 15, D–3400 Goettingen, Germany
Business address: Postfach 35, D–3305 Sickte, Germany
Research center:
Albert Giradin, Maraweg 8, D–4800 Bielefeld 13, Germany, Ph.: 05 21 – 144 35 33
Periodical: Der Deutsche Hugenott (The German Huguenot).

b. Salzburger Verein e. V., Memeler Str. 35, D–4800 Bielefeld, Germany
Research centers:
Harro Janetzke, Knatenserweg 8, D–3062 Bueckeburg, Germany
Herbert Nolde, Am Brachfelde 2, D–3400 Goettingen, Germany

See also: East Prussia 2.1 a.

Periodical: Der Salzburger (The Salzburger)

References:
Heydenreich: Handbuch der praktischen Genealogie (Handbook of practical genealogy)
Reprint: Verlag Degener & Co., Neustadt/Aisch, Germany, 1971, Page 115.

2.4 *Nobility Research*

Deutsches Adelsarchiv, Friedrichsplatz 15, D–3550 Marburg/Lahn, Germany

2.5 *Mennonite Research*

See:
Taschenbuch fuer Familiengeschichtsforschung (Pocket book for family history research)
Verlag Degener & Co., Neustadt/Aisch, Germany, 1975, Page 68

Mennonite research center:
D–6719 Weierhof, Post Marnheim, Germany

Mennonite Records:
Dr. Adalbert Goertz, 12934 Buchanan Trail East, Waynesboro, Pennsylvania 17268, U.S.A.

Literature:
Horst Penner: Die ost- und westpreussischen Mennoniten (The Mennonites of East and West Prussia), Weierhof, Germany, 1978 (see OFK 1979, Page 282).

2.6 *Moravian Research*

Archiv in DDR–8709 Herrnhut, Germany
Baseler Mission – Evangelische Missionsgesellschaft,
CH–4000 Basel, Missionsstrasse 21, Switzerland

Both archives contain church records and other sources of Moravian congregations on the Volga River.

Correction:

Genealogical Guide, p.13
2.7 Emigrant Research

for: Karl-Werner Klüber

new: Mrs.
       Helga Frobeen
       Koppel 17, Haus I

       D-2000 Hamburg 1
       W.-Germany

2.7 *Emigrant Research*

Karl-Werner Klueber, Wittenbergstrasse 4, D–2000 Hamburg 50, Germany

[handwritten: Helga Frobeen, Koppel 17 Haus 1 D 2000 Hbg 1]

Literature:
Handbuch der Genealogie (Handbook of genealogy), Verlag Degener & Co., Neustadt/Aisch, Germany, 1972, Page 216–222

L. G. Pine: American Origins, a handbook of Genealogical Sources throughout Europe, Garden City, N. Y. 1960

M. D. Learned: Guide to the Manuscript Materials Relating to American History in the German State Archives, Washington D. C., 1912

Archives:
Heimatstelle Pfalz, Benzinoring 6, D–6750 Kaiserslautern, Germany

3. Vital Statistics Sources

3.1 *Civil Vital Statistics Books and Records*

(In Prussia since October 1, 1874, in the remainder of Germany since January 1, 1875)

a. West Germany – Federal Republic of Germany including West Berlin, Standesamt I, Berlin (West), Rheinstrasse 54, D–1000 Berlin 41, Germany

Inventory information in:
Verzeichnis der im Standesamt I in Berlin (West) vorhandenen Standesregister und Personenstandsbuecher, Stand 1. Mai 1978 (Index of civil registers and vital statistics books at the civil registry office I in Berlin (West) as of May 1, 1978); Verlag fuer Standesamtswesen GmbH, Frankfurt/Main, Germany

b. Central-Germany – German Democratic Republic (DDR) including East Berlin, Standesamt I, Rueckertstrasse 9, DDR–1054 Berlin N 54, Germany

Partial inventory information in:
Waldemar Klytta: Handbuch der verlagerten Personenstandsregister und Kirchenbuecher der auslaendischen Konsularbehoerden und der Standesaemter mit Sonderaufgaben (Handbook of displaced records of vital statistics and church records of consular offices and registry offices with special duties), second edition, Verlag fuer Standesamtswesen GmbH, Frankfurt/Main, Germany, 1953.

No information is available about records of vital statistics which have found their way to the above registry office since 1953.

c. In Homeland Territories

See listing in Section "B".

3.2 *Church Records*

a. *Protestant Church Records*

Information is supplied by:
Evangelisches Zentralarchiv, Jebenstrasse 3, D–1000 Berlin 12, Germany.

Partial index in:
Verzeichnis der in Berlin (West) vorhandenen ortsfremden Personenstands- und Kirchenbuecher (Index of civil and church records located in Berlin (West), official edition, Verlag fuer Standesamtswesen GmbH, Frankfurt/Main, Germany, 1955.

b. *Roman Catholic Church Records*

Information is given by:
Bischoefliches Zentralarchiv, St. Petersweg 11–13, D–8400 Regensburg, Germany.

Information is also listed in:
Kaps: Handbuch ueber die katholischen Kirchenbuecher in der ostdeutschen Kirchenprovinz oestlich der Oder und der Neisse und dem Bistum Danzig (Handbook of Roman Catholic church records of the East German church district east of the rivers Oder and Neisse and the diocese of Danzig), Muenchen, Germany, 1962.

c. *Military Church Records*

Geheimes Staatsarchiv, Preussischer Kulturbesitz,
Archivstrasse 12–14, D–1000 Berlin 33, Germany

Inventory Information:
Uebersicht ueber die Bestaende des Geheimen Staatsarchivs in Berlin-Dahlem, Part II, VII Main Division, Berlin 1967. (Information of inventories of the Privy State Archives in Berlin-Dahlem).

Katholisches Militaer-Bischofsamt, Adenauerallee 115, D–5300 Bonn 1, Germany.

Inventories mentioned by Klytta see 3.1. b.

d. *Records of Jewish Congregations*

in East Prussia, West Prussia, Pomerania, Lower and Upper Silesia are located at the Bundesarchiv, Am Woellerhof 12, D–5400 Koblenz, Germany.
Amtsblatt der Regierung Breslau 1814 (Breslau government record 1814). Index of 3 755 Jews of the Government District of Breslau as of March 24, 1812, including newly adopted family names.

e. *Mennonite Church Records*

Mennonitische Forschungsstelle, D–6719 Weierhof, Post Marnheim, Germany.
Verzeichnis: A. Goertz, Familiengeschichtliche Quellen der Mennoniten Altpreussens, in: Mennonitische Geschichtsblaetter, 1981, S. 52–65 (Englische Kurzfassung: "Genealogical Sources of the Prussian Mennonites", in: Mennonite Quarterly Review, Oct. 1981, p. 372–380, Goshen, IN 46526 U. S. A.).

f. *Photocopied Church Records*

aa) Zentralstelle fuer Genealogie in der Deutschen Demokratischen Republik, Georgi-Dimitroff-Platz 1, DDR–7010 Leipzig, Germany.
Inventory information is not available to date. In addition to photocopied church records, originals are also kept.

bb) The Genealogical Department of the Church of Jesus Christ of Latter Day Saints (LDS), 50 North Temple, Salt Lake City, Utah, 84150, U. S. A.

The AGoFF (address: Mrs. Heike Brachwitz, Sperlingsstrasse 11a, D–4236 Hamminkeln 4) gives information on whether a microfilm copy of a certain church record is available. Inquiries must include two International postal coupons.

In addition, all microfilms released for usage may be viewed at any local genealogical branch library of the LDS Church. For locations please consult your nearest LDS State Center.

In addition to the more than 200 branch libraries in the USA, there are LDS (Mormon) genealogical libraries in Canada, Australia, Brazil, England, France, Germany, Ireland, Mexico, New Zealand, South Africa, Switzerland and Wales. Before you visit a LDS branch library to research East German sources, you should consult

Ronald Smelser, Thomas Dullien, Heribert Hinrichs (Comp.): "Preliminary Survey of the German Collection" (= Nr. 2 of Finding Aids to the Microfilmed Manuscript Collection of the Genealogical Society of Utah), University of Utah Press, Salt Lake City, 1979.

At the branch library you should study their locality index for call numbers of microfilms as well as the International Genealogical Index (IGI) "Prussia" for family names of interest. Also ask for their list of records in their church record extraction program, which has a number of church records computerized (see also OFK 1981, page 310–311).

4. Gazetteers

4.1 *Published after 1945*

   a. Amtliches Gemeinde- und Ortsnamenverzeichnis der Deutschen Ostgebiete unter fremder Verwaltung (Official gazetteer of German East territories under foreign rule).

   3 volumes, Selbstverlag der Bundesanstalt fuer Landeskunde, Remagen, Germany 1955, now in Bonn-Bad Godesberg, Germany.

   Vol. 1: Official gazetteer of East German territories under foreign rule as of Sept. 1. 1939, including a listing of counties divided by the Oder-Neisse-Line and the Polish-Soviet demarcation line in East Prussia.

   Vol. 2: Alphabetical gazetteer (index of residences) of East Germany under foreign rule as of Sept. 1. 1939, German-foreign language.

   Vol. 3: same as vol. 2, foreign language German.

   b. Gemeindeverzeichnis fuer Mittel- und Ostdeutschland und die frueheren deutschen Siedlungsgebiete im Ausland (Gazetteer for Central- and East Germany and former German settlements in foreign countries), published in cooperation with Statistisches Bundesamt by the President of the Bundesausgleichsamt, Verlag fuer Standesamtswesen GmbH, Frankfurt/Main, Germany 1970.

   c. Muellers Verzeichnis der jenseits der Oder-Neisse gelegenen, unter fremder Verwaltung stehenden Ortschaften (Mueller's Gazetteer of Communities East of the Oder-Neisse-Line), Part I German-foreign language, Part II foreign language-German. Verlag Postmeister a. D. Mueller, D–5600 Wuppertal-Barmen 10, Germany.

   d. Namensaenderungen ehemals preussischer Gemeinden von 1850–1942 (mit Nachtraegen bis 1950) (Name changes of former Prussian communities between 1850 and 1942, with supplements to 1950). A guide to re-naming, annexations and incorporations of towns and rural municipalities over a century. Verlag Degener & Co., Neustadt/Aisch, Germany 1971.

- e. Peter Woerster: Das noerdliche Ostpreussen nach 1945. Deutsch-russisches und russisch-deutsches Ortsnamenverzeichnis mit einer Dokumentation der Demarkationslinie, J. G. Herder-Institut, Marburg/Lahn 1980.
- f. Otto K. Kowallis, Vera N. Kowallis, A Genealogical Guide and Atlas of Silesia. Compiled from Original Maps. Logan, Utah, Everton 1976.

4.2 *Published before 1945*

- a. Several gazetteers of Germany, for instance:
  Muellers Grosses deutsches Ortsbuch (Mueller's great German gazetteer), 1927, 1935, 1938 editions.
  Meyers Orts- und Verkehrs-Lexikon (Meyer's Gazetteer and Traffic Encyclopedia), 1912, 1935, 1937 editions.
  Neumanns Orts- und Verkehrs-Lexikon des Deutschen Reiches (Neumann's Gazetteer and Traffic Encyclopedia of the German Empire), Leipzig, Germany 1905.
- b. Deutsch-fremdsprachiges und fremdsprachig-deutsches Ortschaftsverzeichnis für alle vom Deutschen Reich auf Grund des Versailler Vertrages vom 28.6.1919 abgetrennten Gebiete einschl. Elsass-Lothringen (mit einem Anhang: Ortschaftsverzeichnis der von Oesterreich-Schlesien an Polen abgetretenen Gebiete) (German-foreign language and foreign language-German gazetteer of all territories of the German Empire relinquished by the Treaty of Versailles of June 28, 1919, including Alsace-Lorraine (with an appendix: Gazetteer of territories ceded by Austro-Silesia), Verlag des Preussischen Statistischen Landesamtes, Berlin, Germany 1927.
  (A volume of the above can be found at Johann-Gottfried-Herder-Institut, Gisonenweg 5–7, D-3550 Marburg/Lahn, Germany, a photocopy of same is on file at the AGoFF information center).
- c. L. Krug: Topographisch-statistisch-geographisches Woerterbuch der saemtlichen preussischen Staaten (einschl. Suedpreussen und Neu-Ostpreussen) (Topographic-statistical-geographical dictionary of all Prussian States, including South Prussia and New East-Prussia), 13 volumes, Halle, Germany 1796–1803, available at the University of Goettingen library and at Yale University Library.
- d. L. Krug; A. Muetzell: Neues topographisch-statistisch-geographisches Woerterbuch des Preussischen Staates (New topographic-statistical-geographical dictionary of the Prussian State), 6 volumes, Halle, Germany 1821–1826.
- e. G. F. Krause: Handbuch zu dem Atlas von Preussen, 6 vols., Erfurt 1833–1836.
- f. J. G. Mueller: Vollstaendiges Geographisch-Statistisch-Topographisches Woerterbuch des Preussischen Staats, 4 vols., Erfurt 1836–1837.
- g. G. Koenig: Alphabetisches Verzeichnis saemtlicher Ortschaften und einzeln liegender benamter Grundstuecke des Preussischen Staates, 25 vols. according to Regierungsbezirke, Magdeburg 1833–1835.
- h. Messow: Topographisch-Statistisches Handbuch des Preussischen Staates oder Alphabetisches Verzeichnis saemtlicher Staedte, Flecken, Doerfer ..., 2 vols., Magdeburg 1846–1847.

Outside Germany readers should consult with their local university library regarding the availability of the above listed gazetteers. Many have found their way to them and can be found in the reference sections or the German sections of these libraries. Microfilm copies are available through the LDS (Mormon) library system.

5. **Bibliographies and Literature of Homeland Territories (selective)**

Deutsches Land zwischen Oder und Memel (German Land between the rivers Oder and Memel).
Published by Bund der Vertriebenen, Vereinigte Landsmannschaften und Landesverbaende, Bonn, Germany 1962.

Studien zum Deutschtum im Osten (Studies of the Germans in the East), 8th issue: Deutsche Ostsiedlung im Mittelalter und Neuzeit (German Eastern Colonization during the Middle Ages and Modern Times), Boehlau Verlag, Koeln, Germany 1971.

Robert Mueller-Sternberg: Deutsche Ostsiedlung, Eine Bilanz fuer Europa (German Eastern Colonization, a balance for Europe).
Publisher: Ostdeutscher Kulturrat, Bielefeld, Germany 1969.

Wolfgang Kessler: Ost- und suedostdeutsche Heimatbuecher und Ortsmonographien nach 1945 (East and Southeast German chronicles and monographs of communities after 1945), a bibliography of the regions of expulsion. Published by Stiftung Ostdeutscher Kulturrat (OKR), Saur, Germany 1979.
From this publication the following maps were used: Nr. 6, 9, 13, 15, 18, 23, 25, 28, 29, 34–45.

Manfred Vollack: Ostdeutschland und die ehemaligen deutschen Siedlungsgebiete in Ost- und Suedosteuropa (East Germany and the former German settlements in Eastern and Southeastern Europe), Selbstverlag der Schuelerzeitung "Wir", Stade, Germany 1961.
From this publication the following maps were used: Nr. 5, 7, 8, 10–12, 14, 16, 17, 19–22.

Buecherei des deutschen Ostens, Catalog, Herne 1973.
New edition of 5 volumes presently for sale =
I.   Northeast Germany (1982)
II. Brandenburg, Prussia, Poland, Baltics, Russia (1982)
III. Silesia (1983)
IV. Habsburg Lands (1984)
V.   East and Central Germany, additions (1984).

6. **Archives and Libraries with Source Material of Homeland Territories**

6.1 *In West Germany – The Federal Republic of Germany including West Berlin*

   a. Geheimes Staatsachriv Preussischer Kulturbesitz (Prussian Privy Archives)
      Archivstrasse 12–14, D–1000 Berlin 33, Germany.

      Inventory information:
      Uebersicht ueber die Bestaende des Geheimen Staatsarchivs in Berlin-Dahlem (Summary of inventories of the Privy State Archives in Berlin-Dahlem), Berlin, Germany 1966–1967, 2 volumes.

   b. Bundesarchiv
      Abt. Ostarchiv (Eastern archival section)
      Am Woellerhof 12, D–5400 Koblenz, Germany

      Abt. Zentralnachweisstelle (Central information center)
      Abteigarten 6, D–5100 Aachen-Kornelimuenster, Germany

      Militaerarchiv (Military archives)
      Wiesentalstrasse 1, D–7800 Freiburg, Germany

Inventory information:
Das Bundesarchiv und seine Bestaende (The Federal Archives and its collections), 3rd edition, Boppard am Rhein, Germany 1977 (also see OFK vol. 3, page 249).

c. Johann-Gottfried-Herder-Institut, Gisonenweg 5–7, D–3550 Marburg/Lahn, Germany

Inventory information:
Zentralnachweis ueber Material in anderen Archiven in der Bundesrepublik Deutschland (Information of sources of other archives in the Federal Republic of Germany).

d. Deutsche Dienststelle (WAST) (German armed service center)
Postfach, D–1000 Berlin 52, Germany.

This armed service center has information on nearly 20 million soldiers, members of the Reichsarbeitsdienst (Third Reich's para-military work units), nurses and other members of the armed forces of the Third Reich. The center is in charge of the large register of military identification cards of World War II. In addition to about 24 millions of alphabetically sorted index cards, the center is also in charge of 300 millions of work documents of which one third is computerized.

6.2 *In Central Germany – The German Democratic Republic (DDR) including East Berlin*

In the DDR the Administration for State Archives, a department of the Ministry of the Interior, is in charge of handling inquiries of a genealogical nature which might be directed to any one of the archives under its jurisdiction. After clearing with a particular center about the documents to be inspected, a time for research should be requested from the archives which then will confirm the time requested. We advise to book travel and lodging through Hansa-Tourist GmbH. in Hamburg, Germany (outside Germany researchers are advised to use a reputable travel agency which has connections with the DDR travel bureau.). We definitely do n o t recommend to visit DDR archives without making prior appointments and without supplying the necessary information; rarely will such ventures be successful.

a. Zentrales Staatsarchiv (central state archive)
   aa. Historische Abteilung I (Historical department I)
       Sanssouci-Orangerie, DDR–1500 Potsdam, Germany.
   bb. Historische Abteilung II (Historical department II)
       Koenig-Heinrich-Str. 37, DDR–4200 Merseburg, Germany.

b. Zentralstelle fuer Genealogie in der DDR (Central office for genealogy in the DDR)
   Georgi-Dimitroff-Platz 1, DDR–7010 Leipzig, Germany.

c. Staatsarchiv Greifswald, DDR–2200 Greifswald, Germany.

A permit to use any state archive in the DDR must be obtained from:

Ministerrat der Deutschen Demokratischen Republik, Ministerium des Innern, Staatliche Archivverwaltung, Berliner Strasse 92–101, DDR–1500 Potsdam, Germany

and the following information must be included when application is made:

Place and date of visit to archives, documents to be inspected, for which time period, reasons for the research as well as all data relevant to research.

Permit to use town, county and/or church archives should be obtained from the local authorities.

In general, church archives do not require permits. However, advance notification and contacts are advised.

6.3 *In former Homeland Territories*

See listings in Section "B".

6.4 *In Austria*

a. Oesterreichisches Staatsarchiv, Finanz- und Hofarchiv (Austrian state archive, finance and court archive)
Johannesgasse 6, A—1010 Vienna, Austria.

b. Oesterreichisches Staatsarchiv, Kriegsarchiv (Austrian state archive, war archive)
Stiftsgasse 2, A-1070 Vienna, Austria.

c. Oesterreichisches Staatsarchiv fuer Verkehrswesen (Austrian State Archives for Traffic and Transportation)
Aspangstrasse 33, A—1030 Vienna, Austria.

d. Archiv des evangelischen Oberkirchenrates A. u. H. B. (Archives of the Protestant Supreme Council of Churches)
Severin-Schreiber-Gasse 3, A—1180 Vienna, Austria.

e. Bibliothek der Heraldisch-genealogischen Gesellschaft "Adler"
Haarhof 4 a, A—1010 Vienna, Austria.

6.5 *Libraries*

a. Buecherei des deutschen Ostens (Library of the German East)
Berliner Platz 11, D—4690 Herne, Germany.

Inventory information: Complete catalogue as of April 1, 1974. A new edition is being published and may be purchased (1982, 1983).

This library will make world-wide loans of books in its collection. Lenders are advised to get written confirmation from this library in order to make use of the service which is offered through the "inter-library loan" departments of most libraries.

b. Bibliothek der Stiftung Haus des deutschen Ostens (Library of "Haus des Deutschen Ostens" foundation).
Bismarckstrasse 90, D—4000 Duesseldorf, Germany.

Inventory information: Library catalogue (also for sale).

Part 1: East Prussia, West Prussia, Danzig, Memelland
Selbstverlag, Duesseldorf, Germany 1974.

Part 2: Bohemia-Moravia, Austro-Silesia, Sudeten-Germans, Czechoslovakia, Austria
Selbstverlag, Duesseldorf, Germany 1976.

Part 3: Silesia, Lower and Upper Silesia
Selbstverlag, Duesseldorf, Germany 1978.

This library is a free library. No charges are levied for loaning books. The library is part of the inter-library loan system of Germany. Through this system a well as directly, individual users may borrow books.

Business hours are as follows:

Tuesdays to Fridays	10:00 a. m.–12:30 p. m.
Tuesdays, Wednesdays and Fridays	2:00 p. m.– 5:30 p. m.
Thursdays	2:00 p. m.– 8:00 p. m.
and first Saturdays each month	9:00 p. m.– 1:00 p. m.

c. Niedersaechsische Staatsbibliothek (Library of the State of Lower Saxony)
Waterloostrasse 8, D–3000 Hannover, Germany.

Catalogues: Katalog des Schrifttums ueber den Deutschen Osten (Catalog of Literature of the German East), vol. 1–5 Hannover, Germany 1956–1968; Katalog des Schrifttums ueber Schlesien (Catalog of Literature of Silesia) Additions, Hannover, Germany 1973; Katalog des Schrifttums ueber die baltischen Laender (Catalog of Literature of the Baltic States), vol. 1 and 2, Hannover, Germany 1971; Katalog des Schrifttums ueber die Tschechoslowakei (Catalog of Literature of Czechoslovakia), vol. 1 and 2, Hannover, Germany 1977–78; Continuous publication: Neuerwerbungsliste Niedersachsen/Ostkunde (New acquisitions list Lower Saxony/Eastern Studies) (some volumes are still for sale).

d. Universitaetsbibliothek (University library)
Postfach 1521, D–4400 Muenster, Germany.

e. Johann-Gottfried-Herder-Institut
Gisonenweg 5–7, D–3550 Marburg/Lahn, Germany.

The Johann-Gottfried-Herder-Institut has begun a bibliographical survey of the twenty-five year old press of the expellees. What has been published to date is of considerable documentary and informatory value for historical writers, ethnic research and the cultural index "Veroeffentlichungen ueber Ostmitteleuropa" (Publications of East-Central Europe).

Catalogues: Alphabetischer Katalog (Alphabetical catalogue), vol. 1–5. Additions vol. 1 and 2 Boston, Massachusetts, U. S. A. 1964–1971. Continuous publication: Neuerwerbungen Ostmitteleuropa (New acquisitions East-Central Europe).

f. Bibliothek des Instituts fuer Weltwirtschaft (Library of the institute for world economics) at the University of Kiel, Germany, D–2300 Kiel, Germany.

Inventory listing of East and Southeast European and DDR collections in the Federal Republic of Germany. This makes it possible to locate eastern collections as well as those of individuals.

g. Bayerische Staatsbibliothek (Bavarian State Library)
Ludwigstrasse 16, D–8000 Muenchen 22, Germany.

Periodic publications Osteuropa-Neuerwerbungen 1972ff. (New Acquisitions of Eastern Europe).

h. Wuerttembergische Landesbibliothek (Wuerttemberg State Library)
Kondrad-Adenauer-Strasse 8, D–7000 Stuttgart 1, Germany.

i. Universitaetsbibliothek Freiburg (Library of the University of Freiburg)
Rempartstrasse 15, D–7800 Freiburg, Germany.

j. Badische Landesbibliothek (Baden State Library)
Lammstrasse 16, D–7500 Karlsruhe, Germany.

k. Universitaetsbibliothek Duesseldorf (Library of the University of Duesseldorf)
    Universitaetsstrasse 1, D–4000 Duesseldorf, Germany.

l. Pfaelzische Landesbibliothek (Palatinate State Library)
    Johannesstrasse 22a, D–6720 Speyer, Germany.

m. Bibliothek des Instituts fuer Auslandsbeziehungen (Library of the Institute of Foreign Relations)
    Charlottenplatz 17, D–7000 Stuttgart 1, Germany.

    Periodic publication: Neuerwerbungslisten (Lists of new acquisitions).

n. Forschungsstelle Ostmitteleuropa, Paedagogische Hochschule (Research center East-central Europe, pedagogical university)
    Postfach 500500, D–4600 Dortmund 50, Germany.

o. Nordostdeutsches Kulturwerk, Nord-Ost Bibliothek (North-East German cultural works, North-East library)
    Conventstrasse 1, D–2120 Lueneburg, Germany.

    Catalog: Bestandkatalog (Catalog of inventories), vol. 1 and 2, Lueneburg, Germany 1977–1978.

p. Stiftung Deutschlandhaus (Deutschlandhaus foundation)
    Stresemannstrasse 90, D–1000 Berlin 61, Germany.

q. Universitaet Bremen – Deutsche Presseforschung – (University of Bremen – German press research –)
    Postfach 330 160, D–2800 Bremen 33, Germany.

    The University supervises the Standardkatalog (Union Catalog) of the German press and a collection of micro films, for instance the years 1742–1945 of the "Schlesische Zeitung" (Silesian newspaper). (See also: G. Hagelweide: Deutsche Zeitschriftenbestaende in Bibliotheken und Archiven (Inventories of German periodicals in libraries and archives), Duesseldorf, Germany 1974).

r. Buecherei des "Der Herold" (Library of "Der Herold")
    Archivstraße 12–14, D–1000 Berlin 33, Germany.

    All libraries will furnish photocopies for a fee.

s. See also Richard C. Lewanski: Guide to Polish Libraries and Archives, New York – London 1974.

7. Other Research Aids

7.1 *Homeland Locality Indices*

The homeland locality indices, which grew out of the missing persons bureau of the churches, fulfill important duties of the government of the Federal Republic of Germany. Based on the numerous records of Germans from East of the Oder-Neisse-Line, they can give to various government agencies as well as to individuals, important information in regard do German citizenship, ethnic affiliation, matters relating to the civil status and other points which are often significant. With their resources of 18 1/2 millions of people, alphabetically indexed, they have developed into a directory of Germans from the territories of expulsion.

Today the structure of the missing persons bureau of the churches corresponds to the former Prussian governmental divisions and the national divisions of the countries of origin. Listed persons are indexed alphabetically under their former places of residence as of September 1. 1939. Residents of towns are listed by their former street addresses as well. All changes, with occurred later, for instance: births, deaths, missing in action, moves to and from, are listed under this fixed date and address.

Zentralstelle der Heimatortskarteien (Central office of homeland locality indices)
Lessingstrasse 1, D–8000 Muenchen 2, Germany, Ph.: 089 – 53 00 44 – 46

Addresses of individual "homeland locality indices" are found in Section "B" under the respective research areas.

7.2 *Local Societies*

Bund der Vertriebenen – Vereinigte Landsmannschaften (Federation of expellees – United Local Societies)
Gorch-Fock-Strasse 1, D–5300 Bonn 1, Germany, Ph.: 0228 – 23 20 42.

7.3 *Other Agencies, like homeland information offices, homeland historical societies, foster towns etc.*

See listings in Section "B".

8. Special Hints

8.1 *Genealogical Inquiries*

All inquiries made to Arbeitsgemeinschaft ostdeutscher Familienforscher e. V. (AGoFF), its information and research centers should be, if at all possible, in German and typewritten (poor German will be accepted).

As all AGoFF work is performed free of charge by volunteers and finances to conduct the affaires of the society are raised by annual dues from its members. We request to enclose sufficient return postage; foreign inquiries must include at least t w o International Postal Coupons which are available at your local post office, otherwise information cannot be given. Self-addressed envelopes will eliminate possible typing errors.

8.2 *Research opportunities in Poland*

The Directorate-General of the state archives in Poland does not place archival material for genealogical research at the disposal of researchers. Searches for family documents are solely conducted by the state archives on behalf of and at the expense of researchers after receiving the most accurate information possible concerning the family member one is researching. At this time of writing it is nearly impossible to conduct research with **Protestant church records** personally, because they are deposited exclusively at the state archives. This is true particularly for Protestant church records in Silesia.

Inventory information for the various provincial state archives is listed in the Polish archival guide "Katalog Inventarzy Archiwalnych" (Catalog of archival inventories) published for Naczelna Dyrekcja Archiwów Pánstwowych (Director-General of state archives) by M. Pestkowska and H. Stebelska, Warsaw, Poland 1971 (in the following called: Guide to Polish archives).

Permits to use church archives in Poland are not required presently. However, we recommend to make appointments with parish officials in question prior to embarking on a research trip.

For information on obtaining certificates of civil status from Poland, we advise to contact the Polish embassy in your country. Over the last few years regulations have changed several times, making it difficult to give good information. The embassy will send you current guidelines upon request.

It is useful, when requesting certificates, to use the current Polish place names, which can be taken from German-foreign language gazetteers listed in Section "A" – 4.2.

Schedule of charges made for genealogical research conducted for aliens, regulation # 14 of the Director-General of Polish state archives:

1. Acceptance Fee   § 20.00 US *)
2. Research Fee per Hour   § 10.00 US *)
3. Fee for each copy or photocopy
   of found document   § 10.00 US *)

*) or equivalent in other currencies.

The Polish Embassy Consular Division of your country is the only supplier of civil status certificates for official use from Poland for entries not older than 100 years. Consular fees are levied on them.

Applications for civil status certificates and certificates based on church records older than 100 and more years for **genealogical** purposes are to be forewarded directly to: Naczelna Dyrekcja Archiwów Państwowych, ul. Długa 6 – skrytka pocztowa Nr. 1005, PL 00–950 Warszawa – Polska (Poland).

General Remarks concerning Inquiries

1. Inquiries and correspondence should be conducted in Polish, otherwise translation fees may be expected.
2. One should ask for written duplicates or copies of entries rather than certificates on which information is supplied in abbreviated form.
3. Locality information should give Polish place names, which may be obtained from the above mentioned German-foreign language gazetteers.
4. Give precise questions to shorten research time. Statements such as: before 1845, around 1845 or after 1845 should be avoided. Better: between the years 1845 and 1847 should be used.
5. Two (2) international reply postal coupons – return postage – must be included in your inquiries.

A note about the Microfilm Archives of the Church of Jesus Christ of Latter Day Saints (LDS) at Salt Lake City, Utah, 84150, U. S. A.

Here are found microfilms of church records of Protestant and Roman Catholic parishes of present Poland, in part also of Galicia and Volhynia now situated within the USSR (see also above Section A, 3, 2f, page 14).

Civil Registry Offices in Poland exist

a. since about 1875 in areas of pre-1914 Germany;
b. since 1945 in "old Polish" areas (Central-Poland – Volhynia under Russian jurisdiction; Galicia under Austrian jurisdiction).

The civil registry offices hold church records of the former Protestant parishes and duplicates of Roman Catholic church records from about 1870 and later.

Excerpts of civil registries will be supplied for this time period on a short form. Fees are about US $ 10.00. Applications are to be sent to the local civil registry office.

Protestant Parish Offices

Existing parish offices of the "old Polish" areas keep their own records. Little is known about them.

Roman Catholic Parish Offices

These offices have church records and supply information from them. However, in part these records (older than 100 years) are now deposited at the archives of their respective diocese.

Inquiries are to be directed to the parish office in question or to: Sekretariat Prymasa Polski, ul Miodowa 17, Warszawa I, Poland.

Church offices are not allowed to charge fees, but may accept donations. We suggest to mention intentions to donate (forwarding parcels or the like) and inquire about special needs. Personal research is permitted at parish offices.

According to inquiries made by the Embassy of the Federal Republic of Germany in Warsaw neither civil status certificates will be issued nor personal research permitted in records of local civil registry offices. You may ask for civil status certificates (especially for official purposes) through diplomatic channels of your own country (generally the Department for External Affairs). (Circular letter of the Federal Minister for the Interior of the F. R. G. of December 4. 1975 – #GMBI. page 839).

Only certificates, report cards, attestations etc. will be supplied for present needs (marriages, enclosures to family books, pension purposes etc.). No research possibilities exist in these cases. Exact information is necessary (surname, given name(s), locality, county and dates). Fee is about US. $ 5.00. Genealogical searches cannot be done by the embassies. Some useful information is also found in Polish Genealogical Society Bulletin, 984 N. Milwaukee Avenue, Chicago, Ill. 60622, U. S. A.

8.3 Difficulties with Church Records

Difficulties may often arise when you want to check and confirm certification from **church records**, particularly in **West Prussia** and **Silesia**.

The main difficulty lies in the Roman Catholic Administration of churches. Even before 1945 we did not know where the individual members of Protestant parishes went to document their baptisms, marriages and deaths. No index is available for refugee and border parishes, which were visited after the 1919 border changes by Protestants, as well as the early "prayer houses" during the time of Frederick the Great of Prussia. An index of this kind would make searching for parish documents of these time periods partially possible. However, not all difficulties would be solved, for it is peculiar how poor road conditions, weather, epidemics, floods and sometimes parish vacancies, often pushed official parish recordings into neighbouring parishes, where one would expect them the least. This is also true for West Prussia, which became part of Prussia in 1772; for instance, the county of Grudziadz (Graudenz) where Protestants before 1772 were obliged to document personal status changes at the nearest Roman Catholic parish office. No index or catalogued reference can solve this problem. All you can do here is to search through the neighbouring parish records.

8.4 Compilations of Research Articles

The AGoFF cannot give general information. If you have general questions or want to increase your knowledge, please consult the following publications, general genealogical periodicals, writings and research aids.

1. Wolfgang Ribbe and Eckart Henning: Taschenbuch fuer Familiengeschichtsforschung (Pocket book for family history research). 9th edition. Verlag Degener & Co., Inh. Gerhard Gessner, Neustadt/Aisch, Germany, 1980.

2. Familiengeschichtliche Biographie (Genealogical bibliography), vol. I–VII, XI, XVI (1897–1977), Verlag Degener & Co., Neustadt/Aisch, Germany.

3. Familiengeschichtliche Quellen (Family history sources), volumes 1 to 13. Zeitschrift fuer familiengeschichtliche Quellennachweise (Periodical for family history source information), edited by Oswald Spohr. Verlag Degener & Co., Neustadt/Aisch, Germany, 1950–1959.

4. "Der Schluessel" (The key) – Index for periodicals – 7 volumes. Heinz Reise Verlag, Goettingen, Germany, 1950–1981.

   Volume 5 (1961–1965) lists volumes 1 to 8 of Ostdeutsche Familienkunde (East German Genealogy) published between 1953 and 1960, and Archiv ostdeutscher Familienforscher (Archives of East German family researchers) volumes 1 and 2, 1952–1963.

   Volume 6 lists genealogical-heraldic periodicals of Austria and German speaking Czechoslovakia.

5. Rudolf Dimpfel: Bibliographisches Nachschlagewerk (Bibliographic reference book) 1921, reprint Saendig Verlag, Walluf, Germany 1969. Section 2 lists local references (like: Breslau, Silesia).

6. Deutsches Geschlechterbuch (German Genealogies. Genealogical Handbook of non-noble families, Sources and compilations with Genealogies of German non-noble families. Verlag C. A. Starke, Limburg/Lahn, Germany. Since 1889 182 volumes have been published, for individual information see Section "B".

7. Deutsches Familienarchiv (German Family Archives) (84 volumes to date). Verlag Degener & Co., Neustadt/Aisch, Germany, since 1952.

    Index to volumes 1–50, and 51–75, Verlag Degener & Co., Neustadt/Aisch, Germany, 1980 and 1981.

8. Genealogisches Handbuch des Adels (Genealogical handbook of nobility). Verlag C. A. Starke, Limburg/Lahn, Germany, since 1951.

9. Glensdorfs Internationales Genealogen-Lexikon (Glensdorf's International Directory of Genealogists) volumes 1 and 2. Biographical handbook for family and heraldic researchers. Wilhelm Rost Verlag, Bad Muender am Deister, Germany 1977 and 1979.

10. Familienarchive in oeffentlichem und privatem Besitz (Family archives in public and private collections) edited by H. F. Friederichs, 2 volumes, Neustadt/Aisch. Germany 1972 and 1977 (Volume 1 and 6 of series "Genealogische Informationen" ("Genealogical informations"). Verlag Degener & Co.

8.5 *Maps and Pictorial Materials*

a. Institut fuer Angewandte Geodaesie, Aussenstelle Berlin, D–1000 Berlin 30, Germany, edits and publishes the official map collection "Karte des Deutschen Reiches" (Map of the German Empire) – abbreviated KDR 100 and "Sonderkarten" (Special maps) – abbrevaited SK. Available are the following:

   Brandenburg, East Prussia, Pomerania, Silesia: Price DM 11.00 and Upper Silesia DM 7.50 each.
   As well as 75 "Kreiskarten" (County maps) – abbreviated KK DM 5.00 each.

b. The Bibliothek der Stiftung Haus des deutschen Ostens, Bismarckstrasse 90, D–4000 Duesseldorf, Germany has more than 2 900 maps of our research territories from before May 8, 1945.

c. **Pictorial Materials** (of towns, villages, historical art, portraits, gravestones etc.) are held by: Bildarchiv Foto Marburg, Ernst-von-Huelsen-Haus, Wolfstrasse, D–3550 Marburg, Germany.
   Johann-Gottfried-Herder-Institut, Gisonenweg 7, D–3550 Marburg, Germany has more than 150 000 pictures from east of the Elbe River.
   Goettinger Bildwerk e. V., Waldweg 26, D–3400 Goettingen, Germany.

d. Bundesamt fuer Eich- und Vermessungswesen,
   Krotenthalergasse 3, A–1080 Wien VIII, Austria, has available: Generalkarte von Mitteleuropa (General map of Central Europe) 1:200 000. Price 22 Schillinge and explanation of legend 10 Schillinge. This map collection contains 265 individual maps in coloured print.

   Maps are catalogued by name, such as Wien, and its geographical coordinates.

   Free catalogs may be obtained from a. and from d. upon request. These catalogs are available in **German only**.

8.6   *Rural Genealogy in Prussia*

The land-title-registry (Grundbuecher) and Mortgage Records (Hypothekenbuecher) after 1872 are held by the State Archives or courts. Praestations-Tabellen (for about 1750–1850) are the forerunners of real estate tax lists and are held by the state archives classifield according to Aemter (some are published for East Prussia). Muehlenkonsignationen (list of residents accociated with a grain mill) prior to 1806 list all heads of families for a given location since the royal mills had milling monopoly which nobody could escape by power of penalty. Flurkarten (maps of individual real estate) of the royal Prussian Plankammer often list owners by name before 1912. Some are recently published for the Plankammer of the districts of Frankfurt/Oder, Bromberg, Potsdam, Marienwerder. Messtischblaetter (topographical maps at a scale of 1:25 000) are available from Institut fuer Angewandte Geodaesie in Berlin (see 8.5.a).

ORIGIN OF GERMAN ETHNIC GROUPS EXPELLED FROM THE EAST DURING AND AFTER WORLD WAR II

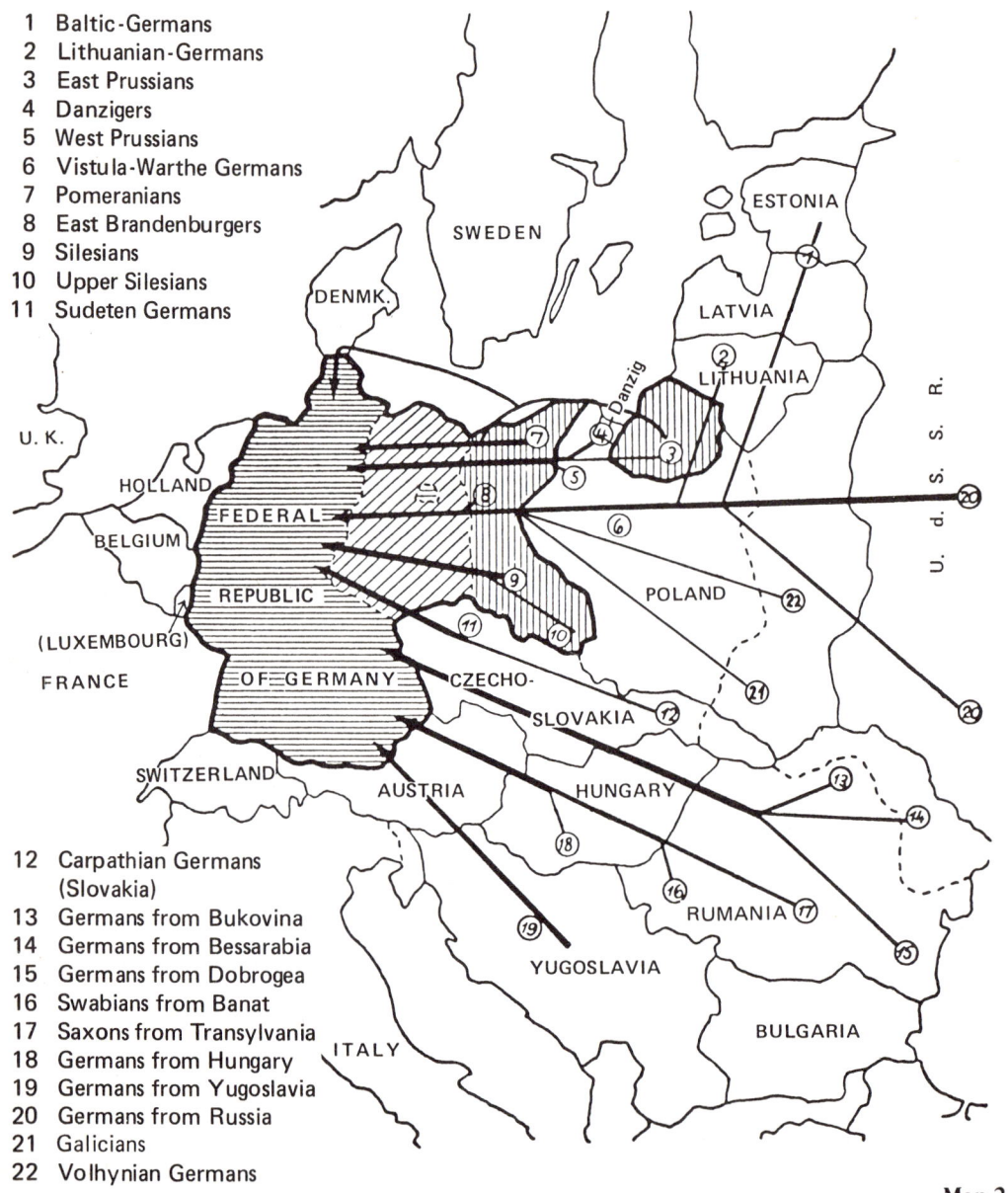

1. Baltic-Germans
2. Lithuanian-Germans
3. East Prussians
4. Danzigers
5. West Prussians
6. Vistula-Warthe Germans
7. Pomeranians
8. East Brandenburgers
9. Silesians
10. Upper Silesians
11. Sudeten Germans
12. Carpathian Germans (Slovakia)
13. Germans from Bukovina
14. Germans from Bessarabia
15. Germans from Dobrogea
16. Swabians from Banat
17. Saxons from Transylvania
18. Germans from Hungary
19. Germans from Yugoslavia
20. Germans from Russia
21. Galicians
22. Volhynian Germans

Map 2

Map taken from:
Die europaeische Bedeutung der Oder-Neisse-Gebiete, Verband der Landsmannschaften
(The European importance of the Oder-Neisse-Territories).

GERMANY AND THE FORMER GERMAN SETTLEMENTS IN EUROPE AS OF DECEMBER 31, 1937 and January 1, 1948.

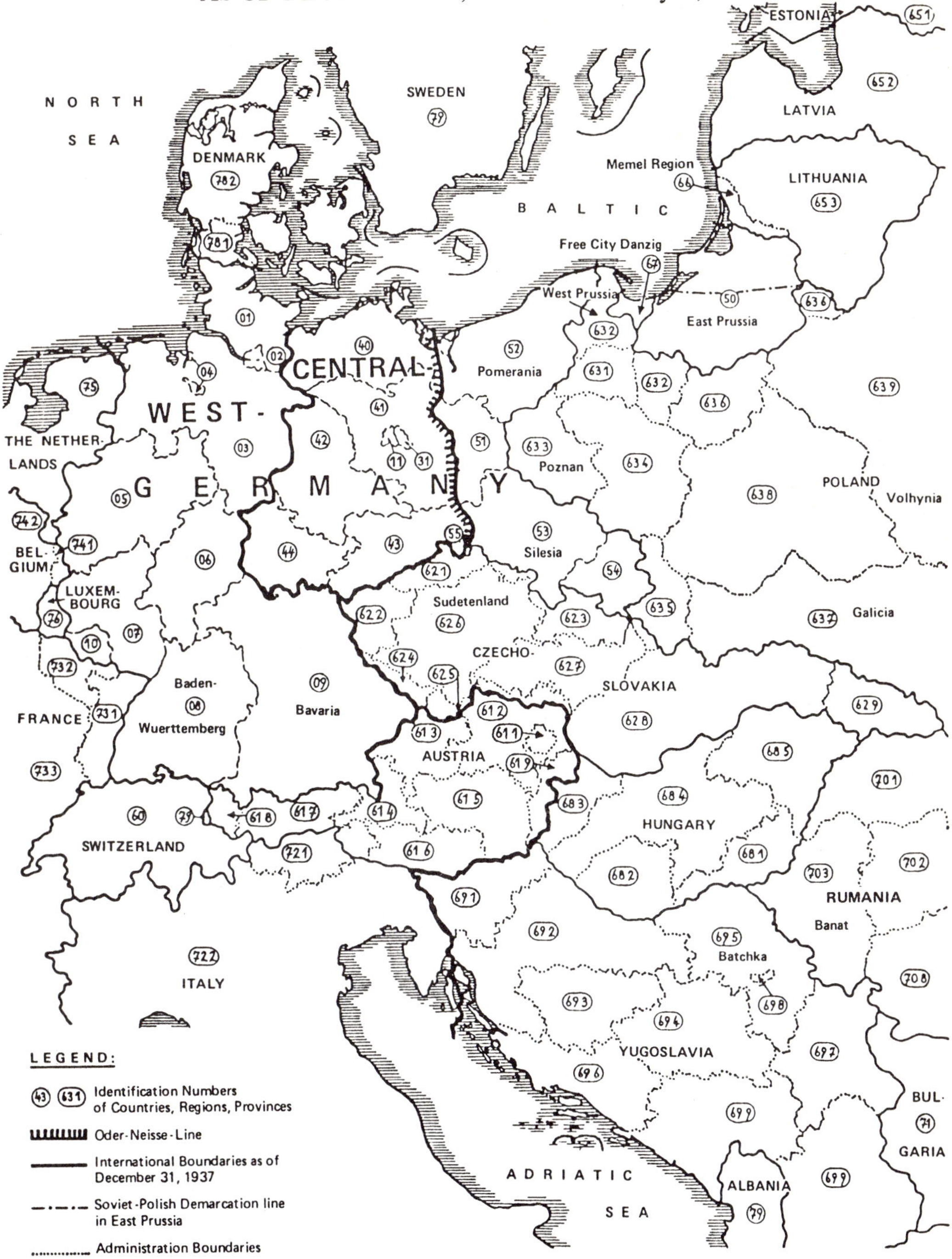

Map 3

Copied from map Nr. 700 47 by Statistisches Bundesamt.

LEGEND:
- ㊸ ⑥³¹ Identification Numbers of Countries, Regions, Provinces
- ⊥⊥⊥⊥⊥⊥ Oder-Neisse-Line
- ——— International Boundaries as of December 31, 1937
- —·—·— Soviet-Polish Demarcation line in East Prussia
- ········· Administration Boundaries

Comments to preceding Map

Following is a listing of territorial names as they would appear in German records with their English equivalent to the right.

50 **Provinz Ostpreussen** — **Province of East Prussia**

    501 Reg.-Bez. Koenigsberg   Adm.-Distr. Koenigsberg
    502 Reg.-Bez. Gumbinnen ⎫ see also #636   Adm.-Distr. Gumbinnen (= Gusev)
    503 Reg.-Bez. Allenstein ⎭   Adm.-Distr. Allenstein (= Olsztyn)

    former Reichsgau Danzig-Westpreussen   *former Administrative District Danzig-West Prussia*

    504 Reg.-Bez. Danzig and Marienwerder see also #632 & 671   Adm.-Distr. Danzig (= Gdansk) and Marienwerder (= Kwidzyn)

51 **Provinz Brandenburg** — **Province of Brandenburg**

    511 Reg.-Bez. Frankfurt/Oder   Adm.-Distr. Frankfurt/Oder

52 **Provinz Pommern** — **Province of Pomerania**

    521 Reg.-Bez. Stettin   Adm.-Distr. Stettin (Szczecin)
    522 Reg.-Bez. Koeslin   Adm.-Distr. Koeslin (= Koszalin)
    523 Reg.-Bez. Schneidemuehl   Adm.-Distr. Schneidemuehl (= Pila)

53 **Provinz Niederschlesien** — **Province of Lower Silesia**

    Reg.-Bez. Breslau   Adm.-Distr. Breslau (= Wroclaw)
    Reg.-Bez. Liegnitz   Adm.-Distr. Liegnitz (= Legnica)

54 **Provinz Oberschlesien** — **Province of Upper Silesia**

    541 Reg.-Bez. Oppeln see also #635   Adm.-Distr. Oppeln (= Opole)
    542 Reg.-Bez. Kattowitz see also #635   Adm.-Distr. Kattowitz (= Katowice)

62 **Tschechoslowakei** — **Czechoslovakia**

    Sudetendeutsche Gebiete   *Sudeten German Regions*

    621 Reg.-Bez. Aussig   Adm.-Distr. Aussig (= Ush-nad-Labem)
    622 Reg.-Bez. Eger   Adm.-Distr. Eger (= Cheb)
    623 Reg.-Bez. Troppau   Adm.-Distr. Troppau (= Opava)
    624 Sudetendeutsche Gebiete des bayerischen Reg.-Bez. Niederbayern und Oberpfalz   Sudeten German regions of the Bavarian adm.-distr. of Lower Bavaria and Upper Palatinate
    625 Sudetendeutsche Gebiete der frueheren Reichsgaue Niederdonau und Oberdonau   Sudeten German regions of the former adm.-districts of Lower Danube and Upper Danube

    former Protektorat Boehmen und Maehren   *former Protectorate of Bohemia and Moravia*

    626 Land Boehmen   Bohemia
    627 Land Maehren   Moravia
    628 Slowakei   Slovakia
    629 Karpato-Ukraine   Carpathian Ukraine

63	**Polen**	**Poland**

former Reichsgau Danzig-Westpreussen — *former Adm.-Distr. Danzig-West Prussia*

- 631 Reg.-Bez. Bromberg — Adm.-Distr. Bromberg (= Bydgoszcz)
- 632 Reg.-Bezirke Danzig und Westpreussen — Adm.-Distr. Danzig and West Prussia

former Reichsgau Wartheland — *former Adm.-Distr. Wartheland*

- 633 Reg.-Bez. Posen — Adm.-Distr. Posen (= Poznan)
- 634 Reg.-Bezirke Hohensalza und Litzmannstadt — Adm.-Distr. Hohensalza (= Inowroclaw) and Litzmannstadt (= Lodz)

former eastern regions assimilated by the Provinzen Oberschlesien und Ostpreussen — *former eastern regions assimilated by the provinces Upper Silesia and East Prussia*

- 635 Reg.-Bezirke Kattowitz und Oppeln (Oberschlesien) — Adm. Distr. Kattowitz (= Katowice) and Oppeln (= Opole) (Upper Silesia)
- 636 Reg.-Bezirke Zichenau, Allenstein und und Gumbinnen (Ostpreussen) — Adm.-Distr. Zichenau (= Ciechanow), Allenstein (= Olsztyn) and Gumbinnen (= Gusev) (East Prussia)

former Generalgouvernement — *former Military Government*

- 637 Distrikte Galizien und Krakau — Districts of Galicia and Krakow
- 638 Distrikte Lublin, Radom und Warschau — Districts of Lublin, Radom and Warsaw

remainder of former Verwaltungsgebiete in Polen — *remainder of former administrative regions in Poland*

- 639 Bezirk Bialystock, Polesien, Wolhynien und Restgebiete — District of Bialystock, Polesje, Volhynia and remaining territories

64 **Sowjetunion (UdSSR)** — **Soviet Union (USSR)**

- 641 Krim (ASSR) — Crimea (ASSR)
- 642 Ukraine (USSR) — Ukraine (USSR)
- 643 Ost-Wolhynien — Eastern-Volhynia
- 644 Don- und Wolgagebiet — Don and Volga Region
- 645 Wolgadeutsche Republik — Volga German Republic
- 646 Nordkaukasus — Northern Caucasus
- 647 Suedkaukasus — Southern Caucasus
- 648 Weissrussland/Weissruthenien — White Russia/White Ruthenia
- 649 uebrige Sowjetunion — remaining USSR

65 **Baltische Staaten (Baltikum)** — **Baltic States**

- 651 Estland — Estonia
- 652 Lettland — Latvia
- 653 Litauen — Lithuania

66 **Memelgebiet** — **Memel Region**

67 **Freie Stadt Danzig** — **Free City of Danzig (= Gdansk)**

former Reichsgau Danzig-Westpreussen — *former adm.-distr. Danzig-West Prussia*

- 671 Reg.-Bez. Danzig — Adm.-Distr. Danzig (= Gdansk)

68 **Ungarn**   **Hungary**
- 681 Oestliches Suedungarn — Eastern South Hungary
- 682 Westliches Suedungarn — Western South Hungary
- 683 Westungarn — Western Hungary
- 684 Mittelungarn — Central Hungary
- 685 Oberungarn — Upper Hungary

69 **Jugoslawien**   **Yugoslavia**
- 691 Draubanschaft — Drave region
- 692 Savebanschaft — Sava region
- 693 Werbassbanschaft — Vrbas region
- 694 Drinabanschaft — Drina region
- 695 Donaubanschaft — Danube region
- 696 Kuestenbanschaft — Adriatic Coast region
- 697 Morawabanschaft — Morava region
- 698 Banschaft Belgrad — Belgrade area
- 699 Wardarbanschaft und Zetabanschaft — Vardar and Zeta regions

70 **Rumaenien**   **Rumania**
- 701 Noerdliches Siebenbuergen mit Sathmar — Northern Transylvania with Satu Mare
- 702 Suedliches Siebenbuergen — Southern Transylvania
- 703 Westrumaenien mit Banat — Western Rumania with Banat
- 704 Bukowina — Bukovina
- 705 Moldau — Moldova
- 706 Bessarabien — Bessarabia
- 707 Grosse Walachei — Vallachia
- 708 Kleine Walachei — Vallachia
- 709 Dobrudscha — Dobrogea

71 **Bulgarien**   **Bulgaria**

SECTION B
REGIONAL INFORMATION

I. Former German Territories east of the Oder-Neisse-Line
within the borders of the Treaty of Versailles of 1920

Map 4

According to the "Potsdam Agreement" of 1945 (in whose deliberations Germany did not participate) Germany continues to exist in her boundaries of 1937. Here it was decided that, "until the completion of a peace treaty with Germany", the northern part of East Prussia would be placed **under the administration** of the Soviet Union, while similarly the remainder of the East Prussia territories would be placed **under the administration** of Poland:

"The heads of the participating three governments agreed that, until the final fixing of Poland's western boundaries, the former German territories east of the line running immediately west of Swinemuende south along the Oder River to the western Neisse River following it south to the border of Czechoslovakia, the part of East Prussia which is not under the administration of the USSR as well as the former Free State of Danzig will come under the administration of Poland, and in this respect are not to be considered to be part of the Soviet Occupation Zone of Germany."

1. **EAST PRUSSIA AND MEMEL REGION (= OSTPREUSSEN)**

Map 5

East Prussia, between 1824 and 1878 united with West Prussia as "Provinz Preussen" (Province of Prussia), included, within the borders of December 31, 1937, apart from the region being dealt with here, the "Regierungsbezirk" (Administrative District) West Prussia", which, after the defeat of Poland in 1939, became part of the newly formed "Reichsgau (Administrative District) Danzig-Westpreussen". The Memel Region – until 1920 a part of the Prussian province of East Prussia – was separated from Germany and, after three years of allied Joint Rule, was occupied by Lithuanian troops in 1923. After the Lithuanian annexation, the Memel Region received autonomous status on May 8, 1924. In 1939 Germany forced the contractual ruling of the return which followed on March 22. In January 1945 the region of the Lithuanian SSR became part of the Soviet Union. The "Regierungsbezirk Zichenau" was formed from sections of the "Wojewodztwo (Administrative District) Warszawa" at the end of 1939 and put under the authority of the "Praesident der Provinz Preussen". In 1945 East Prussia was divided between Poland and the Soviet Union.

1. **Research Areas**

The Prussian province of East Prussia — Administrative districts of Koenigsberg, Gumbinnen and Allenstein (Administrative District of West-Prussia-Marienwerder, which belonged to the province of East Prussia between 1920 and 1939). Memel Region.

Map 6

2. **Genealogical Institutions**

2.1 *Present institutions*

Verein fuer Familienforschung in Ost- und Westpreussen e. V. Sitz Hamburg (Society for family research in East and West Prussia)
President: Dr. R. Farnsteiner, Forstgrund 4, D–2104 Hamburg 92, Germany.

Information available:

a. About East Prussia from:

Dr. Wolf Konietzko, Eichstrasse 6, D–2200 Elmshorn, Germany, Ph. 04121–61856.
General information center and for researches in Eastern Masuren (Masovia).

Bernhard Maxin, Am alten Berg 1, D–6104 Malchen bei Darmstadt, Germany.
Research in Western Masovia.

Guenther Wichman, Surfelln 11a, D–2105 Seevetal 6, Germany, Ph. 04105–52265 and 040–330272.
Research in Northern Masovia.

Walter Merten, Schuetzenstrasse 17, D–5400 Koblenz, Germany.
Research in Ermland (Warmia).

Dr. Rolf Farnsteiner, Forstgrund 4, D–2104 Hamburg 92, Germany, Ph. 040–7962443.
Research in Northeastern East Prussia, Salzburgers.

Dr. Reinhold Heling, In de Kruem 10, D–2104 Hamburg 92, Germany, Ph. 040–70117665.
Altpreussisches Pfarrerbuch (Old Prussian pastors), index Quassowski.

Hans Heinz Diehlmann, Marquardstrasse 6, D–6747 Anweiler am Trifels, Germany.
Nobility.

b. About West Prussia: see Section "B" West Prussia 2.1.

Periodicals:
Altpreussische Geschlechterkunde (Old Prussian genealogy), new series since 1953.
Altpreussische Geschlechterkunde – Familienarchiv – (... family archives) since 1956.

In addition 43 special publications have been published since 1961 which may be ordered from:
Guenther Wichmann, Surfelln 11a, D–2105 Seevetal 6, Germany.

The society library is located at the genealogical society, Alsterchaussee 1, D–2000 Hamburg 13, Germany, business hours are Wednesdays between 4:00 p. m. and 7:00 p. m. only.

Queries on the location of civil registers or church records as well as other genealogical sources of the research territories are answered by the information center of the society (see above Dr. W. Konietzko).

Information about your finds are welcome. Double postage is required when queries are forwarded to other researchers. Queries should include index cards (postcard size) – one surname and its research results per card – having name and address of sender. Queries cannot be handled unless these cards are enclosed. Sample next page.

```
R O D I E S, Maria                         Benkheim, Krs. Angerburg
               *(1820) Surminnen ?, + 10.4.1874 Benkheim
               Schlaganfall, begraben 13.4.1874, Janellen
               oo 7.2.1847 Benkheim Julius Denzer
    "        , Johann Emil, Kürschner in Benkheim
               * 3.9.1796 Pillkallen, get. 5.9.1796 Pillkallen
               + 13.7.1831 Benkheim, begr. 16.7.1831 Benkheim
               oo 8.3.1819 Goldap Elisabeth Regine Faltin
    "        , Jons, Schneider in Koadjuthen, später Pillkallen
               * 14.10.1771 Uszkamohnen, Ksp. Koadjuthen
               get. 17.10.1771 Koadjuthen, + 1.8.1840 Pillkallen,
               begr. 4.8.1840 Pillkallen, Geschwister siehe
               umseitig
    "        , Urbs, Wirt in Uszkamohnen
               * (um 1745), + ?
               oo Marya ...


Dr. Egon Meier, Bauerweg 2, 2000 Hamburg 74
```

2.2 *Former institutions*

Verein fuer Familienforschung in Ost- und Westpreussen, established Nov. 19, 1925 (Society for family research in East and West Prussia).

Periodical:
Altpreussische Geschlechterkunde, 1927 to 1943 (Old Prussian Genealogy).

The following libraries and societies have complete sets of APG from 1927 to 1943:

1. Deutsches Adelsarchiv, Friedrichsplatz 15, D–3550 Marburg/Lahn, Germany.
2. Heraldisch-Genealogische Gesellschaft Adler, Haarhof 4a, A–1000 Vienna, Austria
3. Der Herold, Verein fuer Heraldik, Genealogie und verwandte Wissenschaften, Archivstrasse 12–14, D–1000 Berlin 33, Germany.
4. Johann-Gottfried-Herder-Institut, Gisonenweg 7, D–3550 Marburg/Lahn, Germany.
5. Gesellschaft fuer Familienkunde in Kurhessen und Waldeck ueber die Landesbibliothek, Staendeplatz 8, D–3500 Kassel, Germany.
6. Niedersaechsische Staats- und Universitaetsbibliothek, Prinzenstraße 1, D–3400 Goettingen, Germany.
7. Universitaetsbibliothek, Bispinghof 24–25, D–4400 Muenster, Germany.

Table of contents and surnames index from 1927 to 1943 was published separately as #21/1972 and is available from the Society (see 2.1).

3. **Documents of Vital Statistics**

3.1 *Books and records of vital statistics*

See listings in Section "A" 3.1.

3.2 *Church records*

a. Richard Rose: Die Kirchenbuecher der evangelischen Kirchen Ost- und Westpreussens nebst einem Verzeichnis der Militaerkirchenbuecher der Provinz Westpreussen und der katholischen Kirchenbuecher der Dioezese Ermland, 1909 (Protestant church books of East and West Prussia plus an index of military church books of the province of West Prussia and the Roman Catholic diocese of Warmia, 1909).

b. E. Grigoleit: Neues Verzeichnis ostpreussischer Kirchenbuecher sowie der vor 1874 abgelegten Personenstandsregister (New index of East Prussian church books and register of vital statistics deposited before 1874), Ailringen, Germany 1958.

Note: The listed locations of deposit are only partially correct. For church books in the Federal Republic of Germany the addresses listed in Section "A" 3.2 should be used; for church books in the German Democratic Republic the new depository is: Zentralstelle fuer Genealogie in der Deutschen Demokratischen Republik, Georgi-Dimitroff-Platz 1, DDR–701 Leipzig, Germany.

c. Collection of Warmian church record copies

Bibliothek des Historischen Vereins fuer Ermland, Ermlandhaus, D–4400 Muenster, Germany.

d. Memel church records

see OFK, II (1959/1961), page 162; information available from Evangelisches Zentralarchiv, Jebenstrasse 3, D–1000 Berlin 12, Germany.

4. **Gazetteers**

4.1 *Published after 1945*

a. See Section "A" 4.1.

b. Verzeichnis der amtlichen Gemeinde- und Ortsnamen des Memellandes nach dem Gebietsstand vom 1.6.1939 (Gazetteer of official locality names of the Memel region as of June 1, 1939), edited and published by the Institut fuer Landeskunde in der Bundesforschungsanstalt fuer Landeskunde und Raumordnung, D–5300 Bonn 2, Germany 1968.

4.2 *Published before 1945*

See Section "A" 4.2.

J. F. Goldbeck: Vollstaendige Topographie des Kgr. Preussens (1785) (Complete topography of the Kingdom of Prussia), reprint Hamburg, Germany 1966–1968, East Prussia (3 volumes).

S. G. Wald: Topographische Uebersicht des Verwaltungsbezirks der Kgl. Preussischen Regierung zu Koenigsberg i. Pr. (Topographic survey of the administrative district of the royal Prussian government at Koenigsberg, Prussia), Koenigsberg 1820, reprint Hamburg, Germany 1979.

A. Schlott: Topographisch-statistische Uebersicht des Regierungsbezirks Koenigsberg (Topographic-statistical survey of the administrative district of Koenigsberg), Koenigsberg 1861.

Der Regierungsbezirk Gumbinnen nach seiner Lage, Begrenzung, Groesse, Bevoelkerung und Einteilung (The administrative district of Gumbinnen according to its situation, boundaries, size, population and divisions), Gumbinnen 1818 (reprint Hamburg 1981).

H. Meyer: Topographisch-statistische Uebersicht des Regierungsbezirks Gumbinnen (Topographic-statistical survey of the administrative district of Gumbinnen), Insterburg 1839.

Kuehne: Ortsverzeichnis der Provinz Ostpreussen, Koenigsberg 1893.

4.3 *Landed Estate Directories*

The Buecherei des Bundesministeriums fuer Ernaehrung, Landwirtschaft und Forsten, Rochusstrasse, D–5300 Bonn-Duisburg, holds:

Paul Niekammer: Ostpreussisches Gueteradressbuch (East Prussian directory of landed estates) second edition, Stettin, Germany 1909.

Julius Ernst: Landwirtschaftliches Gueteradressbuch fuer die Provinz Ostpreussen (Agricultural landed estates' directory for East Prussia), Reichenbach'sche Verlagsbuchhandlung, Leipzig, Germany 1920.

Paul Ellerholz: Handbuch des Grundbesitzes des Deutschen Reiches. I. Das Koenigreich Preussen, Volume III, Provinz Ostpreussen (Handbook of landed property of the German Empire. I. The Kingdom of Prussia, Volume III, Province of East Prussia), Nicolaische Verlagsbuchhandlung, Berlin, Germany 1907.

Hans Wehner: Landwirtschaftliches Adressbuch der Domaenen, Rittergueter, Gueter und Hoefe in der Provinz Ostpreussen (Agricultural directory of domains, knights' landed estates, landed estates and farms in the Province of East Prussia), 5th edition, Verlag von Niekammer's Adressbuecher GmbH., Leipzig, Germany 1932.

5. Selective Bibliography and Literature

5.1 *Published after 1945*

Bruno Schumacher: Geschichte Ost- und Westpreussens (History of East and West Prussia), 5th edition, Wuerzburg, Germany 1959.

Ernst Wermke: Bibliographie der Geschichte von Ost- und Westpreussen (Bibliography of the history of East and West Prussia), 4 vols. (reprint 1962, 1964, 1974) and 1979.

Fritz Gause: Geschichte des Preussenlandes (History of the land of Prussia), Leer, Germany 1966.

Buecherei des deutschen Ostens, Catalog, Herne 1973, pages 54–149; new edition vol. 1, Herne 1982, pages 22–217.

6. **Archives, Libraries with Sources of Homeland Regions**

6.1 *In West Germany – Federal Republic of Germany and West Berlin*

Geheimes Staatsarchiv, Preussischer Kulturbesitz, Archivstrasse 12–14, D–1000 Berlin 33, Germany.

Microfilms of genealogical documents from inventories of the Prussian State Archives at Koenigsberg/Prussia (17th to 19th century).

6.2 *In Central Germany – German Democratic Republik (DDR) and East Berlin*

Zentrales Staatsarchiv, Koenig-Heinrich-Strasse 37, DDR–4200 Merseburg 1, Germany.

Die Ost- und Westpreussen betreffenden Teile des ehemaligen Preussischen Geheimen Staatsarchivs (Portions of the former Prussian Privy State Archives pertaining to East and West Prussia).

Inventory published in: Mitteilungen der Preussischen Archivverwaltung 24–25, Leipzig 1934–1935.

6.3 *In homeland territory*

Allenstein/Olsztyn, Wojewódzkie Archiwum Pánstwowe w Olsztynie, Zamkowa 2, Poland, inventory information: Guide to Polish archives, page 422–430 and Section "A" 8.2.

7. **Other Research Aids**

7.1 *Hometown/village directory*

Heimatortskartei fuer Nordosteuropa, Abt. Ostpreussen and Memelland (Hometown/Village directory for Northeastern Europe, Section East Prussia and Memel region), Meesenring 13, D–2400 Luebeck, Germany, Ph. 0451–62 13 88.

7.2 *Society*

Landsmannschaft Ostpreussen (Society of East Prussians),
Parkallee 86, D–2000 Hamburg 13, Germany.

Periodical: Das Ostpreussenblatt (The East Prussian Paper).

7.3 *Homeland information centers for*

    a. Regierungsbezirk Koenigsberg (excluding counties of Koenigsberg, Braunsberg and Heilsberg)
    b. County of Koenigsberg (= Kreis Koenigsberg)
    c. Regierungsbezirk Gumbinnen (and Memel region)
    d. Regierungsbezirk Allenstein (and Soldau region, counties of Braunsberg and Heilsberg)

at: Landesausgleichsamt Schleswig-Holstein, Meesenring 9, D–2400 Luebeck, Germany.

7.4 *Historical Associations*

    a. Historische Kommission fuer ost- und westpreussische Landesforschung (Historical commission for East and West Prussia), Auf dem Muehlenberg 11, D–5358 Bad Muenstereifel-Houverath, Germany.

    Periodical: Preussenland (Prussia) (since 1963)

b. Historischer Verein fuer das Ermland (Historical society for Warmia), Ermlandweg 22, D–4400 Muenster, Germany.

7.5 *Church institutions*

Hilfskomitee fuer evgl. Deutsche aus Ostpreussen (Relief society for Protestant Germans from East Prussia), Haus der helfenden Haende, D–3331 Beienrode, Germany.

8. Other Hints

a. Deutsches Geschlechterbuch (Book of German Genealogy), vol. 61, 68 and 117 (volumes on East Prussia)

b. For family research in East and West Prussia see also Altpreussische Geschlechterkunde, new series vol. 24 (1976) page 407; vol. 25 (1977) pages 96, 99, 195.

c. **Acquisitions of documents from former East Prussian territories now under Soviet rule.**

It is possible to get documents of your ancestors through the Soviet Embassy in your country for scientific purposes.

However, for private individuals only the following types of documents (from civil or church records) may be requested:

a. **Birth Certificates:** your own certificate only. Excepted are parents who request certificates of minors.

b. **Marriage Certificates** may only be requested by the husband – not by children.

c. **Death Certificates** may be requested by immediate relatives, like parents or children.

Birth certificates of deceased persons or certificates for genealogical purposes will not be given.

After the application you receive a proper form which you have to complete and return to the embassy. After about four months, when the appropriate fees are paid, you will receive an answer. Excess money of the fee will be refunded.

The following regions are under Soviet rule:

a. Parts of the former administrative district of Koenigsberg in Prussia.

The City of Koenigsberg and counties of Bartenstein (*), Gerdauen (*), Heiligenbeil (*), Koenigsberg, Labiau, Memel (since 1920 Memel Region), Preussisch Eylau (*), Samland and Wehlau.

b. Parts of the former administrative district of Gumbinnen.

The Cities of Insterburg and Tilsit, the counties of Darkehmen (later Angerapp*), Stallupoenen (later Ebenrode), Elchniederung, Goldap*, Gumbinnen, Heydekrug (since 1920 Memel Region), Insterburg, Pillkallen (later Schlossberg), Tilsit-Ragnit (a portion of the Memel Region since 1920).

* These are counties which were divided by the "Demarcation Line" between Polish and Soviet administrations. Their territories are found on both sides of the line.

Territorial Border Changes of East Prussia 1914-1945

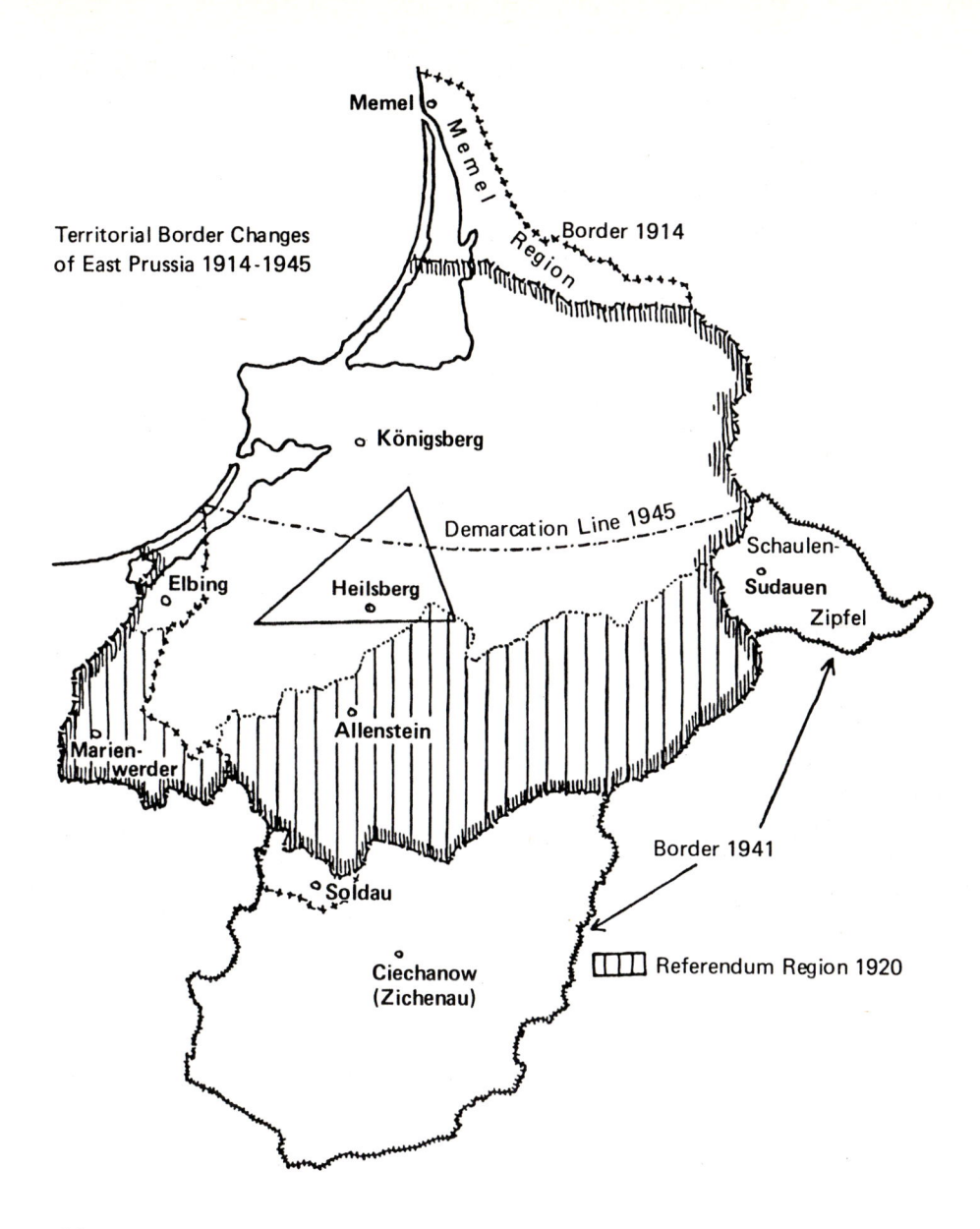

Memel
Memel Region
Border 1914
Königsberg
Demarcation Line 1945
Elbing
Heilsberg
Schaulen-Sudauen Zipfel
Marienwerder
Allenstein
Soldau
Border 1941
Ciechanow (Zichenau)

▯▯▯ Referendum Region 1920

Map 7

2. **WEST PRUSSIA AND DANZIG (= WESTPREUSSEN)**

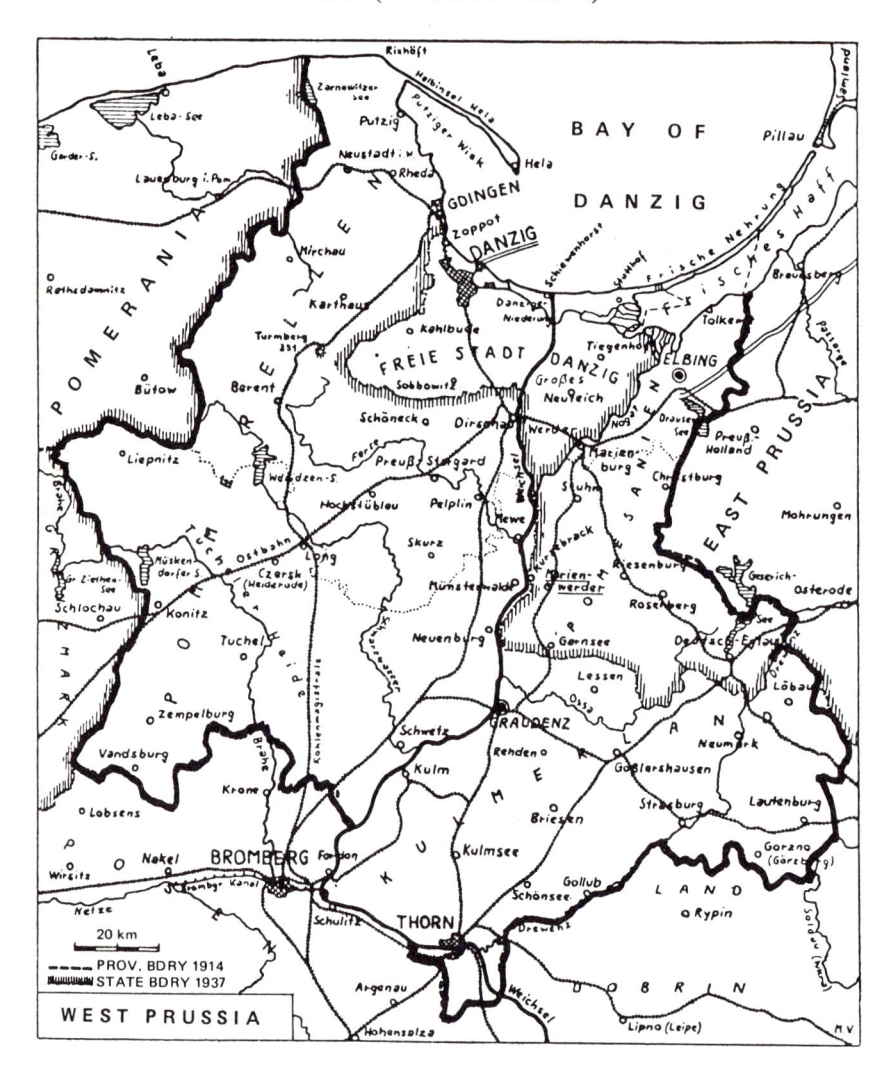

Map 8

The province of West Prussia was formed after the "first partition of Poland" in 1772 within the Prussian section of the partition territory. In 1816, after the Napoleonic Wars, it was re-established without Bromberg and the Netze Region. These formed the basis for the newly created Grand Duchy of Posen. West Prussia received in exchange the counties of Deutsch Krone and Flatow from Pomerania. in 1824 West and East Prussia were combined into the province of Prussia; this union ended in 1878.

After the Treaty of Versailles most of West Prussia was ceded to Poland (Wojewodztwo Pormorze/Pomerellen); Danzig and the surrounding county became the "Free City"; the counties of Regierungsbezirk (administrative district) Marienwerder, which remained in

WEST PRUSSIA AND DANZIG

- —·—·— Border of West Prussia 1878–1920
- — — — Border of Adm. Distr. West Prussia as of Dec. 31, 1937
- ▬▬▬ Border of „Reichsgau" Danzig - West Prussia 1939–1945
- ·········· „Free City" of Danzig
- ········ Border of Adm. Districts as of 1941
- o *Danzig* Seat of a „Regierungspräsident"

Jozo Džambo

Map 9

Germany, formed Regierungsbezirk West Prussia within the province of East Prussia. After the occupation of Poland in September 1939 the Regierungsbezirk West Prussia, the Wojewodztwo (administrative district) Pomorze (Pomerellen) and Danzig were combined to form Reichsgau (administrative district) Danzig-West Prussia.

After World War II all territories of West Prussia and Danzig were taken by Poland.

1. **Research Areas**

   The Prussian province of West Prussia with Danzig. Regions East and West of the lower Weichsel (= Vistula) River.

2. **Genealogical Institutions**

   2.1 *Present institutions*

   Forschungsstelle Westpreussen der AGoFF (Research center West Prussia of the AGoFF) Walter Kapahnke, An der Hellrüsche 24, D–4902 Bad Salzuflen, Germany, Ph. 05222–61866.

   Archives: "Westpreussenkartei" (Index of West Prussia) with 285 000 cards (February 1980).

   Library: About 3.000 titles, among them all volumes of Deutsches Geschlechterbuch 1–182, with 4 vols. on West Prussia.

   2.2 *Former institutions*

   Gesellschaft fuer Familienforschung, Wappen- und Siegelkunde (Society for family research, coats of arms and seals) in Danzig, established in 1919.
   Periodical:
   "Danziger familiengeschichtliche Beitraege" (Danzig family research papers) volumes 1–7, Danzig 1929–1943. Complete sets are held at the Staats- und Universitaetsbibliothek, Goettingen, Germany and the research center West Prussia.

3. **Documents of Vital Statistics**

   See Section "A" 3.

   M. Baer: Die Kirchenbuecher der Provinz Westpreussen (Church books of the province of West Prussia), Danzig 1908.

   A. Goertz: The Mennonite Quarterly Review, Oct. 1981, p. 372–380, Goshen, Indiana 46526, U. S. A., and Mennonitische Geschichtsblaetter 1981, p. 52–65.

4. **Gazetteers**

   4.1 *Published after 1945*

   See Section "A" 3.1.

   4.2 *Published before 1945*

   Gemeindelexikon fuer die Provinz Westpreussen (Gazetteer of the province of West Prussia), Berlin 1898 (also published in other years) with parish and civil registry jurisdictions.
   Available at major libraries.

   E. Jacobson: Topographisch-statistisches Handbuch fuer den Regierungsbezirk Marienwerder (Topographic-statistical handbook of the administrative district Marienwerder), Danzig 1868, 262 pages.

   J. F. Goldbeck: Vollstaendige Topographie des Koenigreichs Preussen (Complete topography of the Kingdom of Prussia) (1789), reprint Hamburg 1969, volume 4: West Prussia.

Topographisch-statistisches Handbuch fuer den Regierungsbezirk Danzig (Topographic-statistical handbook of the administrative district Danzig), Danzig 1869, 382 pages.

Uebersicht ueber die Bestandteile und Verzeichnis aller Ortschaften des Danziger Regierungsbezirks (Survey of compositions and index of all localities of the administrative district of Danzig), Danzig 1820, 233 pages (reprint Hamburg 1981).

Uebersicht saemtlicher Ortschaften in der Provinz Westpreussen, Nachtrag 1–4, Berlin 1900 (Directory of Places in West Prussia).

4.3 *Landed Estate Directories*

The library of Bundesministerium fuer Ernaehrung, Landwirtschaft und Forsten Rochusstrasse 1, D–5300 Bonn-Duisdorf, holds:

Ernst Seyfert: Gueteradressbuch fuer die Provinz Westpreussen, (Directory of landed estates for West Prussia), 12th edition, Reichenbach'sche Verlagsbuchhandlung, Leipzig, Germany 1912.

Landwirtschaftliches Gueteradressbuch fuer die Provinz Grenzmark Posen-Westpreussen sowie Freistaat Danzig, Regierungsbezirk Marienwerder (Agricultural landed estates' directory for the Province Grenzmark Poznan-West Prussia as well as the free state of Danzig, the government district Marienwerder), 3rd edition, Reichenbach'sche Verlagsbuchhandlung, Leipzig, Germany 1932.

5. Selective Bibliography and Literature

5.1 *Published after 1945*

Ernst Wermke: Bibliographie der Geschichte von Ost- und Westpreussen (Bibliography of East and West Prussian history). Covers all titles published to 1974. 4 vols. (reprint 1962, 1964, 1974) and 1979.

Available in major libraries.

Beitraege zur Geschichte Westpreussens (Articles on West Prussian history), a periodical of presently 5 volumes, published by: Copernicus-Vereinigung, Von-Kluck-Strasse 15–23, D–4400 Muenster/Westf., Germany.

This Vereinigung (Society) plans to publish a special volume containing a reprint of the Kontributionskataster Westpreussen (List of taxpayers of West Prussia). The list contains an index of all resident families of West Prussia in 1772. Presently this index is held by Geheimes Staatsarchiv, Preussischer Kulturbesitz, D–1000 Berlin, Germany.

Buecherei des deutschen Ostens, Catalog, Herne 1973, pages 150–193; new edition, vol. 1, Herne 1982, pages 218–308.

6. **Archives, Libraries with Sources of Homeland Regions**

6.1 See Section "A" 6.1.

6.2 See Section "A" 6.2.

6.3 *In Homeland territory*
   a. Bromberg/Bydgoszcz
      Wojewódzkie Archiwum Pánstwowe (Public district archives)
      w Bydgoszczy, ul. Dworcowa 65, Poland

      Inventory information: Guide to Polish Archives, pages 88–130.
   b. Danzig/Gdansk
      Wojewódzkie Archiwum Pánstwowe
      w Gdansku, ul. Waly Piastowskie 5, Poland

      Inventory information: Guide to Polish Archives, pages 131–182 (see "A" 8.2).
   c. Thorn/Toruń
      Wojewódzkie Archiwum Pánstwowe
      w Toruniu, Torun, pl. Rapackiego 4, Poland

      Inventory by K. Ciesielska: Informator o zasobie, Toruń 1977.
   d. Archives of the diocese of Pelplin

      for Roman Catholic church books.
   e. Archives of the county courts often hold probate records and testaments.

      For use of the above archives see Section "A" 8.

7. **Other Research Helps**

7.1 *Hometown/village directory*

   Heimatortskartei Nordosteuropa, Abt. Danzig-Westpreussen
   Meesenring 13, D–2400 Luebeck, Germany, Ph. 0451–62 13 88.

7.2 *Local Societies*
   a. Landsmannschaft Westpreussen (Society of West Prussians)
      Von-Kluck-Strasse 15–23, D–4400 Muenster/Westf., Germany.

      Periodical: Der Westpreusse (The West Prussian)
   b. Bund der Danziger (Society of Danzigers)

      Periodical: Unser Danzig (Our Danzig)

7.3 *Homeland information centers*
   a. Regierungsbezirk Danzig (excluding counties of Danzig and Zoppot)
   b. Counties of Danzig and Zoppot
   c. Regierungsbezirk Bromberg (= Bydgoszcz)
   d. Regierungsbezirk Marienwerder (= Kwidzyn)

   at: Landesausgleichsamt Schleswig-Holstein, Meesenring 9, D–2400 Luebeck 1, Germany.

7.4 *Historical Associations*

Historische Kommission fuer ost- und westpreussische Landesforschung (Historical commission for East and West Prussia),
Auf dem Muehlenberg 11, D–5358 Bad Muenstereifel-Houverath, Germany.

7.5 *Church institution*

Hilfskomitee der Evangelischen aus Danzig-Westpreussen (Relief society for Protestants from Danzig-West Prussia), Baeckerstrasse 3–5, D–2400 Luebeck, Germany.

Periodical: Danzig-Westpreussischer Kirchenbrief (Danzig-West Prussian church bulletin).

8. **Other Hints**

Deutsches Geschlechterbuch (Book of German Genealogy), volumes 126, 132, 133, 182 (Volumes of West Prussia) see Section "A" 2.1.

Area of ,,Free City" of Danzig 1920-1939

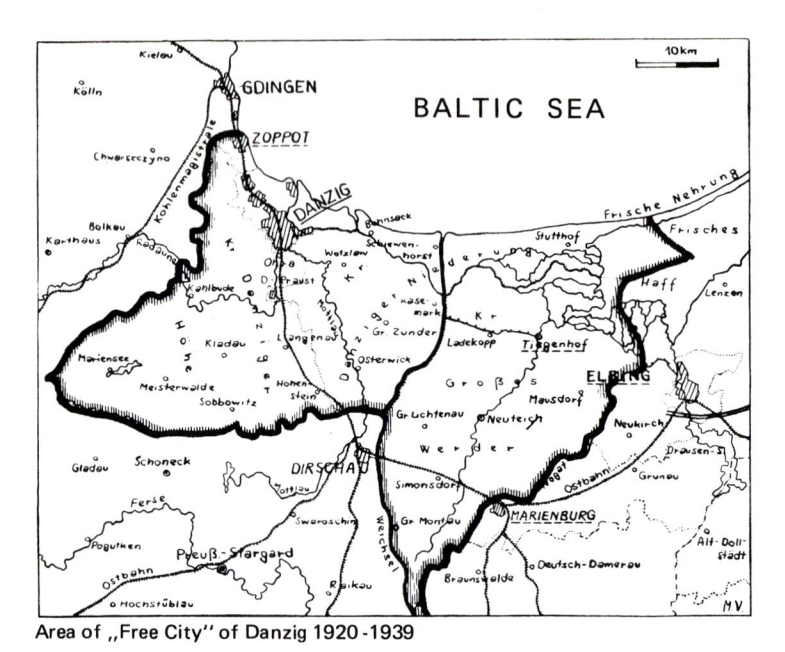

Map 10

West Prussian Border Changes 1914-1945

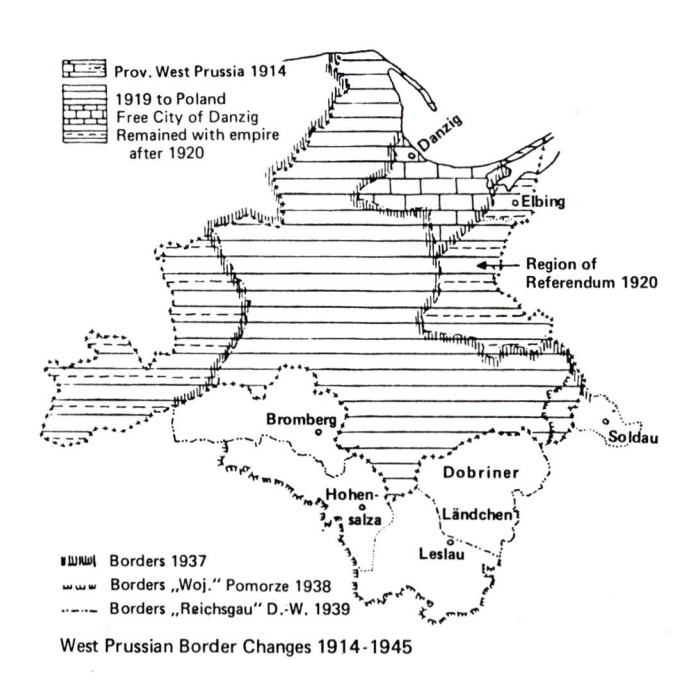

Map 11

3. **POMERANIA (= POMMERN)**

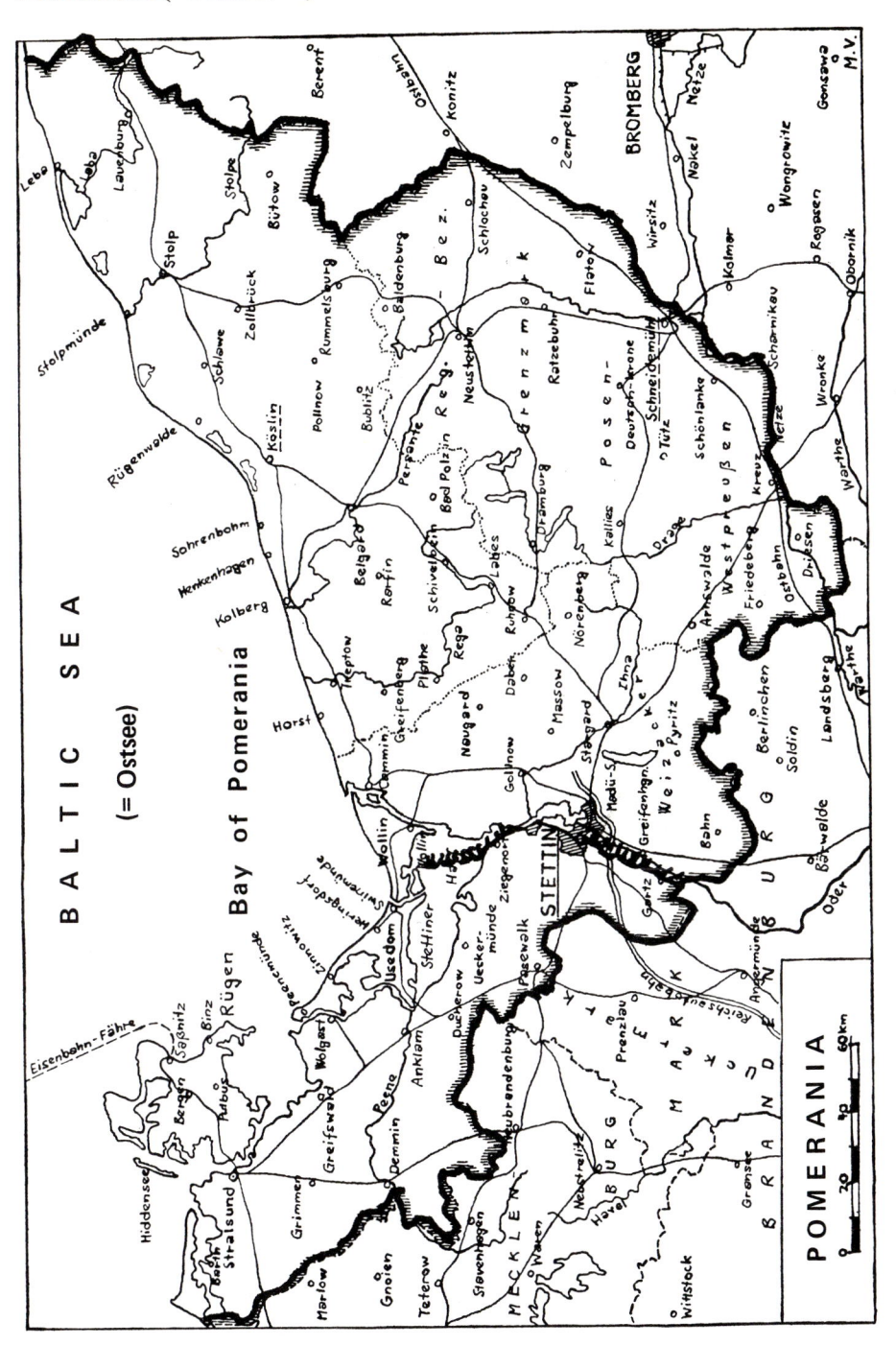

Map 12

Map 13

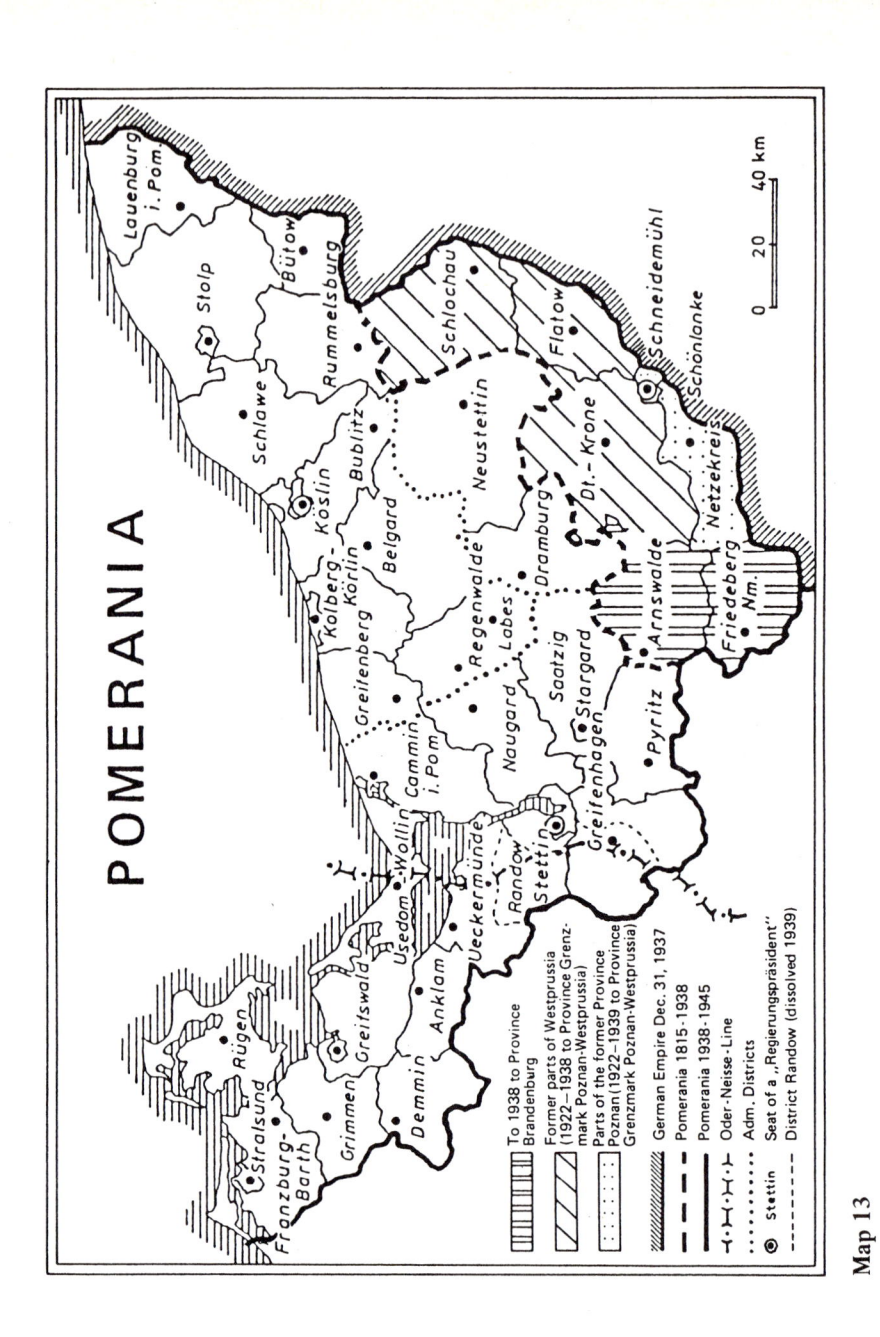

The Prussian province of Pomerania was enlarged in 1938 by the counties of Schlochau, Flatow, Deutsch-Krone and Netze – (1918–1928) as part of the province Grenzmark Posen-West Prussia, as well as the counties of Arnswalde and Friedeberg (Neumark). Eastern Pomerania, mainly that part of Pomerania lying east of the Oder River and historically called "Hinterpommern", was placed under Polish rule in 1945. The western part, "Vorpommern", became part of Mecklenburg within the German Democratic Republic (DDR), now the districts of Rostock and Neubrandenburg.

1. **Research Areas**

    The Prussian province of Pomerania
    (also Western Pomerania, now part of the German Democratic Republic)

    (Regions north of the Netze River which were part of the province of Grenzmark Posen-West Prussia since 1920 were united with Pomerania in 1938. This area was combined with the counties of Friedeberg, Arnswalde, Dramburg and Neustettin to form the Regierungsbezirk (administrative district) of Schneidemuehl (= Pila).

2. **Genealogical Institutions**

    2.1 *Present institutions*

    Forschungsstelle Pommern der AGoFF (Research center Pomerania)
    Director: Dr. Max Bruhn, Ollsener Strasse 24, D–2116 Hanstedt-Nordheide, Germany, Ph. 04182–73 55.

    Periodicals:
    Pommersche Zeitung (Pomeranian Newspaper), Johnsallee 18, D–2000 Hamburg, Germany.

    POMMERN, cultural periodical, Kiel, Germany.

    Sedina-Archiv, published by Pommerscher Zentralverband e. V., Johnsalle 18, D–2000 Hamburg 13, Germany.

3. **Documents of Vital statistics**

    3.1 *Books and records of vital statistics*

    see listings in Section "A" 3.1.

    3.2 *Displaced church records*

    see listings in Section "A" 3.2.

    3.3 *Church records in homeland regions*

    Western Pomerania (Vorpommern):
    Evangelisches Konsistorium, Bahnhofstrasse, 36, DDR–220 Greifswald, Germany.

    Staatsarchiv, Kreishaus, DDR–2200 Greifswald, Germany.

    Parish offices, some will give information, others will not.

    M. Wehrmann: Die Kirchenbuecher in Pommern. Baltische Studien 42, 1892, pp. 201–280.

4. **Gazetteers**

4.1 *Published after 1945*

See Section "A" 4.1.

4.2 *Published before 1945*

Gemeindelexikon fuer die Provinz Pommern, Berlin 1888.

Topographisch-Statistische Uebersicht des Stettiner Regierungsbezirks, Stettin 1842.

Topographisch-statistische Uebersicht des Reg. Bezirks Frankfurt a.d. Oder, Berlin 1820.

Topographisch-statistisches Handbuch des Reg. Bezirks Frankfurt a.d. Oder, Frankfurt a.d. Oder 1867.

4.3 *Landed estates*

The Library of Bundesministerium fuer Ernaehrung, Landwirtschaft und Forsten, Rochusstrasse 1, D–5300 Bonn-Duisdorf, Germany, holds:

Paul Niekammer: Pommersches Gueteradressbuch (Pomeranian directory of landed estates), 2nd edition, Stettin, Germany 1905.

Ernst Seyfert: Gueteradressbuch fuer die Provinz Pommern (Directory of landed estates for Pomerania), 5th edition, Reichenbach'sche Verlagsbuchhandlung, Leipzig, Germany 1920.

Handbuch des Grundbesitzes im Deutschen Reich, Provinz Pommern (Handbook of landed property in the German Empire, Province of Pomerania), 5th edition, Nicolaische Verlagsbuchhandlung, Berlin, Germany 1924.

Ernst Seyfert und Hans Wehner: Landwirtschaftliches Adressbuch der Rittergueter, Gueter und Hoefe der Provinz Pommern (Agricultural directory of knights landed estates, landed estates and farms in the Province of Pomerania), Nicolaische Verlagsbuchhandlung, Berlin, Germany 1924.

W. Kind: Landwirtschaftliches Adressbuch der Provinz Pommern (Agricultural directory of the Province of Pomerania), Verlag von Nietkammer's Adressbuecher GmbH, Leipzig, Germany 1939.

5. **Bibliographies and Literature**

5.1 *Published after 1945*

See listings in Section "A" 5.1.

Dr. Herbert Spruth: Landes- und familiengeschichtliche Bibliographie fuer Pommern (Local and family historical bibliography for Pomerania), Neustadt/Aisch, 1962/1965.

H. Bahlow: Pommersche Familiennamen (Family Names of Pomerania), Neustadt 1982.

5.2 *Published before 1945*

Verzeichnis ueber sippenkundliches Schriftum ueber Pommern (Index of genealogical literature of Pomerania) in vol. 1, page 260 of OFK.

Hans Ziegler: Geschichtliche und landesgeschichtliche Literatur Pommerns (Historical and local historical literature of Pomerania), published in "Pommersche Jahrbuecher" (Pomeranian yearbooks), 1938.

Buecherei des deutschen Ostens, Catalog, Herne 1973, pages 194–245; new edition, vol. 1, Herne 1982, pages 309–416.

Periodicals before 1945

Monthly newsletters of Gesellschaft fuer Pommersche Geschichts- und Altertumskunde, since 1882.

Pommersche Jahrbuecher des Ruegisch-Pommerschen Geschichtsvereins (Pomeranian yearbooks of the Ruegisch-Pomeranian Historical Society), since 1899.

Unser Pommerland (Our Pomerania), 1917–1945, Stettin, Germany.

Veroeffentlichungen der Historischen Kommission fuer Pommern (Publications of the historical commission of Pomerania), since 1926, Stettin, Germany.

Pommersche Sippenforschung (Pomeranian genealogical research), family historical information of the Pommersche Vereinigung fuer Stamm- und Wappenkunde in Stettin, 1925–1943.

6. Archives and Libraries with Sources of Homeland Regions

6.1 *In West-Germany – Federal Republic of Germany including West Berlin*

See listings in Section "A" 6.1.

Stadtbuecherei Luebeck: Collection Grube-Stettin.

Geheimes Staatsarchiv, Preussischer Kulturbesitz, Archivstrasse 12–14, D–1000 Berlin 33, Germany:
Collection Lassahn-Spruth, 110 binders of Pomeranian genealogy, 3000 pedigrees, descendant charts, individual finds etc.

Buecherei (Library) "Der Herold", Archivstrasse 12–14, D–1000 Berlin 33, Germany.

Stiftung Pommern, Schloß Rantzaubau, Daenische Strasse 44, D–2300 Kiel 1, Germany.

Collection Bruhn, Ollsener Strasse 24, D–2116 Hanstedt-Nordheide, Germany:
Genealogical sources, 20 000 index cards.

6.2 See Section "A" 6.2.

6.3 *In homeland territory*

Koeslin (= Koszalin)
Wojewódzkie Archiwum Pánstwowe
w Koszalinie, ul. Zwiazku Walki Mlodych 16, Poland
Inventory information: Guide to Polish Archives, pages 286–295, see "A" 8.2.

Stettin (= Szczecin)
Wojewódzkie Archiwum Pánstwowe
w Szczecinie, ul. sw. Wojciecha 13, Poland
Inventory information: Guide to Polish Archives, pages 537–554, see "A" 8.2.

6.4 *In Sweden*

Riksarkivet, Fack, S–100 26 Stockholm 34, Sweden.

Extensive, for Pomerania every important collections, among them the "Pomeranica" and Gadebusch collections which are described in Hermann Brulin: "Die Gadebusch-sammlung im Stockholmer Reichsarchiv" (The Gadebusch collection at the Stockholm archives). Translated by Prof. Dr. Johannes Paul, Pyritz, 1929, published by Gesellschaft fuer Zeitungskunde Pommerns.

Krigsarkivet, Fack, S–104 50 Stockholm 80, Sweden.

Muster rolls of Swedish-Pomeranian regiments, biography collection etc.

7. Other Research Aids

7.1 *Hometown/village directory*

Heimatortskartei Nordosteuropa, Abt. Pommern (Hometown/village directory for Northeastern Europe, Sect. Pomerania)
Meesenring 13, D–2400 Luebeck, Germany, Ph. 0451–62 73 88.

7.2 *Society of Pomeranians*

Pommersche Landsmannschaft (Society of Pomeranians)
Johnsallee 18, D–2000 Hamburg 13, Germany.

7.3 *Homeland information centers for*

    a. Regierungsbezirk Stettin (= Szczecin)
    b. Regierungsbezirk Koeslin (= Koszalin)
    c. Regierungsbezirk Schneidemuehl (= Pila)

at: Landesausgleichsamt Schleswig-Holstein, Meesenring 9, D–2400 Luebeck, Germany.

7.4 *Historical Associations*

    a. Gesellschaft fuer pommersche Geschichte, Altertumskunde und Kunst (Society for Pomeranian history, science of antiquity and art)
       Dr. Berger, Farinastrasse 42, D–3110 Uelzen, Germany.

    b. Historische Kommission fuer Pommern (Historical commission for Pomerania)
       Rotenberg 16, D–3550 Marburg/Lahn, Germany.

7.5 *Church Institutions*

Konvent ev. Gemeinden aus Pommern (Community of Protestant parishes from Pomerania)
Dudenweg 9, D–4770 Soest, Germany.

8. **Other Hints**

Information available for:

Kreis (County) Regenswalde and Naugard: R. Koehler, Ob.-Rg.-Rt., Septimer Strasse 37, D–1000 Berlin, Germany.

Kreise Greifenberg and Cammin: Hildegard Brehmer, Im Langenfeld, D–3014 Laatzen, Germany.

Kreis Demmin and Western Pomerania (Vorpommern): Dr. Max Bruhn, see this section 2.1.

Deutsches Geschlechterbuch (Book of German Genealogy), vols. 4, 9, 67, 90, 115, 136, 137, 145, 172, the 10th Pomeranian volume is in preparation.

4. **EAST BRANDENBURG (= BRANDENBURG-OST)**

Map 14

"The Land east of the Oder" was called the Neumark (New Mark) (in contrast to the Altmark – Old Mark) since the 15th century. In 1815 the Neumark became a part of the Prussian province of Brandenburg excluding portions of Dramburg and Schivelbein, which were ceded to Pomerania. In 1938 the counties of Arnswalde and Friedeberg Nm. were taken out of the Regierungsbezirk (administrative district) of Frankfurt/Oder and added to Pomerania, the districts of Meseritz and Schwerin came to the province of Brandenburg.

1. **Research Areas**

Brandenburg (East). Portions of Regierungsbezirk Frankfurt/Oder of the Prussian province of Brandenburg situated east of the Oder-Neisse-Line, with the following counties of Neumark and Lower Lusatia:

Forst (Lusatia), Frankfurt (Oder), Guben, Landsberg (Warthe), Crossen (Oder), Koenigsberg (Neumark), Lebus, Meseritz, Oststernberg, Schwerin (Warthe), Soldin, Sorau (Lusatia), Weststernberg, Zuellichau-Schwiebus

according to the administrative division of May 8, 1945 and before.

Map 15

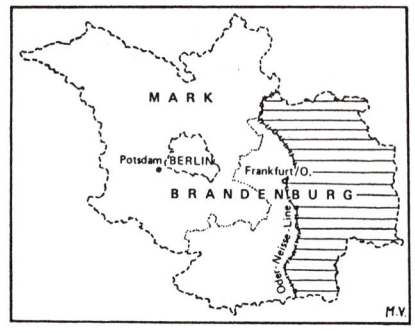

Partition of Brandenburg 1945

Map 16

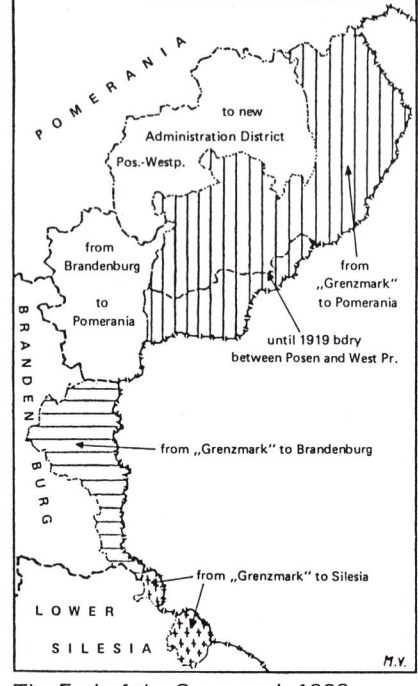

The End of the Grenzmark 1938

Map 17

2. **Genealogical Institutions**

2.1 *Present institutions*

Forschungsstelle Ostbrandenburg-Neumark of AGoFF (Research center East Brandenburg-Neumark of AGoFF)

Director: Dipl.-Ing. Alfred Bley, Im Langewann 65, D–6940 Weinheim-Lü., Germany, Ph. 062 01–5 36 44.

2.2 *Former institutions*

Verein fuer Geschichte der Neumark (Gegr. 1890) (Society for history of the Neumark, est. 1890), Abteilung Familienforschung (department genealogy est. 1933), Landsberg (Warthe).

Publications and periodicals:

"Der Neumaerker", bulletins of genealogy in Neumark, information of the Verein fuer Geschichte of Neumark, supplement to "Die Neumark", vol. I and II, 1933 to 1942, vol. III, 1943.

Sources:

Ahnenlisten mit Ahnenreihen aus der Neumark (Pedigrees of Neumark), vol. I, R. Schmilling, Landsberg (Warthe) 1938.

Neumaerkisches Geschlechterbuch (Deutsches Geschlechterbuch vol. 93) (Genealogies of Neumark) (German Genealogies).

These publications are held by Buecherei des Deutschen Ostens in Herne, Germany as well as by the Bibliothek des Germanischen Nationalmuseums, D–8500 Nuernberg, Germany.

Special institutions:
The library of Verein fuer Geschichte der Neumark with about 12.000 volumes in Landsberg (Warthe) perished in 1945.

3. Documents of Vital Statistics

3.1 *Books and records of vital statistics*

See listings in Section "A" 3.1.
Vital statistics information which survived is found in Polish state archives.

3.2 *Church records*

See listings in Section "A" 3.2.
Paul Schwartz: Die Kirchenbuecher der Mark Brandenburg, vol. 1, Landsberg 1900.

3.3 *Church records in homeland*

Church records which survived are found in Polish state archives or at the office of the Roman catholic parish in question.

4. Gazetteers

4.1 *Published after 1945*

See Section "A" 4.1.

4.2 *Published before 1945*

See Section "A" 4.2.

4.3 *Landed Estate Directories*

The Buecherei des Bundesministeriums fuer Ernaehrung, Landwirtschaft und Forsten, Rochusstrasse 1, D–5300 Bonn-Duisdorf, Germany, holds:

Paul Niekammer: Gueteradressbuch der Provinz Brandenburg (Directory of landed estates of the Province of Brandenburg), Stettin, Germany 1907, 2nd edition of same Leipzig, Germany 1914.

Landwirtschaftliches Adressbuch der Rittergueter, Gueter und Hoefe der Provinz Brandenburg (Agricultural directory of knights landed estates, landed estates and farms in the Province of Brandenburg), Verlag von Niekammer's Adressbuechern GmbH, Leipzig, Germany 1929.

5. **Bibliographies and Literature**

   See Section "A" 5.

   a. Landesgeschichtliche Vereinigung fuer die Mark Brandenburg (State historical society of Mark Brandenburg) e. V. (est. 1884) with its own library.
   Secretary: Hans Axtheim, Britzer Damm 23, D–1000 Berlin 47, Germany.

   Publications and periodicals:

   Mitteilungsblatt und Jahrbuch fuer Brandenburgische Landesgeschichte (Information bulletin and yearbook of Brandenburg local history).

   b. Institut fuer Geschichte an der Deutschen Demokratischen Akademie der Wissenschaften zu Berlin (Ost) (Institute for history at the German Democratic Academy of Sciences in Berlin (East).

   Publications and periodicals:

   Schriften des Instituts fuer Geschichte, Reihe II (Writings of the Institute for history, series II): Landesgeschichte (Local history) vol. 6.

   Bibliographie zur Geschichte der Mark Brandenburg und der Stadt Berlin 1941–1956 (Bibliography of history of Mark Brandenburg und the City of Berlin 1941–1956), Akademie-Verlag Berlin (DDR), 1961.

   Bibliographie zur Geschichte der Mark Brandenburg (Bibliography of history of Mark Brandenburg) section 1 ff.

   Veroeffentlichungen des Staatsarchivs Potsdam, DDR (Publications of the state archives at Potsdam, DDR), Weimar, 110 ff., vol. 8 and others, Hans-Joachim Schrekkenbach.

   c. R. Lehmann: Bibliographie zur Geschichte der Niederlausitz (bis 1926) (Bibliography of history of Lower Lusatia) (prior to 1926), published in: Veroeffentlichungen der Hist. Komm. f. d. Provinz Brandenburg und die Reichshauptstadt Berlin II (Publications of the historical commission of the Province of Brandenburg and the capital city of Berlin) and Brandenburgische Bibliographien (Brandenburg bibliographies) vol. 3, Berlin 1928.

   d. R. Lehmann: Bibliographie zur Geschichte der Niederlausitz (Bibliography of history of Lower Lusatia) vol. 2 (1926–1945 and supplements), Boehlau-Verlag, Muenster-Koeln, Germany 1954, published in: Mitteldeutsche Forschungen (Central German research), published by: Reinhold Olesch, Walter Schlesinger, Ludwig Erich Schmidt, vol. 2.

   e. Writings, bulletins and yearbooks "Die Neumark" of Verein fuer Geschichte der Neumark (Gegr. 1890) may be found at Buecherei des deutschen Ostens in Herne, Germany and Bibliothek des Germanischen Nationalmuseums in Nuernberg, Germany, see also this section 2.2.

   f. Buecherei des deutschen Ostens, Catalog, Herne 1973, pages 246–258; new edition, vol. 2, Herne 1982, pages 1–69.

6. **Archives and Libraries with Sources of Homeland Regions**

6.1 *In West Germany – Federal Republic of Germany including West Berlin*
See Section "A" 6.1.

6.2 *In Central Germany – German Democratic Republic (DDR) including East Berlin*
See Section "A" 6.2.

6.3 *In homeland territory*
  a. With jurisdiction over the counties of Frankfurt/Oder, Landsberg/Warthe, Lebus, Meseritz, Schwerin/Warthe, Soldin, Weststernberg:

  Wojewódzkie Archiwum Państwowe, Gorzow Wielkopolski, Poland (Public state archives at Gorzow Wielkopolski – formerly Landsberg/Warthe).

  b. With jurisdiction over the county of Koenigsberg (Nm): Wojewódzkie Archiwum Państwowe, Szczecin (Stettin), Poland.

  c. With jurisdiction over the counties of Forst (Lausatia), Crossen/Oder, Guben, Oststernberg, Sorau (Lausatia), Zuellichau-Schwiebus: Wojewódzkie Archiwum Państwowe, Zielona Gora (Gruenberg in Silesia), Poland.

  Inventory information: Guide to Polish Archives for Landsberg/Warthe: pages 652–660. For Gruenberg in Silesia: pages 641–648.

  For use of archives see Section "A" 8.2.

7. **Other Research Aids**

7.1 *Hometown/Village directories*
  a. Heimatortskartei Mark Brandenburg (Hometown/village directory for Mark Brandenburg
  Postfach 101420, Auf dem Kreuz 41, D–8900 Augsburg, Germany, Ph. 0821–3156236.

  b. Zentralkartei fuer Stadt- und Landkreis Landsberg/Warthe (General directory for the county of Landsberg/Warthe)
  Irma Krueger, Neuendorfer Strasse 83, D–1000 Berlin 20, Germany.

  c. Heimatkreiskartei fuer Stadt- und Landkreis Koenigsberg (Nm) (Home county directory for the county of Koenigsberg (Nm), City of Braunschweig,
  Eiermarkt 6, D–3300 Braunschweig, Germany.

  d. Zentralkartei fuer Stadt- und Landkreis Sorau (General directory for the county of Sorau)
  Guenther Krause, Osterymweg 3, D–4600 Dortmund 13, Germany.

7.2 *Societies*
Landsmannschaft Berlin-Mark Brandenburg (Society of Germans from Berlin-Mark Brandenburg), Federal business office: Schloss-Strasse 92, D–7000 Stuttgart 1, Germany.

7.3 *Other places*

Heimatauskunftsstelle Regierungsbezirk Frankfurt/Oder (Homeland information center administrative district Frankfurt/Oder) at Landesausgleichsamt Niedersachsen Schoenworth 7, D–3000 Hannover, Germany.

7.4 *Historical Associations*

a. Landesgeschichtliche Vereinigung fuer die Mark Brandenburg (Local historical society of Mark Brandenburg) e. V. (est. 1884) with its own library.
Secretary: Hans Axtheim, Britzer Damm 23, D–1000 Berlin 47, Germany.

Publications and periodicals:

Mitteilungen und Jahrbuecher fuer Brandenburgische Landesgeschichte (Bulletins and yearbooks of Brandenburg local history).

b. Historische Kommission fuer Berlin und die Mark Brandenburg (Historical commission of Berlin and Mark Brandenburg), Kirchwegg 33, D–1000 Berlin 38, Germany.

c. Institut fuer Geschichte an der Deutschen Akademie der Wissenschaften in Berlin (Ost).

d. Bundesarbeitsgemeinschaft Landsberg/Warthe Stadt und Land (Federal research group for Landsberg/Warthe – city and county)
Waldweg 30, D–3101 Hambuehren, Germany.

Publications:

Schriftenreihe der Bundesarbeitsgemeinschaft Landsberg/Warthe Stadt und Land (Publications of the Federal research group of Landsberg/Warthe), Landsberg an der Warthe (Landsberg on Warthe) 1257–1945–1976, 1978, 1980, city and county during the turmoils of history, culture and society over the centuries, agriculture, industry, trades, traffic and administration. Published by Hans Beske and Ernst Handke, editor Karin Bader, Verlag Ernst und Werner Gieseking, Bielefeld, Germany, 3 volumes*)

e. Special institutions

Heimatstube Landsberg/Warthe (Homeland room) with library at Herforder Haus, Elisabethstrasse 9, D–4900 Herford, Germany.

Heimatkreis Koenigsberg (Nm) (Home county Koenigsberg (Nm)), Kreuzstrasse 97, D–3300 Braunschweig, Germany.

Heimatkreis Schwerin (Warthe) (Home county Schwerin), Mittelstrasse 9, D–4320 Hattingen (Ruhr).

Publications:

Kreiskalender fuer den Heimatkreis Koenigsberg-Neumark (County calendar of the home county of Koenigsberg-Neumark), Publisher: Otto Meyer, Kreuzstrasse 97/IV, D–3300 Braunschweig, Germany*.

* at the Buecherei des Deutschen Ostens in Herne, Germany.

7.5 *Church institutions*

Hilfskomitee fuer die ostbrandenburgischen Kirchengemeinden (Relief society for East Brandenburg parishes), Neuendorfer Strasse 83, D–1000 Berlin 20 (Spandau), Germany.

Periodical:

Heimatblatt der ehem. Kirchengemeinden Landsberg/Warthe (Homeland bulletin of former Landsberg/Warthe parishes).

8. **Special Hints**

Genealogical research is particularly difficult in this area, because vital statistics, archival sources and libraries were largely destroyed, and research is expensive. – See Section "A" 8.

Sources:
Ahnenlisten mit Ahnenreihen aus der Neumark, Band 1, R. Schmilling, Landsberg/Warthe, 1938.

Neumaerkisches Geschlechterbuch (Deutsches Geschlechterbuch Band 93).

Publications, Periodicals and Sources are held bei Buecherei des deutschen Ostens in Herne, in Bibliothek der Stiftung Haus des deutschen Ostens in Duesseldorf as well as in Bibliothek des Germanischen Nationalmuseums in Nuernberg.

5. SILESIA, LOWER AND UPPER SILESIA (= SCHLESIEN)

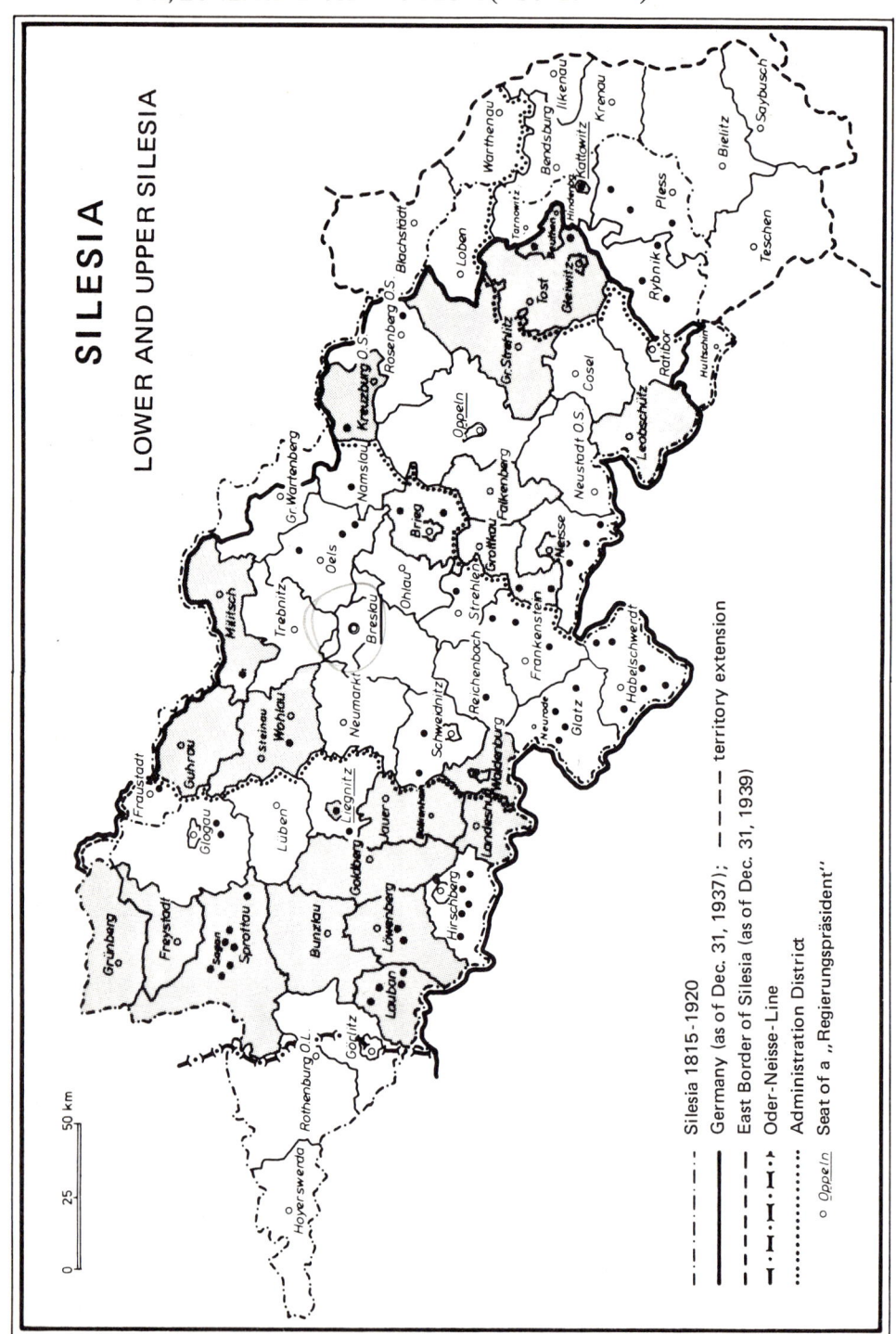

Map 18

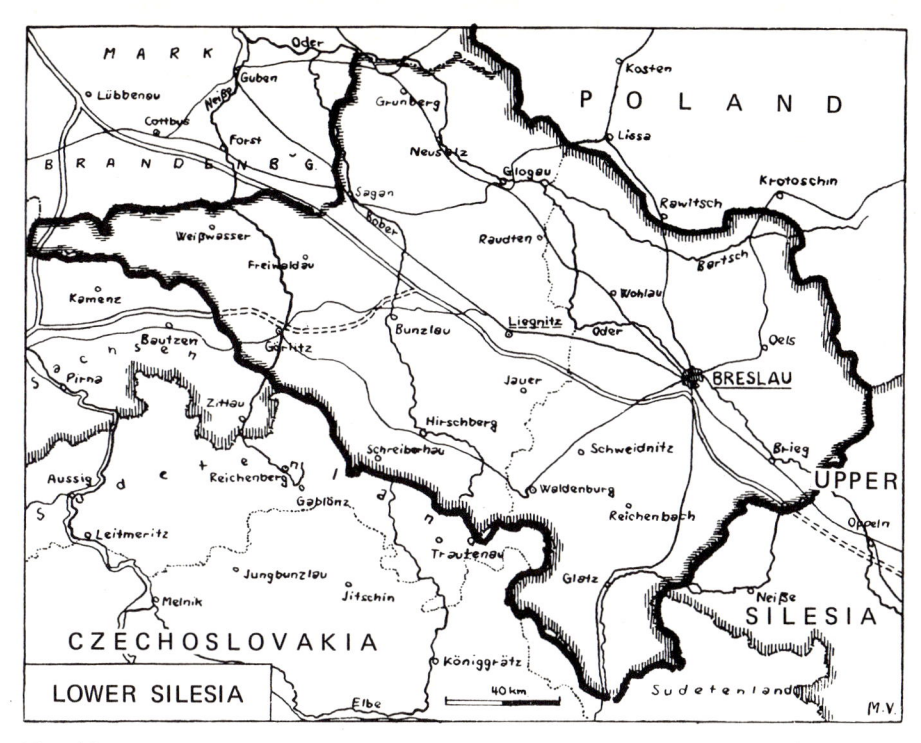

Map 19

The borders of the Prussian province of Silesia (Pol. Slask) remained generally unchanged during the administrative reforms of 1815 and 1919. On October 14, 1919 the Prussian State Assembly, in response to Polish demands for greater autonomy for Upper Silesia, decided to divide the province into the province of Upper Silesia, with the Regierungsbezirk (Administrative district) Oppeln, and Lower Silesia, with the Regierungsbezirk Liegnitz and Breslau. After the Treaty of Versailles Silesia lost in 1920 parts of the counties of Guhrau, Militsch, Gross Wartenberg, and Namslau to Poland and the Hultschin Region of the county of Ratibor to newly created Czechoslovakia. After the referendum of March 20, 1920 and the following decision of partition by the Allied Powers, the counties of Kattowitz, Koenigshuette, Pless and Rybnik as a whole and the counties of Beuthen, Hindenburg (Upper Silesia), Lublinitz, Ratibor, Tarnowitz and Tost-Gleiwitz became part of Poland on July 15, 1922.

In 1938 the Prussian provinces of Lower and Upper Silesia again were united to form the province of Silesia. After the partition of Poland by Germany and the Soviet Union in 1939 and after the military occupation of Poland, the newly created Regierungsbezirk Kattowitz was added to Silesia. This united the territories ceded in 1921 (without the county of Loben), the counties of historical "Congress Poland" (Blachstedt, Warthenau, Bendsburg, Ilkenau und Krenau) and the Teschen-Region of former Czechoslovakia. On April 1, 1941 the province of Silesia again was divided.

The portion of the province of Silesia west of the Lusatian Neisse River (Upper Lusatia) now belongs to the German Democratic Republic (DDR).

1. **Research Areas**

   The Prussian provinces of Lower Silesia and Upper Silesia excluding the regions west of the Neisse River and Austro-Silesia.

2. **Genealogical Institutions**

   2.1 *Present institutions*

   Forschungsstelle Schlesien der AGoFF (Research center Silesia of the AGoff)
   Director: Neithard von Stein, Suedweg 137, D–3064 Bad Eilsen, Germany, Ph. 05722–83 81, 05722–84 349.

   2.2 *Former institutions*

   a. Niederschlesische Arbeitsgemeinschaft fuer Familienkunde, name was changed several times, last to Arbeitsgemeinschaft fuer schlesische Sippenkunde (research group for Silesian genealogy) (AGSS).

      Periodical: Der Schlesische Familienforscher, 1930–1944 (The Silesian Genealogist). This periodical is available at the Research Center (see 2.1) and at Buecherei des deutschen Ostens in Herne, Germany (see Section "A" 6.3).

      In volume 4 of "Der Schluessel" (The Key) the periodicals "Der Schlesische Familienforscher" 1930–1944 and "Der Sippenforscher" (The Genealogist) 1934–1939, supplements to the "Schlesische Zeitung" (Silesian Newspaper), are indexed.

   b. Arbeitsgemeinschaft fuer Familienforschung Liegnitz

   c. Deutscher Kulturbund fuer Polnisch-Schlesien (research group for genealogy Liegnitz, German cultural society for Polish-Silesia), Kattowitz.

      Periodical: Der Kulturwart mit Familienkundlicher Suchecke (The culture warden with genealogical query corner).

   d. Sippenkundliche Arbeitsgemeinschaft Beuthen OS (Genealogical research group Beuthen, Upper Silesia).

   e. Sippenkundlicher Verein Bunzlau (Genealogical society Bunzlau).

   f. Verein fuer Familienforschung Friedeberg a. Qu. (Society for genealogy Friedeberg on Queis) (Branch of AGSS).

   g. Sippenkundlicher Landesverein fuer die Gesamtlausitz, Goerlitz (Local genealogical society for all of Lusatia)

      Periodicals:

      Der Familienforscher in der Oberlausitz, Oberlausitzer sippenkundliche Beitraege (The genealogist in Upper Lusatia, Upper Lusatian contributions).

   h. Neisser Arbeitsgemeinschaft fuer Sippenforschung Oppeln (Neisse research group of genealogy in Oppeln).

   i. Sippenforschungsstelle Oberschlesien in Ratibor (Genealogical research center Upper Silesia in Ratibor).

   k. Arbeitsgemeinschaft fuer Familienforschung in Reichenbach (Eulengebirge) (research group of genealogy in Reichenbach, Owl Mountains).

3. **Documents of Vital Statistics**

3.1 *Books and records of vital statistics*

See listings in Section "A" 3.1 a, b.

In homeland region:

The preserved books of vital statistics of Breslau are held at Urzad Stanu Cywilnego Archiwum, Wrocław, ul. Wlodkowica 21–22, Poland (Civil registry office).

3.2 *Displaced church records*

See listings in Section "A" 3.2.

3.3 *Church records in homeland regions*

    a. Archivum Panstwowe Miasto Wrocławia i Wojewodztwa Wrocławskiego (State archives of the City and administrative district of Wrocław-Breslau), Wrocław, ul. Pomorska 2, Poland.

    Besides holding the preserved archival materials, several church records are also held.

    b. Archiwum Archidiecezjalne (Archives of the archidiocese), Wrocław, ul. Kanonia 12, Poland.

    Held are several church records mentioned in the handbook — see "A" 3.2 b — particularly those which had been moved there previously and those of the Roman Catholic churches of the City of Breslau (= Wrocław).

    Roman Catholic church records of the diocese of Breslau are mostly available. The diocese archives are currently collecting all R. C. church records prior to 1900, in order to have all records of this diocese centrally located. Other dioceses are planning or have begun similar projects.

    At the Buecherei des deutschen Ostens, in Herne, Germany (see Section "A" 6.3) and the Forschungsstelle Schlesien (see 2.1) one can find Randt/Swientek: "Die aeltesten Personenstandsregister Schlesiens" (The oldest vital statistic registers of Silesia), an index of Protestant and Roman Catholic church records located in Silesia **in the year 1937.**

    c. Eberlein-Jungnitz: Die Kirchenbuecher Schlesiens beider Konfessionen, Breslau 1902.

4. **Gazetteers**

4.1 *Published after 1945*

See Section "A" 4.1.

4.2 *Published before 1945*

See Section "A" 4.2.

Schlesisches Ortschaftsverzeichnis, Breslau 1893.

4.3 *Landed Estate Directories*

The Library of Bundesministerium fuer Ernaehrung, Landwirtschaft und Forsten Rochusstrasse 1, D–5300 Bonn-Duisdorf, holds:

Schlesisches Gueteradressbuch, 8th, 11th, 12th, 14th, 15th edition (Silesian directory of landed estates), Verlag Wilhelm Gottlieb Korn, Breslau, Germany.

Amtliches Gueteradressbuch fuer die Provinz Oberschlesien (Official directory of landed estates for Upper Silesia), Ratibor, Germany 1930.

H. Wehner: Landwirtschaftliches Adressbuch der Rittergueter, Gueter und groesseren Hoefe der Provinz Schlesien (Agricultural directory of knights landed estates, landed estates and larger farms in the Province of Silesia), Reichenbach'sche Verlagsbuchhandlung, Leipzig, Germany 1921.

5. **Bibliographies and Literature**

See Section "A" 5.

    a. Geschichte Schlesiens (History of Silesia), published by Historische Kommission fuer Schlesien (Historical commission for Silesia).
        vol. 1: Von der Urzeit bis zum Jahre 1526 (From antiquity to 1526), 3rd edition, Stuttgart, Germany 1961.
        vol. 2: Die Habsburgerzeit 1526 bis 1740 (The time of the Habsburgers 1526 to 1740), Darmstadt, Germany 1973.

    b. Elisabeth Friedrichs: Schlesische Lebensbilder (Silesian biographies), 5 volumes and index, Neustadt/Aisch, Germany 1971.

    c. O. K. Kowallis: A Genealogical Guide and Atlas of Silesia, Everton Publishers, Logan, Utah, 84321, U. S. A.

    d. Buecherei des deutschen Ostens, Catalog, Herne 1973, pages 286–468; new edition, vol. 3, Herne 1983.

6. **Archives and Libraries with Sources of Homeland Regions**

6.1 *In West Germany – Federal Republic of Germany including West Berlin*

See Section "A" 6.1.

Bundesarchiv – Abt. Ostarchiv – (Federal Archives – dept. Eastern Archives), Am Woellershof 12, D–5400 Koblenz, Germany.

Among the inventories are microfilms of Jewish parishes in Silesia and films of card index of Liegnitz residents.

6.2 *In Austria*

Maehrisch-Schlesisches Heimatmuseum (Silesian Homeland museum), Schiesstattgasse, Rostockvilla, A–3400 Klosterneuburg, Austria.

This museum deals with the collection of Silesian homeland treasures of the Habsburg period – including literature.

Archival material from before 1740, when Silesia was part of Austria, are probably held in Vienna archives. Addresses can be found in Taschenbuch fuer Familiengeschichtsforschung (Pocketbook for family history research), Neustadt/Aisch, Germany 1975, page 398, and 1980.

6.3 *In homeland territory*

Breslau (= Wrocław)

Archiwum Pánstwowe Miasto Wrocławia i Wojewodztwa Wrocławskiego, (see 3.3), ul. Pomorska 2, Wrocław, Poland.

Gruenberg (= Zielona Gora)

Wojewódzkie Archiwum Pánstwowe w Zielonej Gorze, Stary Kiselin 31, Zielona Gora, Poland (District state archives in Gruenberg = Zielona Gora).

Oppeln (= Opole)

Wojewódzkie Archiwum Pánstwowe w Oplu, ul. Zamkowa 2, Opole, Poland (District state archives in Oppeln/Opole).

Kattowitz (= Katowice)

Wojewodzkie Archiwum Panstwowe w Katowicach, ul. Jagiellonska 25, Katowice, Poland (District state archives in Kattowitz/Katowice).

Inventory information:	Guide to Polish Archives (see "A" 8.2):	
	for Breslau/Wrocław	pages 589–640
	for Gruenberg/Zielona Gora	pages 641–668
	for Oppeln/Opole	pages 431–436
	for Kattowitz/Katowice	pages 183–232

7. Other Research Aids

7.1 *Hometown/village directories*

Heimatortskartei – Abt. Niederschlesien (Hometown/village directory – section Lower Silesia)
Postfach 2187, Luitpoldstrasse 16, D–8600 Bamberg, Germany, Ph. 0951– 26 716.

Heimatortskartei – Abt. Oberschlesien-Breslau (. . . section Upper Silesia-Breslau)
Steinweg 2, D–8390 Passau, Germany, Ph. 0857–34 011.

7.2 *Society of Silesians*

a. Landsmannschaft Schlesien, Nieder- und Oberschlesien e.V. (Society of Silesians), Bundesgeschaeftsfuehrung, Haus Schlesien, Heisterbacherrott, D–5330 Koenigswinter 41, Germany.

Periodical: Der Schlesier (The Silesian).

b. Landsmannschaft der Oberschlesier (Society of Upper Silesians), Bahnhofstrasse 67–69, D–4030 Ratingen 6 (Hösel), Germany.

Periodical: Unser Oberschlesien (Our Upper Silesia).

7.3 *Homeland information centers*

a. Regierungsbezirk Breslau (Administrative district Breslau) (without city and county of Breslau).

b. City and county of Breslau.

c. Regierungsbezirk Liegnitz (including county of Fraustadt and parts of the county of Zittau east of the Neisse River).

   for all above at Landesausgleichsamt Niedersachsen
   Schoenworth 7, D–3000 Hannover, Germany.

   d. Regierungsbezirk Oppeln (including Hultschin Region and excluding the industrial area of Western Upper Silesia).

   e. Industrial area of Western Upper Silesia, with cities of Beuthen, Gleiwitz, Hindenburg and counties of Beuthen-Tarnowitz and Tost-Gleiwitz.

   f. Industrial area of Eastern Upper Silesia, Regierungsbezirk Kattowitz including counties of Bielitz, Chrzanow (Krenau), Olkusz (Ilkenau), Sosnowiec (Sosnowitz), Bedzin (Bendsburg), Blachownia (Blachstedt), Zawiercie (Warthenau), Saybusch, Teschen und Olsa Region.

   for above at Landesausgleichsamt Nordrhein-Westfalen
   Bankstrasse 1, D–4000 Duesseldorf, Germany.

7.4 *Historical Associations*

   a. Historische Kommission fuer Schlesien (Historical commission for Silesia)
   Am Weisel 42 II, D–6500 Mainz 21, Germany.

   b. Stiftung Kulturwerk Schlesien (Cultural foundation Silesia), Sitz Wuerzburg, Postfach 32, Kardinal-Doepfnerplatz 1, D–8700 Wuerzburg, Germany.

   Periodical:
   Schlesien (Silesia), quarterly for art, science and ethnic studies (Lower, Upper and Sudeten Silesia).

7.5 *Church institutions*

   a. Gemeinschaft evangelischer Schlesier (Hilfskommission) (Union of Protestant Silesians) (Relief society) e. V., Meesenring 15, D–2400 Luebeck 1, Germany.

   Periodical: Schlesischer Gottesfreund (Silesian friend of God).

   b. Heimatwerk schlesischer Katholiken (Homeland work of Silesian Catholics), Stresemannstrasse 21, D–4000 Duesseldorf 1, Germany.

   Periodical: Heimatbrief der Katholiken des Erzbistums Breslau (Homeland bulletin of Catholics of the Archdiocese Breslau).

   c. Verein fuer Schlesische Kirchengeschichte (Society for Silesian church history), Siplingerstrasse 5, D–8972 Sonthofen, Germany.

   Periodical: Jahrbuch fuer Schlesische Kirchengeschichte (Yearbook for Silesian church history) (volume 56 published in 1977).

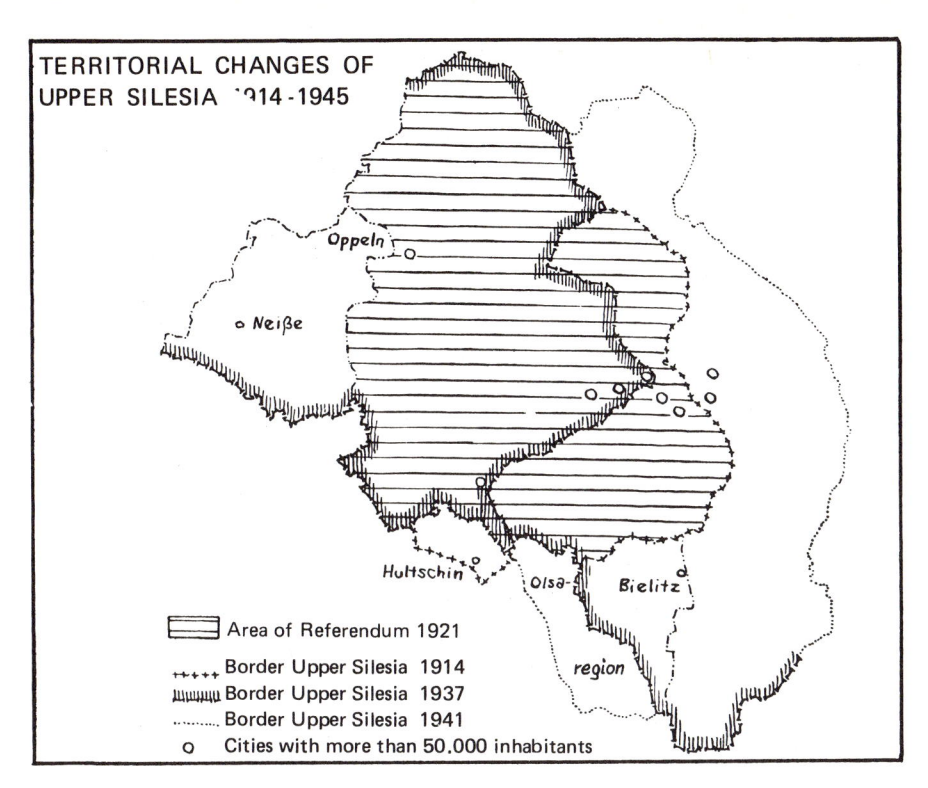

Map 20

8. **Other Hints**

   Deutsches Geschlechterbuch (Book of German Genealogy), volumes 73, 112, 153 and 175 (Erstes, Zweites, Drittes und Viertes Schlesisches Geschlechterbuch – first, second, third and fourth Silesian book of genealogy), (with Western Upper Silesian part of former county of Tarnowtz).

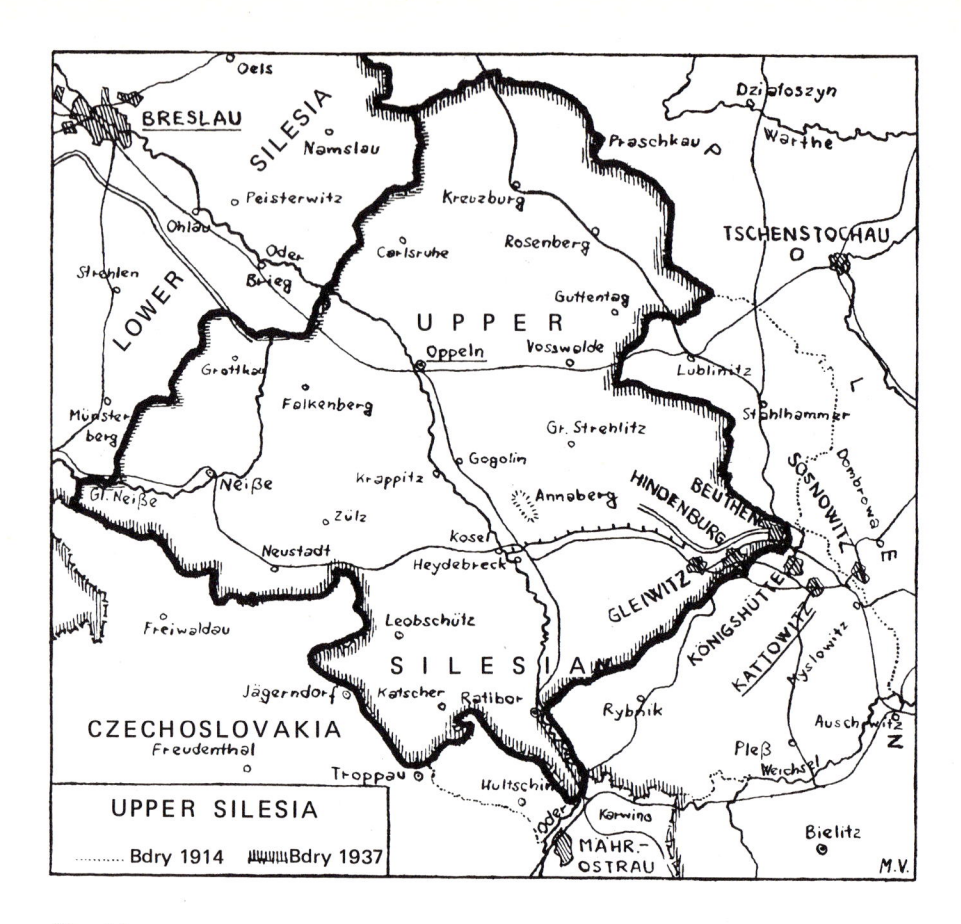

Map 21

6. POSEN (= POZNAN)

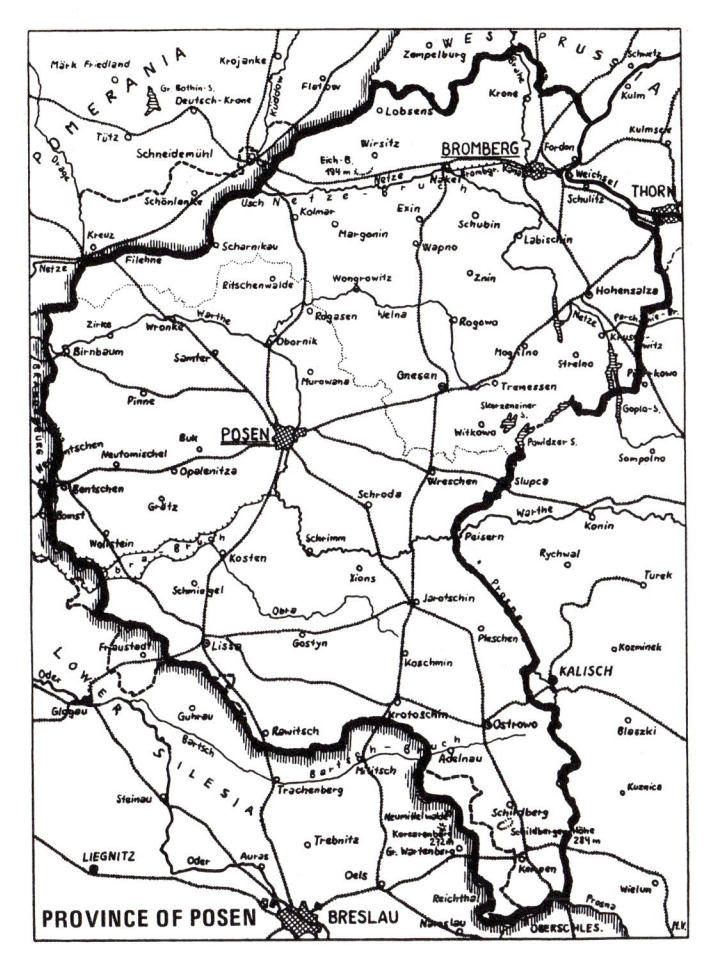

Map 22

In 1815 that part of Poland, which between 1793 and 1807 had been under Prussian rule, was returned to Prussia as "Grand Duchy of Posen" after the Congress of Vienna. Since 1850 Provinz Posen was the core territory of historical Greater Poland. With the exeption of the counties of Fraustadt, Meseritz and Schwerin (Warthe), which were added to Grenzmark (Border territory) Posen-West Prussia, all of the province of Posen was ceded to Poland in 1920. In 1939 Reichsgau (administrative district) Posen, later named Reichsgau Wartheland, was formed of the ceded territory and of several counties of "Congress Poland". The counties of Wirsitz and Bromberg were added to "Reichsgau Danzig-West Prussia". Posen was part of South Prussia in 1793–1807.

POSENER LAND

```
Border of province Posen 1818-1918
Border of „Deutsches Reich" 1920-1939
Border of „Reichsgau Posen (Wartheland)" 1939-1945
Administration District
```

Map 23

1. **Research Areas**

   Prussian province of Posen (prior to 1920) (1939 to 1945 Reichsgau Wartheland).

   Netze River district (1772 to 1807–1815) with the counties of Bromberg, Schubin, Wirsitz, Kolmar, Czarnikau, Filehne and Hohensalza.

2. Genealogical Institutions

2.1 *Present institutions*

Forschungsstelle Posen der AGoFF (Research center Posen) of AGoFF. **Director: Otto Firchau, Nachtigallenweg 6, D–4902 Bad Salzuflen, Germany, Ph. 05222–13 661.** Director for family research for the province of Posen and Germans in Poland of Forschungsstelle Ostmitteleuropra (research center East Central Europe) in the state of Nordrhein-Westfalen.

2.2 *Former institutions*

Historische Gesellschaft im Wartheland, Posen (Historical society in Wartheland, Posen).

Series of publications:

Deutsche Sippenforschung in Polen (German genealogy in Poland), later Deutsche Sippenforschung im Osten (German genealogy in the East), new series. Publisher: Dr. Alfred Lattermann, Posen.

Unsere Heimat (Our Homeland), Publisher: K. Lueck and A. Lattermann.

3. Documents of Vital Statistics

3.1 *Books and records of vital statistics*

See listings in Section "A" 3.1.

3.2 *Displaced church records*

See listings in Section "A" 3.2.

Photocopies of the church records of the Roman Catholic parish of Bromberg (Bydgoszcz) 1648 to 1772, with baptisms and marriages of Protestants are held at the Research Center Posen, see 2.1 above.

3.3 *Church records in homeland*

See Section "A" 3.3.

Meyer: Die Kirchenbuecher im Regierungsbezirk Bromberg (in: Jahrbuch der Historischen Gesellschaft des Netzedistriktes, 1898).

H. Freiherr von Cornberg: Die Kirchenbuecher der evangelischen Kirche der Provinz Grenzmark Posen-Westpreussen, Schoenlanke 1934.

W. Volkmann: Die Kirchenbuecher der katholischen Pfarreien in der frueheren Provinz Grenzmark Posen-Westpreussen, Schneidemuehl 1939.

4. **Gazetteers**

4.1 *Published after 1945*

See listings in Section "A" 4.1.

4.2 *Published before 1945*

See listings in Section "A" 4.2.

Verzeichnis saemtlicher Ortschaften der Provinz Posen (Gazetteer of the province of Posen), Berlin 1907, 172 pages.

Verzeichnis aller Ortschaften des Bromberger Regierungsbezirks (Gazetteer of the administrative district of Bromberg), Bromberg 1833, 164 pages.

Ortsverzeichnis der Provinz Posen (Gazetteer of the province of Posen) 1900, held at the Research Center Posen, see 2.1 above (LDS Film Nr. 476, 277).

Baeck: Die Provinz Posen in geographischer, statistischer und topographischer Beziehung, Berlin 1847.

Gemeindelexikon der Provinz Posen, Berlin 1888.

Kirstein: Handbuch des Grundbesitzes in der Provinz Posen, Berlin 1895.

Verzeichnis saemtlicher Ortschaften des Reg. Bez. Posen, Posen 1845.

5. **Selective Bibliography and Literature**

5.1 *Published after 1945*

Wartheland-Nachrichten (Wartheland-News); Publisher: Landsmannschaft Wartheland im Berliner Landesverband der Vertriebenen (Society of Warthelanders in the Berlin State Association of Expellees) e. V., Stresemannstrasse 90–102, D–1000 Berlin 61, Germany. 23 yearly volumes published to date. Published twice a month.

Jahrbuch Weichsel-Warthe (Yearbook Vistula-Warta); Publisher: Landsmannschaft Weichsel-Warthe, Bundesverband (Society of Vistula Warthelanders, Federal association) e. V., Koenigswoerther Strasse 2, D–3000 Hannover, Germany.

Der Kulturwart, Beitraege zur deutsch-polnischen Nachbarschaft (The Warden Culture, contributions to German-Polish neighbourhood); publisher: same as Jahrbuch Weichsel-Warthe above; present editor: Albert Rentz, Postfach 531, D–4410 Warendorf (Westf.), Germany.

Altburgunder Heimatbote – Schubiner Kreisblatt (Oldburgundian Homeland Messenger – publication of the county of Schubin); 24th annual volume is being published by: Verlag Heimatkreis Altburgund (Schubin) e. V., editor: Willy Eilmes, D–3101 Mueden/Oertze, Germany, supplement: Altburgunder Familienarchiv (Oldburgundian family archives).

Birnbaum Jahreshefte (Birnbaum year books). To date 5 editions with genealogical material have been published. Available from: Mrs. Kate Heening, Gartenweg 2, D–3005 Hemmingen 1, Germany.

Verzeichnis des deutschsprachigen Schrifttums ueber das Bromberger Land (Index of writings on the Bromberg region); Bidegast-Vereinigung 1977, editor: Hans Juergen Grund, Oberbilker Allee 57, D–4000 Duesseldorf 1, Germany.

Bromberg, published three times a year, Bidegast-Vereinigung e. V., editors: Hans Juergen Grund, Oberbilker Allee 57, D–4000 Duesseldorf 1, Germany, and Gerhard Ohlhoff, D–4502 Bad Rothenfelde, Germany.

Bromberg, Ein Buch der Erinnerung (Bromberg, a book of remembrance), with maps of surroundings of 1772 and county. Articles of Bromberg's past, a chronicle, 553 pages. Publisher: Bidegast-Vereinigung e. V. 1973.

Verlag Boehlau GmbH, Postfach 60 01 80, D–5000 Koeln 60, Germany has published "Die Plankammer der Regierung Bromberg" (The maps chamber of the government of Bromberg) Spezialinventar 1772–1912 (Special inventory 1772–1912). This publication contains a wealth of information for local, colonization and family history. Cologne 1978.

Czarnikau; 2 volumes; available from: LWW-Berlin, Wilhelm Luening, Harzer Strasse 32, D–1000 Berlin 44, Germany.

Eichenbruck-Wongrowitz: Heimatbuch (chronicle); available from: Heinrich Gabbert, Am Raden 3, D–3141 Wendisch Evern, Germany.

Exin 1262–1962; Eine Festschrift (An anniversary publication); 160 pages with map. Publisher: Heimatkreis Schubin, Bergen.

Hermstal Heimatbuch (Hermstal chronicle).

Kolmarer Heimatbrief (Kolmar Bulletin). 12 bulletins have been published so far. Publisher: Heimatkreisgemeinschaft Kolmar; editor: Arthur Schuetz, Gantesweilerstrasse 13, D–4230 Wesel 1, Germany.

"Antlitz und Geschichte des Kreises Kolmar/Posen" (Face and history of the county of Kolmar/Posen), a chronicle; publisher: Heimatkreis Kolmar.

Margonin-Heimatbuch (Margonin chronicle).

Obornik – Eine koenigliche Stadt an der Warthe (Obornik – A royal city on Warta River); publisher: Landsmannschaft Weichsel-Warthe, see address above.

Buecherei des deutschen Ostens, Catalog, Herne 1973, pages 259–285; new edition, vol. 2, Herne 1982, pages 125–281.

Posener Evangelische Kirche – ihre Gemeinden und Pfarrer (The Protestant Church of Posen – its parishes and ministers), detailed personal names and dates for all ministers, 148 pages.

Posener Stimmen, Heimatbrief (Voices of Posen, a homeland news letter); address: Bernhard-Riemann-Strasse 30, D–2120 Lueneburg, Germany.

Schmiegel, Geschichte einer deutschen Handwerkerstadt im Osten (Schmiegel, a history of a German craftsmen city in the east); with many source indices and pedigree charts. Available from: Dr. Oskar Matzel, D–2130 Rotenburg (Wuemme), Germany.

Der Kreis Schubin (The county of Schubin); publisher: Heimatkreis Schubin, 1975, 349 pages, a chronicle with genealogical contributions.

Der Kreis Wirsitz, Ein westpreussisches Heimatbuch (The county of Wirsitz, a West Prussian chronicle) – 1973; 460 pages, with many maps, illustrations and genealogical material, including some before 1772. Several thousand family names.

6. **Archives and Libraries with Sources of Homeland Regions**

6.1 *In West Germany – Federal Republic of Germany including West Berlin*

See Section "A" 6.1.

Posener Archiv (Archives of Posen) at the D.-Paul-Blau-Haus, D–2120 Lueneburg, Germany.

Archiv der Gemeinschaft Evangelischer Posener (Hilfskomitee) e. V. (Archives of the union of Protestants of Posen) (Relief society), Bernhard-Riemann-Strasse 30, D-2120 Lueneburg, Germany.

6.2 *In Central Germany – German Democratic Republic including East Berlin*

See Section "A" 6.2.

An index of civil status registers and church records of Grenzmark from before 1874, now held at Zentralstelle fuer Genealogie in Leipzig, Germany (see Section "A" 6.2 for address), was published in OFK I, pages 163, 204, 1953–1957.

6.3 *In homeland territory*

a. Archiwum Pánstwowe, ul. Dluga 6, PL–00–850 Warszawa, Poland (Public archives).

b. Wojewódzkie Archiwum Pánstwowe Bydgoszcz, ul. Dworcowa 65, PL–83–009 Bydgoszcz, Poland.

Inventory information: Guide to Polish Archives, pages 88–130, see "A" 8.2.

Archival material: Documents of state organizations, offices, departments, self governing bodies, schools, political organizations and private archives.

Presumably the Archiv der Forschungsstelle Posen-Bromberg (Archives of the research center Posen-Bromberg) and the Familienarchiv Colbe (Family archives Colbe) and the original burger lists of the city of Bromberg, 1772 to 1855.

c. Archiwum Pánstwowe Torun, pl. Rapackiego, PL–87–Torun, Poland.

See Section "B" 3.

Inventory information: Guide to Polish Archives, pages 116–123, see "A" 8.2.

d. Wojewodztwo árchives in Poznan:

Archiwum Pánstwowe Miasta Poznanina i Wojewodztwa Poznanskiego (City of Posen and administrative district of archives in Posen), ul. 23 Lutego 41/43, PL–61–744 Poznan, Poland.

Inventory information: Guide to Polish Archives, pages 436–499, see "A" 8.2.

Archiwum Pánstwowe miasta Poznania i Wojewodztwa Poznanskiego, Warsaw 1969, 771 pages

e. Archiwum Archidiecezalne (Archives of the archdiocese), 62–200 Gniezno-Katedra, Poland.

These archives will give information on the location of individual parish records of Roman Catholic parishes, for instance:

Bialosliwie	89–340, ul. Kosciuszki 14, Poland
Kcynia	89–240, ul. Farna 1, Poland
Mrocza	89–360, Poland
Naklo	89–100, ul. Piotra Skargi 6, Poland
Sipiory	89–242, Poland

7. **Other Research Aids**

7.1 *Hometown/village directories*

Heimatortskartei Deutsche aus dem Wartheland und Polen (Hometown/village directory of Germans from the Wartheland and Poland), Gross Barlinge 4, D–3000 Hannover, Germany, Ph. 0511–81 66 36.

7.2 *Societies*

Landsmannschaft Weichsel-Wartheland (Society of Vistula-Warthelanders), Koenigswoertherstrasse 2, D–3000 Hannover, Germany.

7.3 *Homeland informations*

Heimatauskunftstelle fuer Posen (Homeland information center for Posen), at Landesausgleichsamt Hamburg, Hamburger Strasse 47, D–2000 Hamburg 76, Germany.

Heimatauskunftsstelle fuer den Regierungsbezirk Bromberg (Homeland information center for the administrative district Bromberg), Meesenring 9, D–2400 Luebeck, Germany.

7.4 *Historical Assiciations*

Historisch-Landeskundliche Kommission fuer Posen und Deutschtum in Polen (Commission of historical studies for Poznans and Germans in Poland), Prof. Dr. Gotthold Rhode, Saarstrasse 21, D–6500 Mainz, Germany.

7.5 *Church institutions*

Gemeinschaft Evangelischer Posener (Hilfskomitee) e. V. (Union of Protestants from Posen) (Relief society), Marienstrasse 30, D–3000 Hannover 1, Germany.

Monthly periodical: Posener Stimme (Voice of Poznan).

8. **Special Hints**

Genealogical research results – pedigree lines – are published in Deutsches Geschlechterbuch (Book of German Genealogy) vol. 62, 78, 116, 140 and in Altburgunder Familienarchiv (Oldburgundian family archives), supplement to Altburgunder Heimatbote (Oldburgundian homeland messenger).

II. GERMAN SETTLEMENTS IN CENTRAL-, EAST- AND SOUTH-EASTERN EUROPE.

German settlements in Eastern Europe stretched to the endless reaches of Russia. Closed German settlement regions existed in the Baltic States (Estonia, Latvia, Lithuania); in Poland (Central Poland, Galicia, Volhynia; after the Treaty of Versailles: the Polish Corridor Region, the Poznan Region, Eastern Upper Silesia), in Russia (along the Volga River, along of the Black Sea, on the Crimean Peninsula, in the Caucasus), in Slovakia (Zips or Spi and Hauerland), in Rumania (Transylvania, Banat, Bukovina, Bessarabia, Dobrudscha or Dobrogea) and in Yugoslavia (Banat, Bácska, Slavonia, Srem or Srijem). In Hungary one could distinguish between three large, mostly closed (Swabian Turkey, Transdanubian Central Highlands or Dunántulikoezéphgység, Eastern Burgenland with Heideboden or Fenyér) and several small settlement regions.

In the central Danube region the German ethnic enclaves were often part of several countries, like Banat (between the Tisa and Danube Rivers and the Carpathian Mountains), was partially in Yugoslavia, Rumania and Hungary like Bačka (between the Tisa and Danube Rivers) which was partially in Yugoslavia and Hungary.

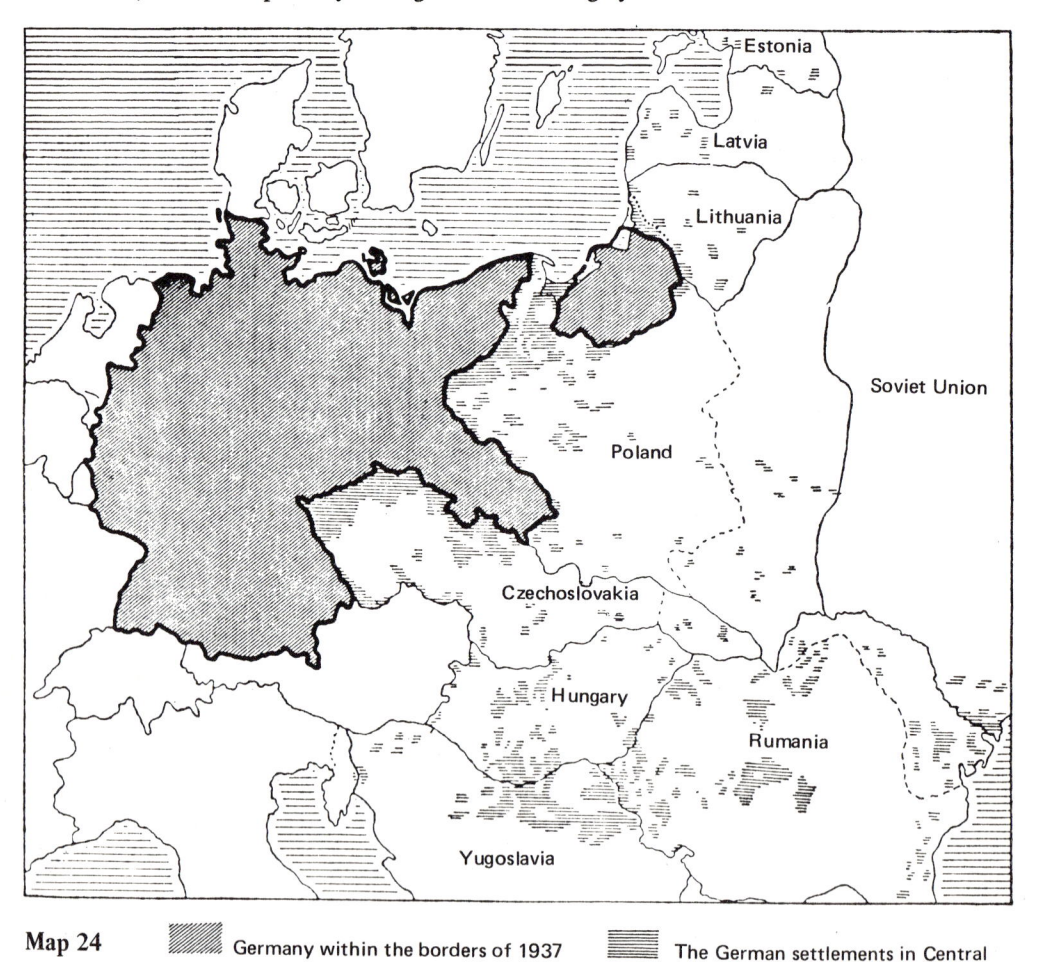

Map 24   ▨ Germany within the borders of 1937   ≡ The German settlements in Central and Eastern European regions of expulsion

1. **POLAND**
   a) **Central Poland and Volhynia**

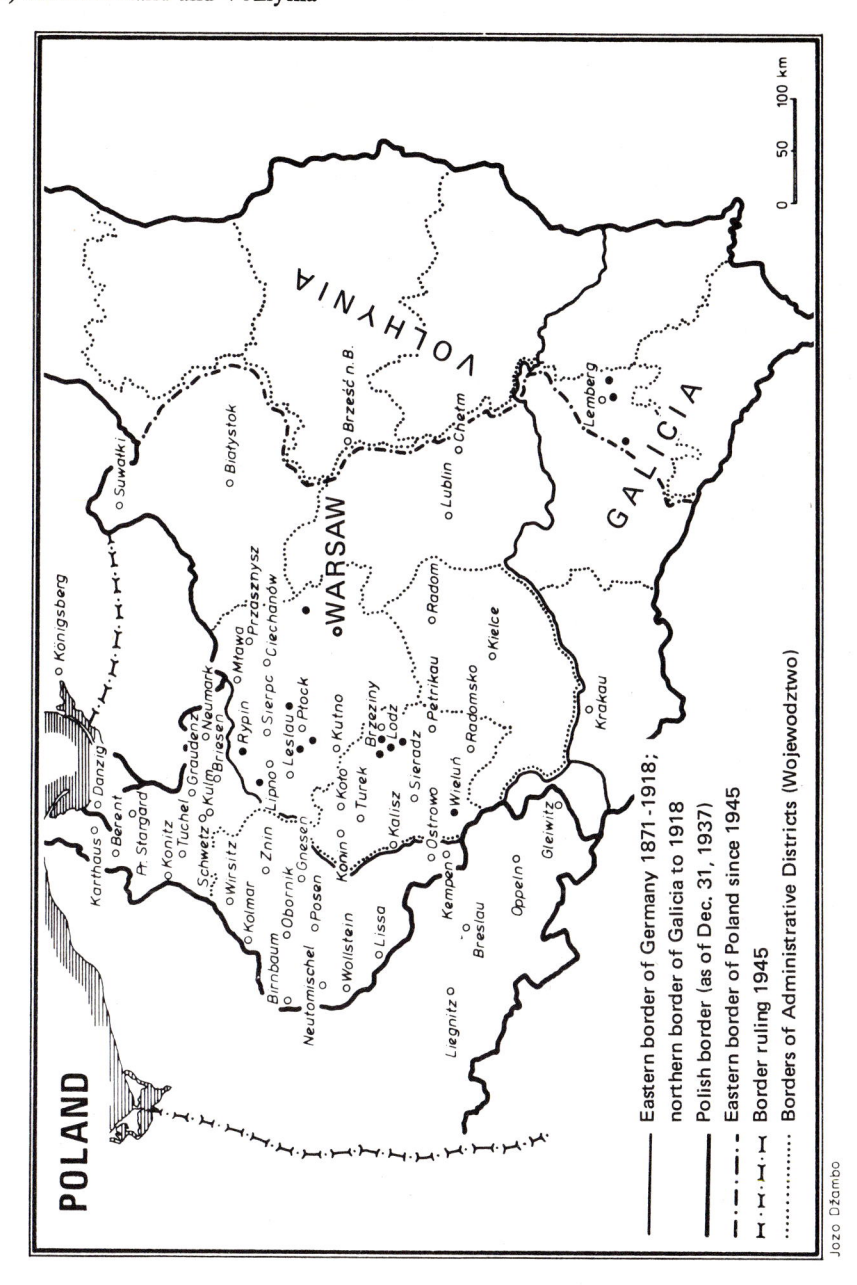

Map 25

The geographical borders of German territories in Poland can only clearly be given for specific periods of time. After the loss of Polish sovereignty in 1795 the historical Polish territory was divided among Prussia, the Habsburg Monarchy and Russia. After the Treaty of Versailles in 1920, East-Upper-Silesians, West Prussians and Posen Germans remained within Poland. After the occupation of Poland in 1939 portions of Poland became parts of "Reichsgau Wartheland" and of the province of East Prussia that had not been German in a political nor ethnic sense.

In the context of this book Polish territories are those regions which did not belong to Germany in 1914. Historical "Congress Poland", Galicia and Volhynia, i. e. Russian Poland.

1. Research Areas

The Wojewodztwos (Administrative district) of: Białystok, Kielce, Łodz, Lublin and Warsaw as well as the wojewodztwos formed in 1975:

Biała Podlaska, Chełm, Ciechanòw (Zichenau), Czestochowa (Northern Section), Kalisz, Konin, Łomzà, Ostrołeka (Scharfenwiese), Piotrkòw Trybunalski (Petrikau), Płock (Schroettersburg), Radom, Siedlce, Sieradz, Skierniewice, Suwalki (Sudauen Southern Section), Tarnobrzeg, Włocławek (Leslau), Zamość, along with the Eastern portion of the USSR, formerly Poland, and Volhynia.

2. Genealogical Institutions

2.1 *Present institutions*

Forschungsstelle Mittelpolen-Wolhynien der AGoFF (Research center Central Poland-Volhynia of AGoFF)
Rudolf Peiker, Ostpreussenring 138, D–2400 Luebeck 14, Germany, Ph. 0451–30 25 40.

3. Documents of Vital Statistics

3.1 *Books and records of vital statistics*

No civil record offices existed in Central Poland or Volhynia. Priests, pastors and rabbis served as record officers.

3.2 *Displaced church records*

A small number is held in West Berlin, church records of Lipno and Rypin at the Bundesarchiv (Federal archives) (see OFK III, page 249, 1962–1964). Information is given by the research center (see above 2.1).

3.3 *Church records in homeland*

The preserved church records are held at the present parishes, otherwise at the local civil record offices and archives of the administrative district, Catholic church records at parish offices, older ones at the diocese archives, copies of Volhynian records possibly at the archives in Warsaw.

4. Gazetteers

Slownik: Geograficzny Ziem polskich, 15 vols., Warsaw 1880–1900.

5. **Bibliographies and Literature**

5.1 Alfred Lattermann: Einfuehrung in die deutsche Sippenforschung in Polen (Introduction to German genealogy in Poland), Posen 1938.

Dr. Eduard Kneifel: Geschichte der evangelisch-augsburgischen Gemeinden in Polen (History of Protestant-Augsburgian churches in Poland), privately published, D–8061 Vierkirchen b. Muenchen, Germany.

Pastoren der evangelisch-augsburgischen Kirche in Polen (Pastors of Protestant-Augsburgian churches in Poland) – Literaturnachweis (a bibliography), privately published.

Die Lodzer deutsche evangelische Kirche im Wartheland (The Lodz German Protestant church in Wartheland), 1939–1945, privately published.

Otto Heike: 150 Jahre Schwabensiedlung in Polen 1795–1945 (150 years of Swabian settlement in Poland 1795–1945), Leverkusen, Germany 1979, available from: R. Beilstein, An der Kreuzkapelle 9, D–4052 Korschenbroich, Germany.

Dr. Otto Kossmann: Die Deutschen in Polen seit der Reformation (Germans in Poland since the reformation), Johann-Gottfried-Herder-Institut, Marburg/Lahn, Germany 1978.

Mennonitisches Lexikon, Band 4 "Wolhynien" (Mennonite Encyclopedia, vol. 4, "Volhynia"), Karlsruhe, Germany 1967; also see English edition, Scottdale 1959.

Buecherei des deutschen Ostens, Catalog, Herne 1973, pages 469–478; Herne 1982, vol. 2, pages 125–281.

6. **Archives and Libraries with Source Material of Homeland Regions**

6.1 *In West Germany – Federal Republic of Germany including West-Berlin*

Archiv der Deutschen aus Mittelpolen und Wolhynien (Archives of Germans from Central Poland and Volhynia), Stadthaus, Mozartstrasse 19, D–4050 Moenchengladbach, Germany.

6.3 *In homeland territory*

State archives are in all capitals of administrative districts (see 1. above). Inventory information: Guide to Polish Archives, see "A" 8.2.

Richard C. Lewanski: Guide to Polish Libraries and Archives, New York-London 1974.

State archives of the Lodz region
(from: Glos Robotniczy – Voice of the Worker – Sept. 8, 1973: Compilation of inventories of the archives of old documents, archives of the City of Lodz and state archives of Piotrkow.)

The archives at Łódź have royal and princely documents of the 14th century as well as collections of the families of Potocki and Ostrowski.

Old parchments beginning 1520, register of jurors of the 17th century, counselors and jurors of Pabjanice 17th and 18th century, administrative and police documents of "Russian" times (Gubernia Piotrkowska and Kališka 1852–1914), court documents 1808–1914, land title documents 1864–1917, school administrative documents 1817–1918, factory inspections 1886–1914, court documents 1914–1918, citizen committee of the city of Łódź 1914–1915, wojewodztwo documents 1918–1939, state police documents 1920–1939, land registers 1919–1933, city documents 1939–1945, index of „Preferred" citizens of the "Third Reich" in the City and Wojewodztwo Łódz, Ghetto documents, repatriation documents 1945–1951, city documents 1794–1949, suburbs 1816–1940, spinning-mills 1834–1945, banks and companies 1870–1946.

The archives at Pabjanice have old city and state documents from 1802–1969, burgher registers, notary documents, plans and maps of development, photographs of Old-Pabjanice, seals, merchandise collections of the Kindler company as well as the archives of Dr. Ing. chem. E. Lot.

County archives in Leczyca, Łodz, Pabjanice, Sieradz, Tomaszow and Skierniewice.

The local archives at Piotrkow have become wojewodztwo archives with a local branch at Tomaszow Mazowiecki.

The wojewodztwo archives for Skierniewice are located at Rawa Mazowiecki, a branch at Zyrardow and a branch at Lowicz.

Inventory information: Guide to Polish Archives, page 14, see "A" 8.2.

7. Other Research Aids

7.1 *Hometown/village directories*

Heimatortskartei Deutsche aus dem Wartheland und Polen (Hometown/village directory of Germans from the Wartheland and Poland), Gross Barlinge 4, D–3000 Hannover, Germany, Ph. 0511–81 66 36.

7.2 *Societies*

Landsmannschaft Weichsel-Warthe (Society of Vistula-Warta region), Koenigswoerther Strasse 2, D–3000 Hannover, Germany, Ph. 0511–71 60 58.

Monthly periodical as a supplement to the newsletter of the Hilfs-Komitee: Mitteilungen Weichsel-Warthe (Bulletins Vistula-Warta).

Yearbooks of Landsmannschaft Weichsel-Warthe.

7.3 *Homeland informations*

Central Poland

Heimatauskunftstelle Polen I, Bereich Łodz (Homeland information center Poland I, Łodz region), Bankstrasse 4, D–4000 Duesseldorf, Germany.

Central Poland and Galicia

Heimatauskunftstelle Polen II (Homeland information center Poland II), Schoeneworth 7, D–3000 Hannover, Germany.

7.4 *Historical Associations*

Historisch-Landeskundliche Kommission fuer Posen und das Deutschtum in Polen (Commission of historical studies of Poznan and ethnic Germans in Poland), Prof. Dr. Gotthold Rhode, Saarstrasse 21, D–6500 Mainz, Germany.

Historischer Verein fuer Wolhynien (Historical society for Volhynia), Hugo Schmidt, Pastor i. R., Breslauer Strasse 10, D–8540 Schwabach, Germany.

Periodical: Wolhynische Hefte (Volhynian notes).

7.5 *Church institutions*

Hilfskomitee der evangl. luth. Deutschen aus Polen (Relief society of evang.-luth. Germans from Poland), Koenigswoerther Strasse 2, D–3000 Hannover, Germany.

8. **Special Hints**

Heimatarchiv Forschungsgruppe der Wolhyniendeutschen: Kartei der Deutschen im Raume Białystok in Privathand (Homeland archives research group of Germans from Volhynia: Index of Germans from the Białystock region) (in private possession).

b) Galicia (= Galizien)

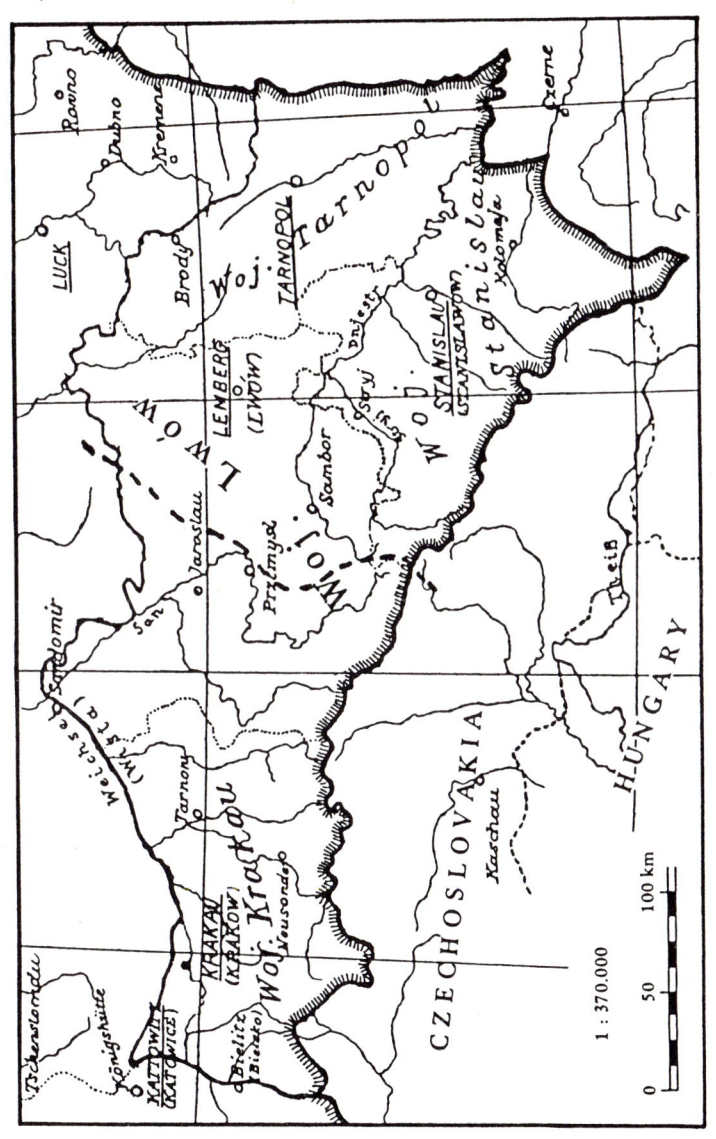

Map 26

The map shows Galicia of 1921–1939, the dashed line is the present border between Western and Eastern Galicia (Polish – Soviet border).

1. **Research Areas**

   Western Galicia (now Poland), Eastern Galicia (now Ukrainian SSR).

2. **Genealogical Institutions**

   2.1 *Present institutions*

   a. **Forschungsstelle Galizien der AGoFF** (Research center of AGoFF)
      Ernst Hexel, Im Gries 20, D–5300 Bonn 2 (Bad Godesberg), Germany, Ph. 0228–34 55 20.

   b. **Sippenkundliche Arbeitsgemeinschaft des Hilfskomitees der Galiziendeutschen** (Genealogical group of the relief society of Germans from Galicia)
      Ernst Hexel, address see 2.1 above,
      Rudolf Peiker, Ostpreussenring 138, D–2402 Luebeck, Germany, Ph. 0451–30 25 40.

3. **Documents of Vital Statistics**

   3.1 *Books and records of vital statistics*

   No civil records offices existed in Galicia before 1939. Priests, pastors and rabbis served as record officials.

   3.2 *Displaced church records*

   Only the church records of the Makowa branch of the Protestant church of Bandrow is held at Evangelisches Zentralarchiv, Jebenstrasse 3, D–1000 Berlin 12, Germany.

   A copy of the church records of the Mennonite church of Kiernica-Lemberg is held at D–7150 Backnang, Germany; another at the Warsaw State Archives.

   The registration book of the Protestant church of Stanislau is held at Galiziendeutsches Heimatarchiv (Homeland archives of Germans from Galicia) presently held by Ernst Hexel, address see 2.1 above.

   3.3 *Church records in homeland regions and the remainder of Poland*

   a. Eastern Galicia

      Protestant church records, partly in original, partly copies with entries prior to about 1870, are held in Warsaw at the "Archives of old Documents" – Archiwum Główne Akt Dawnych, ul. Długa, 7, PL–00–950 Warszawa, skrytka pocztowa Nr. 1005, Poland –.
      for entries after about 1870, at the Central-Warsaw record office – Urząd Stanu Cywilnego, Warszawa-Šródmiescie, Poland. –

      Roman Catholic church records, which were taken out of Galicia during the resettlement of Poles, are at the archives of the Western Galician dioceses or at the wojewodztwo of Lublin. A very small number is held by the University of Lublin.

      Greek Orthodox church records remained in Eastern Galicia and are probably held by the respective record offices or archives.

b. Western Galicia

Protestant church records are held at the respective record offices or archives.

Roman Catholic church records are held by the respective record offices or diocese archives.

Greek Orthodox church records are held at the wojewodztwo archives.

4. Gazetteers

4.1 Indices of German settlements in Polish or Ukrainian villages in Galicia with information on respective church offices: in preparation. Ernst Hexel, address see 2.1 above.

4.2 Gazetteer of Galicia with information on respective church offices, manuscript at Ernst Hexel, address see 2.1 above.

4.3 Gazetteer of Galicia – "Gemeindelexikon von Galizien", Vienna 1906.
Spezial-Ortsrepertorium von Galizien, Vienna 1893.

4.4 Gazetteer of Western Galicia and administrative divisions of Poland:
Rozdział Administracyjny Polskiej Rzeczypospolitej Ludowej – Warsaw.

5. Bibliographies and Literature

5.1 *Published after 1945*

Sepp Mueller: Schrifttum ueber das Deutschtum in Galizien (Literature on Germans in Galicia), Johann-Gottfried-Herder-Institut, Marburg, Germany, 1962.

Sepp Mueller: Die galiziendeutschen Sippen Mueller und Mang (The Galician-German families Mueller and Mang), Landsmannschaft Weichsel-Warthe 1967.

Rudolf Peiker: Familienforschung der Galiziendeutschen, in "Aufbruch und Neubeginn", Heimatbuch II der Galiziendeutschen (Family research of Germans from Galicia, in „Departure and New Start", chronicle of Germans from Galicia) 1977.

Ernst Hexel: Galiziendeutsche Familienforschung seit 1970 (Family research of Germans from Galicia since 1970), 1978 yearbook Weichsel-Warthe.

Genealogical Tables of Galician Mennonites, Backnang 1983.

5.2 *Published before 1945*

Ludwig Schneider: Das Kolonisationswerk Joseph II in Galizien (Colonisation of Joseph II in Galicia), Hirzel-Verlag, Leipzig 1939.

Wilhelm und Kallbrunner: Quelle zur Siedlungsgeschichte in Suedosteuropa (Source on settlement history in Southeastern Europe), Muenchen 1932.

Alfred Lattermann: Einfuehrung in die deutsche Sippenforschung in Polen (Introduction to German genealogy in Poland), Posen 1938.

Peter Bachmann: Mennoniten in Kleinpolen (Galizien) (Mennonites in Galicia) with pedigree charts, Lemberg (Lwow) 1934 (reprint 1980, 1983).

Gedenkbuch zur Erinnerung an die Einwanderung der Deutschen in Galizien vor 150 Jahren (Book of commemoration of immigration of Germans to Galicia 150 years ago), Posen 1937.

6. Archives and Libraries with Sources on Homeland Territories

6.1 *In West Germany – The Federal Republic of Germany including West-Berlin*

Galiziendeutsches Heimatarchiv in der Heimatstelle Pfalz (Galician-German home archives at the homeland center Palatinate), Benzinoring 6, D–6750 Kaiserslautern, Germany, Ph. 0631–68 091–93.

The genealogical material is presently held by Ernst Hexel, address see 2.1 above.

6.2 *In Austria*

Oesterreichisches Staatsarchiv, Finanz- und Hofkammerarchiv (Austrian state archives, finances and court department archives), Johannesgasse 6, A–1010 Vienna, Austria.

6.3 *In homeland territory*

See Guide to Polish Archives, section "A" 8.2.

Wojewodztwo archives in Kraków
Wojewódzkie Archiwum Pánstwowe w Krakówie
PL 32–700 Kraków, ul. Kanoniczna 1
         ul. Grodzka 54
         ul. Sienna 16, Poland

Branches in Bochnia
ul. Kazimierza Wielliego 31, P 32–700 Bochnia, Poland.

in Tarnów
ul. Kniewskiego, PL 33–100 Tarnów, Poland

Wojewodztwo Archives in Nowy Sącz
Wojewódzkie Archiwum Pánstwowe w Nowym Sączu
ul. Królowej Jadwigi 10, PL 94–400 Nowy Targ, Poland

Branch in Nowy Sącz
ul. Szwedzka 2, PL 33–300 Nowy Sacz, Poland

Wojewodztwo Archives in Przemysl
Wojewódzkie Archiwum Pánstwowe w Przemyslu
ul. Polskiego Czerwonego Krzyża 4, PL 37–700 Przemysl, Poland

Wojewodztwo Archives in Rzeszów
Wojewódzkie Archiwum Pánstwowe w Rzeszówie
ul. Boźnicza 4, PL 35–064, Poland

Branch in Jasło
ul. Sniadeckich 15, PL 38–200 Jasło, Poland

Wojewodztwo Archives in Tarnobrzeg
Wojewódzkie Archiwum Pánstwowe w Tarnobrzegu
ul. Batosza 4, PL 27–600 Sandomierz, Poland

from "Archiwa Pánstwowe w Polsce" – Informator 1979 –.

7. Other Research Aids

7.1 *Hometown/village directories*

Heimatortskartei Deutsche aus dem Wartheland und Polen (Hometown/village directory of Germans from the Wartheland and Poland), Grosse Barlinge 4, D–3000 Hannover, Germany, Ph. 0511–61 66 36.

7.2 *Societies*

Landsmannschaft Weichsel-Warthe (Society of Vistula-Warta Germans), Koenigswoerther Strasse 2, D–3000 Hannover, Germany, Ph. 0511–71 60 58.

Monthly periodical as a supplement to the relief society "Mitteilungen Weichsel-Warthe" (Bulletins Weichsel-Warta).

Yearbooks of Landsmannschaft Weichsel-Warthe.

7.3 *Information centers*

Heimatauskunftstelle Polen II (Homeland information center Poland II), Schoeneworth 7, D–3000 Hannover, Germany.

7.4 *Historical Associations*

Historisch-landeskundliche Kommission fuer Posen und das Deutschtum in Polen (Commission of historical studies for Posen and ethnic Germans in Poland), Prof. Dr. Gotthold Rhode, Saarstrasse 21, D–6500 Mainz, Germany.

Heimatkundliche Arbeitsgemeinschaft beim Hilfskomitee Galiziendeutscher (Group for homeland studies, division of the relief society for Germans from Galicia), Dipl. Ing. Erwin Gerlach, Lange Wiese 21, D–4800 Bielefeld, Germany.

7.5 *Church institutions*

Hilfskomitee der Galiziendeutschen, A. u. H. B. (Relief society of Germans from Galicia), Arnold Jaki, Pastor i. R., Theodor-Veiel-Strasse 55, D–7000 Stuttgart 50 (Bad Cannstatt), Germany, Ph. 0711–56 66 37.

Monthly bulletin: Das heilige Band (The Holy Bond)

Calender: Zeitweiser (Guide to Time)

Memorial books: I. Heimat Galizien (Homeland Galicia)
                  II. Aufbruch und Neubeginn (Departure and New Start).

8. Other Hints

Genealogical questionaires of re-settlers from Galicia 1939/40 are held – incomplete – at Bundesarchiv, Am Woellerhof 1, D–5400 Koblenz 1, Germany.

Several genealogical papers were published at "Das heilige Band" and "Zeitweiser".

Administrative Divisions of Poland since 1795
Wojewodztwos

Map 27

Northern Poland

Szczecin (Stettin), Koszalin (Koeslin), Slupsk (Stolp), Gdańsk (Danzig), Elblag (Elbing), Olsztyn (Allenstein), Suwałki.

Western Poland

Gorzów Wielkopolski (Landsberg/Warthe), Zielona Góra (Gruenberg), Jelenia Góra (Hirschberg), Legnica (Liegnitz).

Southern Poland

Wałbrzych (Waldenburg), Wrocław (Breslau), Opole (Oppeln), Katowice (Kattowitz).

Great Poland

Piła (Schneidemuehl), Bydgoszcz (Bromberg), Toruń (Thorn), Poznań (Posen), Leszno (Lissa), Konin, Kalisz (Kalisch), Włocławek (Leslau).

Central Poland

Łódź (Lodsch) Błock, Sieradz, Czestochowa, Piotrków-Trybunalski, Skierniewice, Ciechanów (Ziechenau) Warszawa (Warschau), Radom.

Eastern Poland

Ostrołęka, Łomźa, Białystok, Siedlce, Biała Podlaska, Lublin, Chełm, Zamość.

Southeastern Poland

Kielce, Tarnobrzeg, Kraków (Krakau), Tarnów, Rzeszów, Przemyśl, Krosno, Nowy Sącz (Neu Sandez), Bielsko-Biała, (Bielitz-Biala).

2. **BALTIC STATES – LITHUANIA, LATVIA, ESTONIA.**

BALTIC STATES

- Borders (as of 1937)
- Border changes 1939 and 1945
- Border between Poland and USSR (1945)
- Border of Memel Region 1920-1938

Map 28

The Baltic Germans, i. e. the ethnic German populations of the former Russian Baltic Sea provinces Estonia, Livonia and Courland, after 1918 the republics of Estonia and Latvia, did not form an uniform population until the German re-settlement in 1941. Exceptions were individual rural colonies such as Hirschenhof in Livonia. The Baltic Germans formed, although numerically small, a cultural and upper class. Although there is a large number of family histories and genealogies, there are no chronicles published.

The German population group of Lithuania is not considered to be a part of the Baltic Germans.

1. **Research Areas**

   The former countries

   Latvia

   consisting of the former Baltic Sea provinces of Czarist Russia, Courland including Semgallen and Southern Livonia, and Lettgallen or Polish Livonia.

   Estonia

   consisting of the former Baltic Sea provinces of Estonia, Oesel and Northern Livonia.

   Lithuania

   Nobody is in charge of this research region. Some research opportunities are listed below.

2. **Genealogical Institutions**

   2.1 *Present institutions*

   Forschungsstelle Baltikum der AGoFF (Research center for Baltic States of AGoFF) **Winno von Loewenstern, Parkstrasse 45, Frankenforst, D–5060 Bergisch Gladbach, Germany, Ph. 02204–64 121.**

   The genealogists of the societies of knights of Courland, Livonia, Estonia and Oesel in the association of societies of knights, their addresses as well as those of many other genealogists and historians, may be contacted through Forschungsstelle Baltikum (see 2.1 above). Their listing would require more space than is available here.

   2.2 *Former institutions*

   are being succeeded by the above named institutions and individuals.

3. **Documents of Vital Statistics**

   3.1 *Books and records of vital statistics*

   See listings in Section "A".

   3.2 *Displaced church records*

   Excerpt copies "Koerbersche Kirchenbuchabschriften" (Koerbers church book copies) of Reval, Narwa and individual localities of Estonia are held by Forschungsstelle Baltikum (see 2.1 above).

Further photocopies are held by Archiv der Estlaendischen Ritterschaft (Archives of the Estonian society of knights), c/o Georg von Krusenstjern, Weitlstrasse 81, D–8000 Muenchen 45, Germany.

Individual documents are held at Archiv der Kurlaendischen Ritterschaft (Archives of the Courland society of knights) at Hessisches Staatsarchiv Marburg, Friedrichsplatz 15, D–3550 Marburg/Lahn, Germany.

3.3   *Church records in homeland territory*

are presently not available. Inquiries are to be addressed to the State Archives Riga, Latvian Socialist Soviet Republic, and may be successful in the future.

4.   **Gazetteers**

    a. M. Friederichsen: Finland, Estonia, Latvia and Lithuania with 16 maps, 144 pages, Breslau 1924, available at the Buecherei des deutschen Ostens (see Section "A", 6.3 a.).

    b. Verzeichnis lettlaendischer Ortsnamen (Gazetteer of Latvia) in co-operation with H. Meyer and G. von Pantzer published by Hans Feldmann (before 1945, reprint 1963), available at Forschungsstelle Baltikum (see 2.1 above).

5.   **Selective Bibliographies and Literature**

5.1   *Published after 1945*

Gerhard von Pantzer: Personen- und Familienkundliche Literatur in baltischen Zeitschriften 1948 bis 1960 (Personal and genealogical literature published in Baltic periodicals 1948 to 1960), Baltic pedigree charts, special edition No. 10., Cologne 1970, available at Forschungsstelle Baltikum (see 2.1 above).

Olaf Welding: Das baltische genealogische Schrifttum 1700 bis 1939, Schrifttumsberichte zur Genealogie, 11. Literaturbericht (Baltic-genealogical literature 1700 to 1939, bibliographic report of genealogy, 11th bibliographic report), Neustadt/Aisch 1958, available at Forschungsstelle Baltikum (see 2.1 above).

Erik Thomson: Baltische Bibliographie 1957 bis 1961 and Nachtraege 1945 bis 1958 (Baltic bibliography 1957 to 1961 and supplement 1945 to 1958), available at Buecherei des deutschen Ostens (see Section "A" 6.3 a.).

Helmut Weiss: Baltische Bibliographie (Baltic bibliography) published annually in Zeitschrift fuer Ostforschung, Marburg.

Additional works have been published. Information is available from Carl-Schirren-Gesellschaft: Manager Baroness Vera von Sass, Am Berge 35, D–2120 Lueneburg, Germany.

Buecherei des deutschen Ostens, Catalog, Herne 1973, pages 484–520; Herne 1982, vol. 2, pages 282–375.

5.2   *Published before 1945*

See Carl-Schirren-Gesellschaft above and the archives and libraries listed below.

6. **Archives and Libraries with Sources on Homeland Regions**

6.1 *In West Germany – The Federal Republic of Germany including West-Berlin*

Archiv der Kurlaendischen Ritterschaft im Hessischen Staatsarchiv Marburg (Archives of the Courland society of knights), address see 3.2 above.

Archiv der Estlaendischen Ritterschaft bei Georg von Krusenstjern (Archives of the Estonian society of knights) address see 3.2 above.

Inventories of the Livlaendischen Ritterschaft (Livonian society of knights) are also held at the Hessian State Archives; address see 3.2 above.

Bibliothek, Archiv und Karten- und Bildersammlung der Carl-Schirren-Gesellschaft (Library, archives and map and picture collection of the C.-S.-G.); address see 5.1 above.

Additional inventories are in private hands; information available from Carl-Schirren-Gesellschaft (see 5.1 above) and Forschungsstelle Baltikum (see 2.1 above).

6.2 *In Central Germany – German Democratic Republic (DDR) including East-Berlin*

Small collections are held at the state archives in Potsdam; address see Section "A" 6.2 a.

6.3 *In homeland territory*

State archives Riga, no contacts have been established to date (see 3.3 above).

Central state archives of Tartu (Dorpat).

7. **Other Research Aids**

7.1 *Hometown/village directories*

Heimatortskartei Nordosteuropa, Abteilung Deutschbalten (Hometown/village directory Northeastern Europe, Baltic-German section), Estonia-Latvia, Meesenring 13, D–2400 Lübeck, Germany, Ph. 0451–62 13 88.

Heimatortskartei Nordosteuropa, Abteilung Litauen (Hometown/village directory Northeastern Europe, Lithuanian section), Waldstrasse 1, D–2224 Burg, Dithmarschen, Germany, Ph. 04825–23 24.

7.2 Deutsch-Baltische Landsmannschaft im Bundesgebiet (German-Baltic society in West Germany) e. V., Chairman: Harro von Hirschheydt, Wichmannstrasse 20, D–3000 Hannover, Germany, Ph. 0511–83 04 50.

Landsmannschaft der Litauendeutschen (Society of Lithuanian-Germans), Burgstrasse 17, D–5760 Arnsberg 1, Germany, Ph. 0293–22 68 58.

7.3 *Other agencies*

Heimatauskunftstelle Baltikum (Litauen, Lettland und Estland) (Homeland information center Baltic States – Lithuania, Latvia and Estonia), at: Landesausgleichsamt Hessen, Luisenstrasse 13, D–6200 Wiesbaden, Germany.

7.4 *Historical Associations*

Baltische Historische Kommission (Baltic historical commission), Chairman: Prof. Dr. Georg von Rauch, Birkenweg 2a, D–2300 Kiel-Kronshagen, Germany.

7.5 *Church institutions*

    a. Deutsch-Baltischer Dienst (German-Baltic service) E. V. (Relief society of Luth. Baltic-Germans), Kastanienallee 23, D–3000 Hannover-Doehren, Germany.

    Archives and library at Schloss Gestorf, D–3257 Springe, Germany.

    b. Hilfskomitee der ev. Deutschen aus Litauen (Relief society of Germans from Lithuania), D–3511 Atzenhausen, Germany.

7.6 *Selective Periodicals*

Jahrbuch des baltischen Deutschtums (Yearbook of Baltic Germans), published by: Carl-Schirren-Gesellschaft, address 5.1 above.

Baltische Hefte (Baltic bulletins), publisher: Harro von Hirschheydt, address see 7.2 above.

Baltische Briefe mit Beilagen fuer die Landsmannschaft, die Baltische Historische Kommission, die Carl-Schirren-Gesellschaft und andere Einrichtungen (Baltic letters for the society of Baltic Germans, the Baltic historical commission, Carl-Schirren-Gesellschaft and other institutions), Wolf von Kleist, Grosshansdorf/Hamburg, Germany.

Die Raute, cultural and news letter of Germans from Lithuania, editor: Albert Unger, Burgstrasse 17, D–5760 Arnsberg 1, Germany.

Above periodicals and others are available at Forschungsstelle Baltikum, address see 2.1 above.

8. **Special Hints**

Most Baltic family researchers work more or less on specific families, groups, cities or regions. Listings are found in the membership list of the AGoFF. Information is available from Forschungsstelle Baltikum, address see 2.1 above.

3. **SOVIET UNION**

RUSSIA / USSR

Former areas of German Settlements
USSR 1922-1939
USSR since 1945

Map 29

The Germans in Russia, including the Baltic German intelligentsia, and that of old St. Petersburg, migrated, like the Mennonites in the 18th and 19th centuries, for religious reasons to Volhynia (see also Poland), the Volga Region, the Russian Black Sea coast and Bessarabia (see Southeastern Europa). In addition, they migrated to the Asiatic regions of Southern Caucasus and Siberia. The Volga-Germans were forced out after 1941. They now reside in Soviet Asia, notably in Kazakhstan and Siberia.

1. **Research Areas**

   Volga-German autonomous region
   Black Sea-Germans – Odessa/Nikolajev – Crimea – Rostov – Stalino – Dnepropetrovsk – Saporoshje – Northern and Southern Caucasus.

   Map 30

2. **Genealogical Institutions**

   2.1 *Present institutions*

   Forschungsstelle Russlanddeutsche der AGoFF (Research center of Germans from Russia in AGoFF)
   Dr. Paul Edel, Bischof-Fischer-Strasse 114, D–7080 Aalen, Germany, Ph. 07361–61 485.

   American Historical Society of Germans from Russia, P.O. Box 1424, Greeley, Colorado 80631, USA.

3. **Documents of Vital Statistics**

   3.1 *Church records in homeland territories*

   Parts of the archives of the Consistorium-General of the Lutheran Church in Russia with copies of records of all churches, are now held at the Central State Historical Archives, Leningrad, Naberezhnaya Krasnogo Flota 4, USSR.

For information see Section "B" East Prussia 8. c.

For information of Protestant church records of the Ukraine and Bessarabia see OFK 1977 pages 23–24.

5. **Bibliographies and Literature**

Dr. K. Stumpp: Die Auswanderung aus Deutschland nach Russland in den Jahren 1763–1862 (The Emigration from Germany to Russia between 1763 and 1862), privately published, 1018 pages with about 22 000 families.

Die Russlanddeutschen – 200 Jahre unterwegs – Ein Bildband (Germans from Russia – 200 years on the move – a pictorial).

Das Schrifttum ueber das Deutschtum in Russland. Eine Bibliographie (Bibliography of the Germans from Russia), privately published.

Buecherei des deutschen Ostens, Catalog, Herne 1973, pages 479–483; Herne 1982, vol. 2, pages 376–427.

7. **Other Research Aids**

7.1 *Hometown/village directories*

Heimatortskartei Suedosteuropa-Ostumsiedler, Abteilung Deutsche aus Russland, Bessarabien, Bulgarien und Dobrudscha (Hometown/village directory Southeastern Europe-Eastern resettlers, Dept. Germans from Russia, Bessarabia, Bulgaria and Dobrogea), Rosenbergstrasse 50, D–7000 Stuttgart, Germany.

7.2 Landsmanschaft der Deutschen aus Russland (Society of Germans from Russia), Schlossstrasse 92, D–7000 Stuttgart 1, Germany.

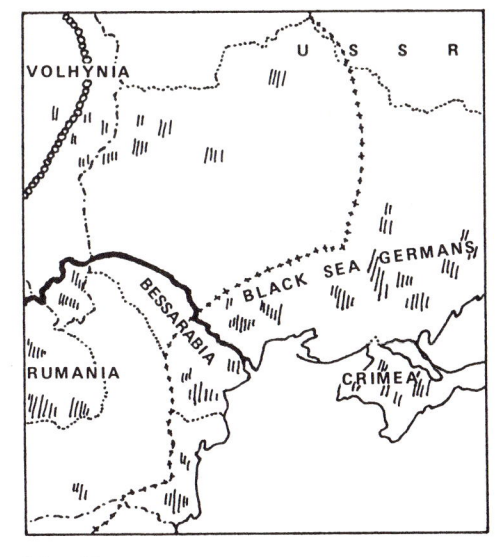

Map 31

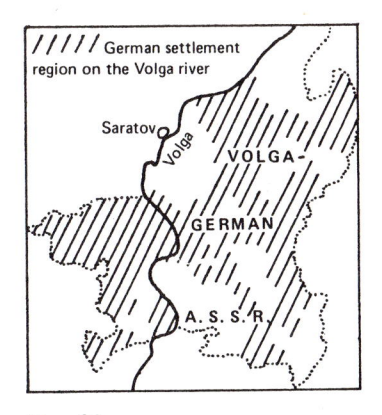

Map 32

7.3 *Other agencies*

Heimatauskunftstelle Sowjetunion, Bulgarien, Bessarabien und Dobrudscha (Homeland information center Soviet Union, Bessarabie, Bulgaria and Dobrogea) at: Landesausgleichsamt Baden-Wuerttemberg, Schloss-Strasse 92, D–7000 Stuttgart 1, Germany.

7.4 *Church institution*

Kirchliche Gemeinschaft der evangelisch-lutherischen Deutschen aus Russland (Church group of Lutheran Germans from Russia), Postfach 41 03 08, D–3500 Kassel, Germany.

4. **SUDETEN GERMAN REGIONS — BOHEMIA, MORAVIA, AUSTRO-SILESIA**

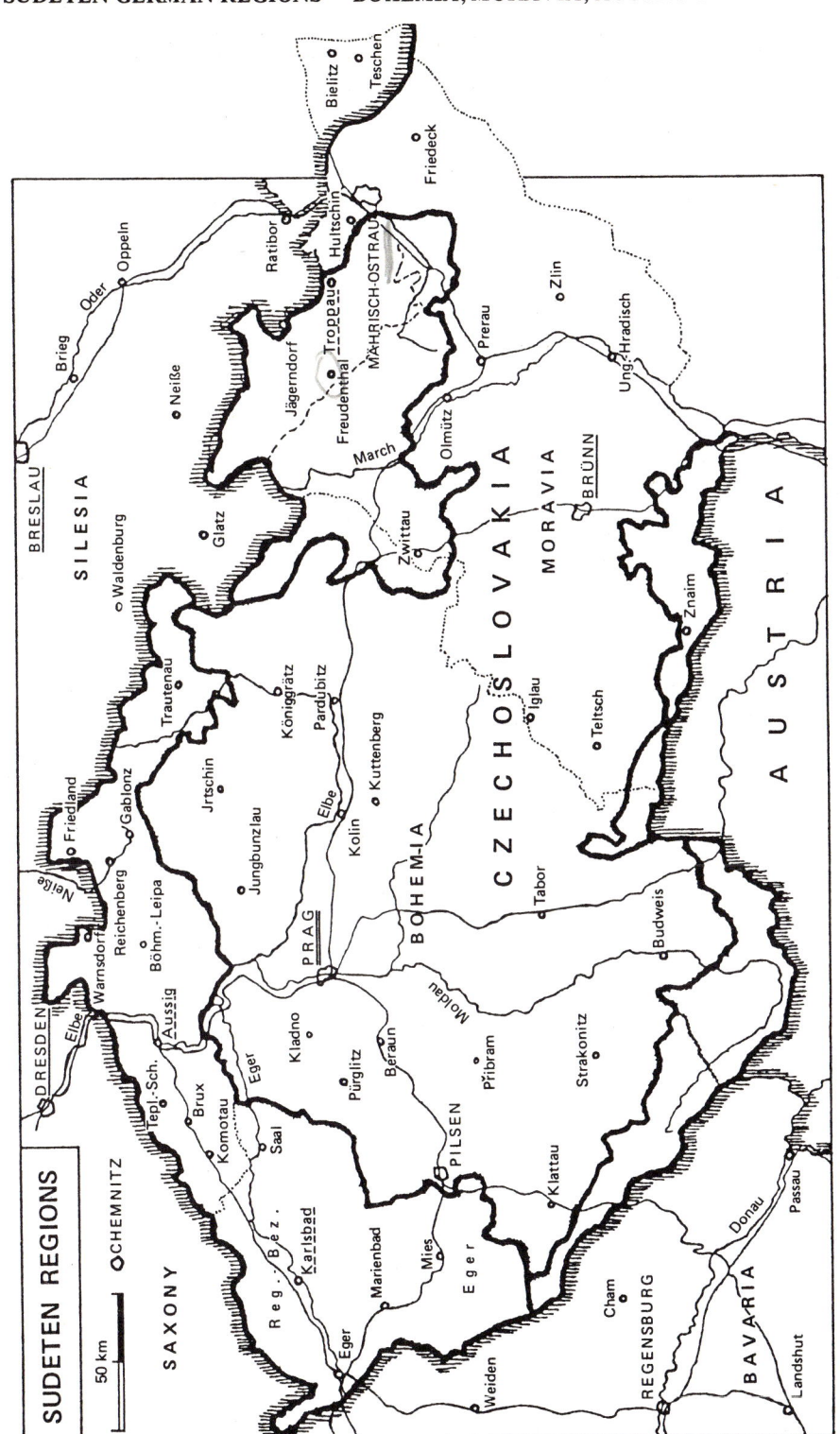

Map 33

The term "Sudeten-Germans" was coined by Franz Jesser in 1902 referring to the German speaking population of the crown territories of Bohemia, Moravia and Silesia of the Habsburg Monarchy. This term became popular in 1918 for the German population of newly created Czechoslovakia.

In 1938 Czech border territories facing Germany and Austria, which were mainly settled by Sudeten-Germans, were ceded to Germany by the Munich Agreement and formed mostly "Reichsgau Sudetenland" (Administrative district). In March of 1939 the German government forced the "Protectorate Agreement" on the Czech government. The remaining Czech territories of Czechoslovakia were occupied by German troops in violation of the Munich Agreement, and declared "Protectorate Bohemia and Moravia". The Teschen region, which had fallen to Poland in 1918, was added to the province of Silesia after the conquest of Poland in 1939.

1. **Research Areas**

   Sudeten-German Territories (Bohemia, Moravia, Silesia – 1917 Crown Territories).

2. **Genealogical Institutions**

    2.1 *Present institutions*

    a. **Forschungsstelle Sudetenland der AGoFF** (Research center Sudetenland in AGoFF)
       Sudetendeutsches Genealogisches Archiv (Sudeten-German genealogical archives) (Research center of the latter see b. below)
       Director: Adolf Fischer, Juttastrasse 20, D–8500 Nuernberg, Germany, Ph. 0911–40 965.

       Periodicals:
       Quellen und Namennachweis fuer die sudetendeutsche Familiengeschichtsforschung – Beilage zur Zeitschrift "Archiv ostdeutscher Familienforscher" (Sources and addresses of Sudeten-German family history, research-supplement to the periodical "Archives of Eastern German Family Researchers").

    b. **Sudetendeutsches Genealogisches Archiv** (Sudeten-German genealogical archives)
       Information center: Lore Schretzenmayr, Erikaweg 58, D–8400 Regensburg, Germany, Ph. 0941–21 814.

    c. **Vereinigung sudetendeutscher Familienforscher (VSFF)**, Society of Sudeten-German family researchers.
       Business office: Juttastrasse 20, D–8500 Nuernberg, Germany, Ph. 0911–40 965.

       Since 1972 all genealogical societies, institutions and institutes interested in Bohemia, Moravia and Austro-Silesia have been merged in the VSFF.

       The institutions and research groups of "Research Center Sudetenland" of AGoFF and VSFF are mostly headed by one person.

       Periodicals: Sudetendeutsche Familienforschung (Sudeten-German family research) (new series since 1970), since 1973 annual publications.
       Publisher: VSFF
       Editor: Dr. Gert Reiprich, Viktor-Scheffel-Strasse 15, D–8000 München, Germany.

BOHEMIA, MORAVIA, SILESIA

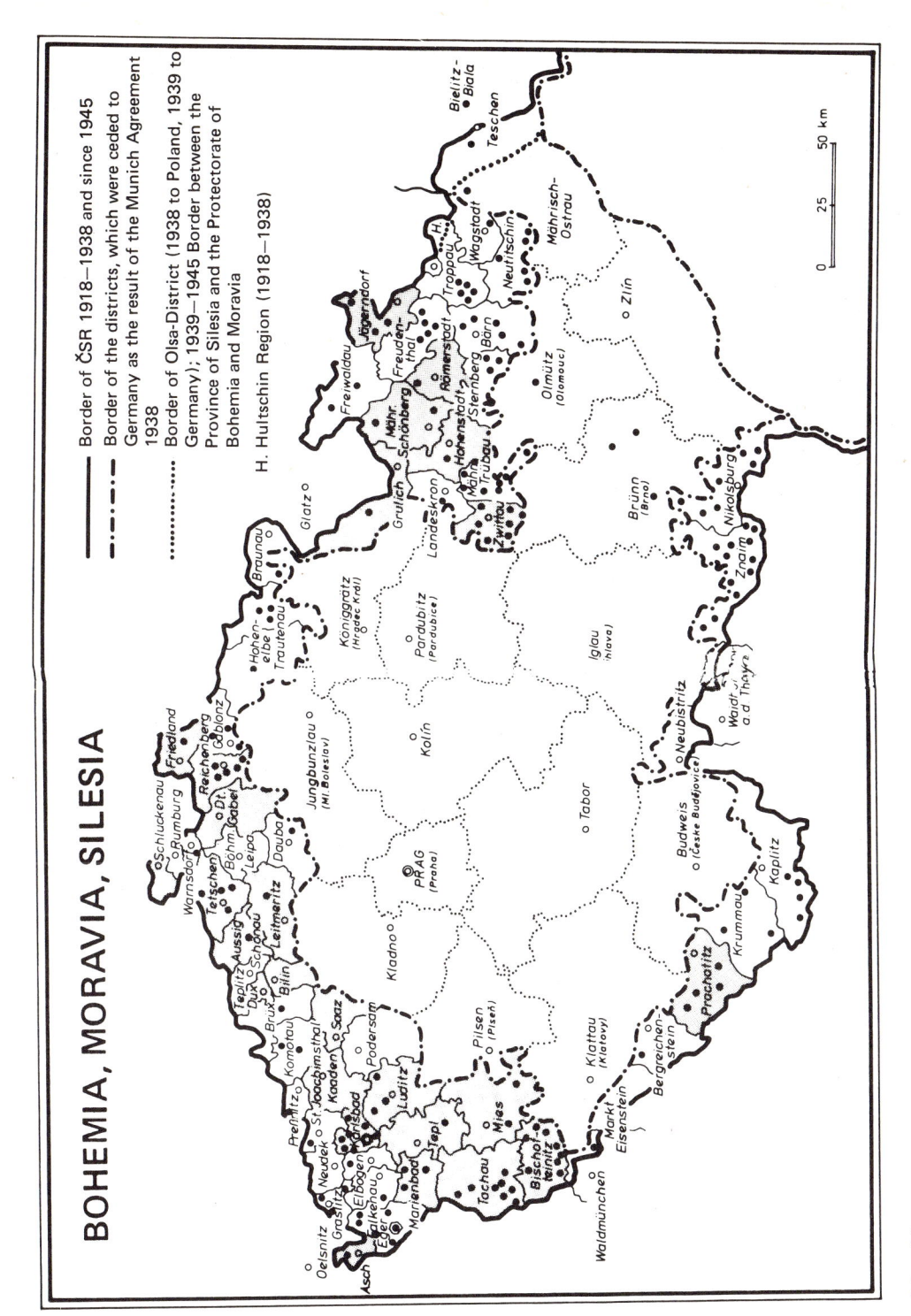

— Border of ČSR 1918–1938 and since 1945
—·—·— Border of the districts, which were ceded to Germany as the result of the Munich Agreement 1938
·········· Border of Olsa-District (1938 to Poland, 1939 to Germany); 1939–1945 Border between the Province of Silesia and the Protectorate of Bohemia and Moravia
H. Hultschin Region (1918–1938)

Map 34

Research groups

(as per the last German administrative division of 1941)

1. *Western Bohemia (former Reg.-Bez. – Administrative District – Aussig)*
   (Arbeitskreis Egerlaender Familienforscher – AEFF – Group of Egerland genealogists)

Asch	Archiv des Kreises Asch (Archives of the county Asch) Director: Helmut Klaubert, Postfach 4, Wichernstrasse 10, D–8672 Selb 4, Germany, Ph. 09287–20 31
Bischofteinitz	Eberhard Croy, Eschenweg 21, D–4000 Duesseldorf 30, Ph. 0211–42 40 59
Eger	Adolf Fischer see above 2.1 a.
Elbogen	Gustav Erlbeck, Fabrikweg 12, D–7959 Kirchberg a. d. Iller, Ph. 07354/73 83
Falkenau	Karl-Heinz Kriegelstein, Pustetstrasse 13, D–8416 Hemau, Ph. 09491–18 45, office: 0941–49 550
Graslitz	Horst R. Uebelacker, Erikastrasse 86 D–8031 Groebenzell, Ph. 03142–51 495
Kaaden	Richard Hellmessen, Ingelheimer Strasse 16, D–6000 Frankfurt/Main 71
Karlsbad	Gustav Erlbeck, see above
Luditz	Gertrud Traeger, Pirkheimer Strasse 10, D–8000 Muenchen 70, Ph. 089–53 05 69
Marienbad	Franz Huettl, Im Bahnhof, D–7151 Burgstetten 1, Ph. 07191–68 158
Mies	Robert Froeschl, Eberhartstrasse 36, D–7031 Holzgeilingen, Ph. 07031–41 950
Neudeck	Gustav Erlbeck, see above
Podersam	Alfred Sykora, Gotenstrasse 10, D–7501 Karlsbad 1, Ph. 07202–82 95
Pressnitz	Richard Hellmessen, see above
Saaz	Sigwalt Kaiser, Mespelbrunner Strasse 13, D–8500 Nuernberg, Ph. 0911–30 23 30
St. Joachimsthal	Viktor Makasy, Frauenberg 43, D–7060 Schondorf, Ph. 07181–32 37
Tachau	Oswald Froetschl, Meraner Strasse 3, D–8904 Friedberg, Ph. 0821–60 36 33
Tepl	Dr. Gert Reiprich, Viktor-Scheffel-Strasse 15 D–8000 Muenchen 40, Ph. 089–33 31 71

2. *Northern Bohemia (former Reg. Bez. Aussig)*

Aussig	Lore Schretzenmayr, Erikaweg 58, D–8400 Regensburg, Ph. 0941–2 18 14
Bilin	Friedrich Kriemer, Gustav-Mahler-Strasse 36, D–4010 Hilden, Ph. 02103–4 22 89
Boehmisch Leipa	Hilde Marianne Lerche, Dunantstrasse 1, D–8450 Amberg, Ph. week: 09624–362, weekend: 09621–8 31 02
Braunau	Herbert Birke, Auf der Rheide 6, D–4000 Duesseldorf 30
Bruex	Gustav Erlbeck, see above

	Dauba	Hilde Marianne Lerche, see above
	Deutsch Gabel	Sudetendeutsches Genealogisches Archiv, information see 2.1 b.
	Dux	Friedrich Kriemer, see above
	Friedland/Iserg.	Erhard Marschner, Hoenlestrasse 60, D–8000 Muenchen 21, Ph. 089–56 56 97
	Gablonz	Bruno Reckziegel, Klopfinger Strasse 5, D–8358 Vilshofen (Ndb), Ph. 08541–50 41
	Hohenelbe	Heinrich Tham, Saebener Strasse 7 D–8000 Muenchen 90
	Komotau	Annemarie Giessel-Dienel, Gutenbergstrasse 50, D–7000 Stuttgart 1, Ph. 0711–62 01 25
	Leitmeritz	Sudetendeutsches Genealogisches Archiv, information see 2.1 b.
	Reichenberg	the same
	Rumburg	Erhard Marschner, see above
	Schluckenau	Erhard Marschner, see above
	Teplitz-Schoenau	Friedrich Kriemer, see above
	Tetschen-Bodenbach	Sudetendeutsches Genealogisches Archiv, information see 2.1 b.
	Trautenau	Heinrich Tham, see above
	Warnsdorf	Erhard Marschner, see above
	Nordboehmisches Niederland	Erhard Marschner, see above
3.	*Northern Moravia (former Reg. Bez. Troppau)*	
	Baern	Karl Roessner, Lilienthalstrasse 35, D–3500 Kassel
	Freiwaldau	Dr. Lothar Wieland, Petersbergerstrasse 18 D–5300 Bonn 2 (Bad Godesberg), Ph. 0228–36 61 18
	Freudenthal	Helmut Roessler, Ziegeleistrasse 5, D–7056 Weinstadt
	Grulich	Sudetendeutsches Genealogisches Archiv, information see 2.1 b.
	Hohenstadt	Sudetendeutsches Genealogisches Archiv, information see 2.1 b.
	Jaegerndorf	Wilfried Gesierich, Altvaterstrasse 2 D–8411 Zeitlarn (Oberpf.)
	Landskron	Sudetendeutsches Genealogisches Archiv, information see 2.1 b.
	Maehrisch-Schoenberg	Kurt Dolleschel, Bahnhofstrasse 4, D–3545 Usseln/Waldeck, Ph. 05632–305
	Maehrisch Truebau	Sudetendeutsches Genealogisches Archiv, information see 2.1 b.
	Neutitschein	Hans-Hugo Weber, Leipziger Platz 5 D–8500 Nuernberg, Ph. 0911–56 49 89
	Roemerstadt	Helmut Roessler, see above
	Sternberg	Gottfried Melles, Schleichweg 15, D–6141 Winterkasten
	Troppau und Hultschiner Laendchen	Josef Heinz, Fuerstenstrasse 21, D–8301 Ergolding
	Wagstadt	Hans-Hugo Weber, see above
	Zwittau	Sudetendeutsches Genealogisches Archiv, information see 2.1 b.
	Kuhlaendchen	Hans-Hugo Weber, see above
	Schoenhengstgau	Sudetendeutsches Genealogisches Archiv, information see 2.1 b.
4.	*Bohemian Forest*	Guenther Burkon, Eichendorffstrasse 1 Neu-Esting, Post 8031 Olching, Ph. 08142–1 21 16

5. *Southern Bohemia*   Archiv fuer Suedboehmen in der Adalbert-Stifter-Gesellschaft
Gumpendorfer Strasse 15 II, A–1060 Vienna, Austria
(Archives for Southern Bohemia at the Adalbert-Stifter-Society).

6. *Southern Moravia (Arbeitskreis suedmaehrischer Familienforscher) (Group of Southern Moravian Genealogists)*

Neubistritz	Walfried Blaschka, Kleistrasse 6
Nikolsburg	D–7552 Durmersheim
Znaim	

7. *Language enclaves within Moravia and Austro-Silesia*

Bielitz, Teschen, Maehr. Ostrau	Hans-Hugo Weber, see above
Bruenn	Heinz Wamser, Gauguschgasse 29,
Iglau	A–2380 Percholdsdorf, Austria
Wischau	
Olmuetz	Karl Roessner, see above

8. *Central Bohemia*   Heinz Wamser, see above

9. *Prague*   Erhard Petrzilka, Waldparkdamm 8,
D–6800 Mannheim 1, Ph. 0621–82 12 89

Inquiries are to be sent directly to the respective research groups.

2.2 *Former institutions*

2.2. a. 1. *Zentralstelle fuer sudetendeutsche Familienforschung (Central office for Sudeten-German Genealogy)*

Head Office Aussig, established in Dux in 1926.
Transfered in 1939 to

Arbeitsgemeinschaft fuer Sippenkunde (Group for genealogy), Head Office Reichenberg,
which disappeared along with the German administration of the Sudeten territories in 1945.

2. *Deutscher Verein fuer Familienkunde fuer die Tschechoslowakische Republik (German society of genealogy for Czechoslovakia), Head Office Prague, 1929 to 1939.*

3. *Deutsche Gesellschaft fuer Familienkunde und Eugenik fuer die Tschechoslowakische Republik (German society for genealogy and eugenics for Czechoslovakia), Head Office Prague, 1932 to 1939.*

At the Aussig central office and at the local societies there existed resource and research centers for certain areas of family research between 1929 and 1944.

2.2. b. *Periodicals*:

Sudetendeutsche Familienforschung (Alte Folge) (Sudeten-German family research) (Old series)
published by: Aussiger Zentralstelle, 1929 to 1939.

Volk und Familie (People and family), weekly genealogical Saturday supplement of Sudetendeutsche Tageszeitung (Sudeten-German daily newspaper), beginning about 1933.

Familienforschung (Family research), supplement of the periodical of Deutscher Verein fuer die Geschichte Maehrens und Schlesiens (German society for the history of Moravia and Silesia), Bruenn, 1929 to 1944.

Zeitschrift fuer die Geschichte der Juden in der Tschechoslowakei (Periodical for the history of Jews in Czechoslovakia), Bruenn, 1930 to 1938.

2.2. c. *Special editions*

Sudetendeutsches Sonderheft (Sudeten-German special edition) of "Kultur und Leben" (Culture and Life), monthly for culture-historical and biological genealogy,
published by: Willy Hornschuch, editor: Dr. F. J. Umlauft, Schorndorf (Wuerttemberg), July 1926.

German-Bohemian volume of "Mitteilungen des Roland" (Bulletin of Roland), Dresden, vol. 5/6 1923.

Yearbook 1930 of Deutscher Verein fuer Familienkunde fuer die Tschechoslowakische Republik, Prague, 1931.

2.2. d. *The above periodicals are available at:*

Sudetendeutsches Genealogisches Archiv, see 2.1. a. above.

Bibliothek des Germanischen Nationalmuseums in Nuernberg,
Kartaeusergasse 1, D–8500 Nuernberg, Germany.

Bibliothek des Bayerischen Landesvereins fuer Familienkunde e. V.,
Winzererstrasse 68, D–8000 Muenchen 40, Germany.

Niedersaechsische Staats- und Universitaetsbibliothek Goettingen
Prinzenstrasse 1, D–3400 Goettingen, Germany.

Bibliothek der heraldisch-genealogischen Gesellschaft "Adler"
Haarhof 4a, A–1010 Vienna, Austria.

Bayerische Staatsbibliothek, Postfach 150, D–8000 Muenchen 35.

3. Documents of Vital Statistics

3.1 *Books and records of vital statistics*

The German marriage and civil status laws were introduced in the Sudetenland in 1939 including civil record offices.

3.2 *Displaced church records (including photocopies) – none known*

3.3 *Church records in homeland territory*

Inventory indexes of Roman Catholic church records of German and mixed-language churches of the following dioceses were published in "Sudetendeutsche Familienforschung" (Old series)

Prague	vol. 1 (1928/29) page 18, New Series 3 (1976) page 251
Budweis	vol. 1 (1928/29) page 62
Leitmeritz	vol. 2 (1929/30) page 152

Olmuetz	vol. 2 (1929/30) pages 7, 123, 153
Schoenhengster Sprachinsel	vol. 3 (1930/31) pages 9, 78, 99

A complete inventory of all vital statistics of the former Bohemian Kingdom was taken by Statistische Zentralkommission (Statistical central commission) of Vienna in 1887. The questionaire documents, containing some blanks, were indexed alphabetically by locality and are now held at the Oesterreichisches Staatsarchiv, Abt. Allgemeines Verwaltungsarchiv (Austrian state archives, dept. general administrativ archives) Wallnerstrasse 6a, A–1010 Vienna, Austria. A portion of these sources namely the register inventories from Abertham to Leskau were published in the Vienna technical periodical "Die Matrikel" (The Register) (1935, pages 24–35, 43–47, 51–52, 55, 1936, pages 1–4). A complete survey of church records in former Protectorate Bohemia and Moravia is found in a book published in Prague 1940 by Dr. Anton Blaschka "Die Personenstandsregister im Protektorat Boehmen und Maehren" (Records of vital statistics in the protectorate of Bohemia and Moravia). For parts of Upper Silesia which had fallen to Czechoslovakia after World War I, Erich Randt's and Horst-Oskar Swientek's "Die aelteren Personenstandsregister Schlesiens" (The older records of vital statistics of Silesia), Goerlitz, 1938, gives important hints on pages 138–144. Available at Forschungsstelle Schlesien (Research center Silesia) address see section "B" 2.1. Regarding Prague, one should refer to Roman von Prochaska's "Die Prager Pfarrmatriken" (Parish records of Prague), published in 1976 at "Sudetendeutsche Familienforschung", pages 251–258.

As there were about fifty parish offices in Prague the work of Dr. Hilde Lebeda about "Die Pfarrsprengel der Hauptstadt Prag" (The parishes of the capital of Prague) is important. Although not completed, it was published in "Sudetendeutsche Familienforschung" vol. 8, pages 9–11, 49–51, 91–94, vol. 9, pages 125–129 and vol. 10, pages 7–11. The assignments of conscription numbers of Prague houses and streets to parish offices are included in it.

After the church records had been taken over by the Czechoslovakian Government in 1952, they were turned over to the state archives. At first this new regulation included all records prior to about 1870, and later records remained with local civil record offices. At the end of 1979 additional inventories were turned over to the state archives, and since spring of 1980 all records prior about 1900 are held at the state archives.

The above mentioned listings of records naturally do not agree with modern inventories. World War II and its aftermath destroyed or lost a sizeable number of church records. Duplicates of records after 1800 are mostly available. Their location may be found through the state archives in Prague (see 6.3 below). Duplicates of church records of 1780–1820 for Western Bohemian localities belonging to the diocese of Regensburg are now held at Bischoefliches Zentralarchiv (Central episcopal archives) in Regensburg (St. Petersweg 11–13, D–8400 Regensburg 1, Germany).

For Czechoslovakian archives see 6.3 below.

4. Gazetteers

4.1 *Published after 1945*

Sudetendeutsches Ortsnamenverzeichnis (Sudeten-German gazetteer), official gazetteer of Sudeten-German territories which came to Germany by the Munich Agreement of 1938, published by Institut fuer Landeskunde at Bundesanstalt fuer Landeskunde und Raumforschung, Bad Godesberg, Germany, 1963.

Ortslexikon der boehmischen Laender 1910–1965 (Gazetteer of Bohemia states 1910–1965), published by Heribert Sturm for Collegium Carolinum by Oldenbourg Verlag, Muenchen, Trier, Germany, 1977.

Statistický lexikon obcí ČSSR 1974, Prague, Czechoslovakia, 1976.

4.2 *Published prior to 1945*

Ortsbuch fuer die Sudetengebiete (Gazetteer for the Sudeten areas) (Addendum to the 7th edition of Muellers Grosses Deutsches Ortsbuch), Wuppertal-Naechstebreck, 1939, 3rd edition 1944.

Amtliches Deutsches Ortsbuch fuer das Protektorat Boehmen und Maehren (Official gazetteer for the Protectorate Bohemia and Moravia), published by Reichsprotektor in Boehmen and Maehren, Prague, 1944.

"Ortsrepertorium fuer das Koenigreich Boehmen" or "Spezialrepertorium von Boehmen" (Inventory of localities of the Kingdom of Bohemia) or (Special inventory of Bohemia), several issues were published between 1878 and 1918 by k. k. Statthalterei fuer Boehmen (Imperial-royal government office for Bohemia) or k. k. Statistische Zentralkommission (Imperial-royal central commission).

Gemeindelexikon von Boehmen (Gazetteer of Bohemia), published by k. k. Statistische Zentralkommission, Vienna, 1904.

Statistický lexikon obcí v Republice Československe (Gazetteer of the Republic of Czechoslovakia), part I Bohemia, Prague, 1934.

Crusius, Ch.: Topographisches Post-Lexikon aller Ortschaften der K. K. Erblaender, T. 1: Boehmen, Maehren, Schlesien. Wien 1798.

Topographisches Lexikon von Boehmen, Prag 1852.

J. Schaller: Topographie des Koenigreichs Boehmen, 16 parts, Prag 1785–1791.

C. E. Rainhold: Verzeichnis aller im Koenigreich Boehmen befindlichen Ortschaften, Prag 1820.

F. J. Schwoy: Topographie vom Markgrafentum Maehren, 3 vols., Wien 1793–1794.

J. G. Sommer: Das Koenigreich Boehmen, statistisch-topographisch dargestellt, 16 vols., Prag 1833–1849.

Alphabetisches Verzeichnis saemtlicher im Markgrafentum Maehren befindlichen Ortschaften, Bruenn 1855.

Vollstaendiges topographisches Ortslexikon der Markgrafschaft Maehren, Bruenn 1855.

G. Wolny: Die Markgrafschaft Maehren, topographisch, statistisch und historisch geschildert, 6 vols., Bruenn 1835–1842.

G. Wolny: Kirchliche Topographie von Maehren, 10 vols., Bruenn 1855–1866.

5. **Bibliographies and Literature**

Genealogical and homeland study sources

Published after 1945

1. Der Schluessel (The key), complete index with local source information for genealogical, heraldic and historical series of publications, vol. 6, summary of genealogical-historical periodicals in Austria and German speaking Czechoslovakia 1871–1944, edited by Hanns Jaeger-Sunstenau, published by Heinz Reise in co-operation with Genealogisch-Heraldische Gesellschaft Goettingen, 1970.
2. Quellen- und Namennachweis fuer die sudetendeutsche Familienforschung (Source and name information for Sudeten-German genealogy), see 2.1. a. above.
3. Adolf Fischer, Bibliographie der Sudetendeutschen Familienforschung im Jubilaeumsjahr 1976 (Bibliography of Sudenten-German genealogy in the jubilee of 1976), in Sudetendeutsche Familienforschung 1977, see 2.1. b. above.
4. Adolf Fischer, Veroeffentlichungen Egerlaender Familienforscher in Fachblaettern (Publications of Egerland genealogists in genealogical periodicals), in Jahrbuch der Egerlaender (Yearbook of Egerlanders), Egerland-Verlag, Marktredwitz-Nuernberg, 1971 page 136, 1974 page 138, 1976 page 135, 1978 page 137.
5. Adolf Fischer, Egerlaender Heimatblaetter (Egerland homeland bulletins), in the yearbook of Egerlanders, Egerland-Verlag Marktredwitz-Nuernberg, 1964 page 99, 1965 page 138.
6. Adolf Fischer, Publikationsmoeglichkeiten fuer die Egerlaender Familienforscher (Publication opportunities for Egerland genealogists), in OFK vol. III page 184, 1962.
7. Rudolf Hemmerle, Heimat im Buch (Homeland in literature), published by Sudetendeutsches Archiv and Adalbert-Stifter-Verein, Muenchen, 1970.
8. A current index of all Sudeten-German homeland newsletters is found in the pocketbook of members of the executive of the Sudeten-German Society which is published yearly by Verlagshaus Sudetenland GmbH, Arnulfstrasse 71, D–8000 Muenchen, Germany.
9. Valentin Maenner, Index fuer Egerlaender Volks- und Heimatkunde (Index for Egerland ethnic and homeland studies), published by Egerer Landtag, Amberg 1971.
10. Ernst Schwarz, Sudetendeutsche Familiennamen des 15. und 16. Jhdts. (Sudeten-German Names of the 15th and 16th century), Muenchen 1973.
11. Buecherei des deutschen Ostens, Herne. Catalog, 1973, pages 521–643.

6. **Archives and Libraries with Sources on Homeland Regions**

6.1 *In West Germany – Federal Republic of Germany including West-Berlin*

Bibliothek des Germanischen Nationalmuseums (Library of the German National Museum) in Nuernberg, Kartaeusergasse 1, D–8500 Nuernberg 1, Germany.

Sudetendeutsches Archiv e. V. (Sudeten-German archives) established 1955:

Chairman: Anton F. Wuschek, Senatspraesident, Munich.
Secretary, archives, offices, library: Thierschstrasse 11–17, D–8000 Muenchen 22, Germany, Ph. 089–29 42 31.

Arbeitsstelle fuer sudetendeutsche Landeskunde und Zeitgeschichte (Office for Sudeten-German territorial studies and modern history): Alois Harasko
Forschungsstelle fuer Gegenwartsfragen der Tschechoslowakei (Research center for contemporary questions of Czechoslovakia); Dr. Heinrich Kuhn
Sudetendeutsche Bildstelle (Sudeten-German picture center): Hannes Kuehnel
Heimatarchive (Homeland archives): Ilse Dreiseitel

The library includes more than 55 000 volumes. The picture archives 35 000 photographs and 20 000 negatives are one of the largest for any ethnic group.

The Sudeten-German archives collect archival estates of prominent people in politics, arts and sciences (like Lodgman von Auen, Hans-Christoph Seebohm, Wenzel Jaksch).

The Sudeten-German archives are the central collecting agency for documents of the Sudeten-German Society and other Sudeten-German associations.

Arbeitsgemeinschaft fuer kulturelle Heimatsammlungen bei dem Sudetendeutschen Archiv e. V. (Group for cultural homeland collections at the Sudeten-German archives), established 1974 in Regensburg, head office in Munich, Germany.

The group includes seventy-one owners, directors and curators of homeland archives, homeland museums and libraries.

Adlergebirge, Heimatstube und Archive (Homeland room and archives);
Rathaus, D–8264 Waldkraiburg
Curator: Fritz Pischel, Schichtstrasse 2, D–8264 Waldkraiburg, Germany

Boehmerwald-Museum (Bohemian forest museum)
Passau-Oberhaus
Curator: Josef Buerger, Schulrat a. D., D–8391–Hutthurm bei Passau, Germany

Egerland-Museum und Egerland Buecherei (Egerland museum and Egerland library)
Egerland-Kulturhaus, D–8590 Marktredwitz, Germany

Egerland Heimatkartei (Egerland homeland directory): Head office Wendlingen:
Altes Rathaus, D–7317 Wendlingen
Curator: Herbert Schneider, Goethestrasse 3, D–7401 Dusslingen, Germany, Ph. 67072–346

Kuhlaendler Arcchiv und Heimatstube (Kuhland archives and homeland room):
Stuttgarter Strasse 62, D–7140 Ludwigsburg, Germany
Curator: Heinz Kohlbaum, Hirsener Strasse 1, D–7140 Ludwigsburg-Eglosheim, Germany, Ph. 67141–34 41

Riesengebirgsmuseum und -archiv (Museum and archives):
Martinsheim, Eberle-Koegl-Strasse 11, D–8952 Marktoberdorf, Germany
Curator: Richard Floegel, Woerishofener Strasse 27, D–8950 Kaufbeuren, Germany

Schoenhengster Archiv und Heimatstube (Archives and homeland room):
Noerdliche Ringstrasse 33, D–7320 Goeppingen, Germany

Suedmaehren, Heimatstube und Landschaftsarchiv (Southern Moravia homeland room and area archives):
Hauptstrasse 19, D–7340 Geislingen, Germany
Director: Franz Sprinzl, Silberburgstrasse 44, D–7000 Stuttgart, Germany

Altrohlauer Stube (Altrohlau room):
Curator: Rudolf Zettl, Postfach 1322, Saarlandstrasse 49, D–6806 Viernheim, Germany

Altenauer Heimatstube (Altenau homeland room):
Bergstraesser Heimatmuseum, D–6140 Bensheim, Germany

Archiv des Kreises Asch (County of Asch archives):
Director: Helmut Klaubert, Wichernstrasse 10, D–8762 Selb 4, Germany

Ascher Heimatstube (Asch homeland room):
Director: Adolf Kuenzel, Unlitzstrasse 24, D–8673 Rehau, Germany

Aussiger Archiv und Heimatstube (Aussig archives and homeland room):
Liebherrstrasse 4/III Rgb., D–8000 Muenchen 22, Germany
Director: Herbert Engl, Frauenstaedtstrasse 6, D–8000 Muenchen 40, Germany

Baerner Heimatstube (Baern homeland room):
Jahnstrasse 30, D–6306 Langgoens, Germany
Director: Rudi Polzer

Bielitz-Biala Heimatstube (Bielitz-Biala homeland room):
Stadtpalais, D–4780 Lippstadt, Germany
Director: Anni Schlueter, Lang Strasse 15, D–4780 Lippstadt, Germany

Bischofteinitz Heimatmuseum (Bischofteinitz homeland museum):
Schlossplatz, D–8492 Furth im Wald, Germany

Braunauer Heimatmuseum (Heimatarchiv) (Braunau homeland museum and archives):
Paradeplatz 2, D–8550 Forchheim, Germany
Museum director: Rudolf Streubel, Ulmenstrasse 21, D–8500 Nuernberg, Germany
Archives and library: Dr. Erhard Meissner, Rothofweg 17, D–8602 Bischberg, Germany

Bruch-Ladung Wiesa Heimatstube (Bruch-Ladung Wiesa homeland room):
Ewald-Schule II, D–4353 Oer-Erkenschwick, Germany

Bruenner Heimatmuseum (Bruenn homeland museum):
Prediger, D–7070 Schwaebisch Gmuend, Germany

Bruex: Archives of the homeland municipality at the city archives of Erlangen
Cedernstrasse 1, D–8520 Erlangen, Germany
Administrator: Archivrat Dr. Helmut Richter

Bruexer Heimatstube (Bruex homeland room):
Marktplatz 1, Palais Stutterheim, D–8520 Erlangen
Director: Peter Wesselovsky, Leipziger Strasse 3, D–8709 Ochsenfurt, Germany
Administrator: Lidy Wurzberger, Bissinger Strasse 2, D–8520 Erlangen, Germany

Buchauer Heimatstube (Buchau homeland room):
Mittelfranken, D–8843 Pappenheim, Germany

Chodauer Heimatstube (Chodau homeland room):
D–8595 Waldsassen, Germany
Curator: Franz Procksch, Mitterteicher Strasse 5/7, D–8595 Waldsassen, Germany

Heimathaus Kreis Dux (Gaeste- und Wohnheim) mit Duxer Heimatarchiv (Homeland house for county of Dux with Dux homeland archives):
Duxer Strasse 10, D–8760 Miltenberg, Germany

Elbogener Heimatstube (Elbogen homeland room):
Rathaus, D–7918 Illertissen, Germany
Curator: Herbert Schneider, Goethestrasse 3, D–7410 Dusslingen, Germany, Ph. 07072–34 68

Freiwaldau-Graefenberger Archiv und Museum (Freiwaldau-Graefenberg archives and museum):
Elly Hackenberg, Bismarckstrasse 56, D–7312 Kirchheim/Teck, Germany

Freudenthal Archiv und Museum (Freudenthal archives and museum):
Zwangmeisterstrasse, D–8940 Memmingen, Germany
Curator: Dipl. Ing. Robert Kube, Schulweg 7, D–8941 Memmingerberg, Germany

Friedland im Isergebirge Heimatarchiv (Friedland homeland archives):
Friedlandstube: Am Anger, D–6418 Huenfeld 1, Germany
Administrator: Dr. Oskar Kroemer, Danziger Strasse 18, D–6400 Fulda, Germany

Fulnek und Umgebung Heimatarchiv (Fulnek regional archives):
Fritz Eichler, Dantestrasse 8, D–6900 Heidelberg, Germany

Gablonzer Archiv und Museum e. V. (Gablonz archives and museum):
(Gablonzer Haus), D–8950 Kaufbeuren-Neugablonz, Germany
Chairman: Oswald Wondrak
Library, archives, museum: Karl Zenkner
Gablonz gallery: Director: Otto Pohl

Giebauer Heimatstube (Giebau homeland room):
Alte Karolinger Schule Lorsch,
Curator: Paula Braun, Oberstrasse 42, D–6143 Lorsch, Germany

Glasmuseum Rheinbach (Glass museum Rheinbach):
with homeland rooms for the glass cities of Haida, Steinschoenau und surroundings
Postfach 1227, Vor dem Voigtstor 23, D–5380 Rheinbach 1, Germany

Iglauer Heimatstube (Iglau homeland room):
Schloss Hellenstein, D–7920 Heidenheim, Germany

Jauerniger Archiv und Heimatstube (Jauernig archives and homeland room):
Josef Thanheiser, Kehlstrasse 68, D–7143 Vaihingen/Enz, Germany

Kaaden-Duppau Heimatstube und Archiv (Kaaden-Duppau homeland room and archives):
Postfach 248, Am Hof 23, D–8832 Weissenburg, Germany, Ph. 09141–36 25

Heimatstube Kaltenbach Kreis Prachatitz (Homeland room Kaltenbach county of Prachatitz):
Alte Schule, D–8391 Roehrnbach, Germany
Director: Kilian Heigl, Thurwieser Strasse 12, D–8000 Muenchen 45, Germany

Karlsbader Archiv und Museum (Karlsbad archives and museum):
Sonnenberger Strasse 14, D–6200 Wiesbaden, Germany
Curator: Franz Kraus, Goethestrasse 1, D–6277 Camberg/Taunus, Germany

Komotau-Archiv (Komotau archives):
Otto v. Streitberg, Helmholtzstrasse 25, D–8520 Erlangen, Germany
Homeland room at: Marktplatz 1.

Leipa-Haida-Dauba Heimatarchiv (Leipa-Haida-Dauba homeland archives):
Curator: Elisabeth Scholz, Sperberweg 1, D–7530 Pforzheim-Buckenberg, Germany, Ph. 07231–61 888

Leitmeritzer Archiv (Leitmeritz archives):
Habsburgergasse 2, D–6400 Fulda, Germany
Administrator: Gottfried Jaksch

Lichtenstadt Heimatstube (Lichtenstadt homeland room):
in Zirndorf
Director: Alfred Reichmann, Klampferstrasse 5, D—8502 Zirndorf, Germany

Liebnau
Homeland room at the Bauernmuseum, D—8901 Koenigsbrunn, Germany
Curator: Prof. Richard W. Eichler, Steinkirchner Strasse 15, D—8000 Muenchen 71, Germany

Luditzer Heimatstube (Luditz homeland room)
(Hochzeitshaus) D—3437 Bad Sooden-Allendorf
Director: Alfred Roedling, Sudetenstrasse 27, D—3437 Bad Sooden-Allendorf, Germany

Maehrisch Neustadt Heimatmuseum (Maehrisch Neustadt homeland museum):
Altes Schloss, Limburg/Lahn, Germany
Curator: Kurt Nigratschka, Sindersbacher Strasse 4, D—6257 Huenfelden 1-Kirchberg, Germany

Maehrisch Schoenberg Heimatstube, Archiv und Museum (Maehrisch Schoenberg homeland room, archives and museum):
"Haus Maehrisch Schoenberg", Neumarkt 38, D—6430 Bad Hersfeld, Germany

Marienbader Archiv und Museum (Marienbad archives and museum):
Franz Pany, Schleissheimer Strasse 165, D—8000 Muenchen 40, Germany

Mies-Pilsner Heimatmuseum (Mies-Pilsen homeland museum):
Postfach 127 (Rathaus), D—8804 Dinkelsbuehl, Germany

Heimatstube Landkreis Neudek (Homeland room county of Neudek):
Bgm.-Aurnhammer-Strasse 6 (Jahn-Schule), D—8900 Augsburg 22-Goeggingen, Germany

Niederebersdorfer (Kreis Tetschen-Bobenbach) Archiv und Heimatstuben (Niederebersdorf archives and homeland rooms):
Altes Feuerwehrhaus, Oskar-Schoeler-Strasse, D—8132 Tutzing, Germany

Niederlaender Heimatstube und Archiv (Niederland homeland room and archives):
Foster City Boeblingen
Curator: Heinz Bendel, Lichtensteinstrasse 3, D—7030 Boeblingen, Germany

Niemeser Heimatstube (Niemes homeland room):
Curator: Oskar Strzala, Theresienstrasse 13, D—8070 Ingolstadt, Germany

Odrau und Umgebung Heimatarchiv (Odrau regional archives):
D—8859 Neuburg/Donau-Feldkirchen 2, Germany

Plan-Weseritzer Heimatstube mit Archiv (Plan-Weseritz homeland room and archives):
Hochwartstrasse 1, D—8593 Tirschenreuth, Germany
Director: Willi Junker, Woertherstrasse 9, D—8059 Hoerlkofen, Germany

Reichenberger Archiv und Heimatstube (Reichenberg homeland room and archives):
Konrad-Adenauer-Allee 55/I, D—8900 Augsburg, Germany, Ph. 6821—51 14 92

Heimatstube Roemerstadt (Roemerstadt homeland room):
Director: Gustav Koehler, Hofgut Winnerod, D—6301 Reiskirchen, Germany, Ph. 06408—82 86

Schlackenwerther Zimmer (Archiv) (Schlackenwerth room — archives)
at Heimatmuseum der Stadt Rastatt (Homeland museum of the City of Rastatt)
Director: Arch. Josef Hubatschek, Bessarabienstrasse 3, D—7317 Wendlingen, Germany

Heimatstube und Archiv Schluckenau (Schluckenau homeland room and archives):
Schulstrasse 4, D—7912 Weissenhorn, Germany

Sternberger Archiv und Heimatstube (Sternberg homeland room and archives):
Gerhard Wolf, Geiselhardstrasse 5, D–8870 Guenzburg, Germany

Tauchauer Heimatstube (Tachau homeland room):
Postfach 1651, Pfarrplatz 4, D–8480 Weiden, Germany
Kulturzentrum "Haus Bauer".

Teplitz-Schoenauer Museum (Teplitz-Schoenau museum):
D–6000 Frankfurt/M.-Hoechst
Museum and information Director: Josef Richter, Gerlachstrasse 29a, D–6230 Frankfurt/M-Hoechst, Germany

Tetschen-Bodenbacher Heimatmuseum (Tetschen-Bodenbach homeland museum)
Neues Stadtmuseum, D–8860 Noerdlingen
Heimatverband Tetschen-Bodenbach e. V., Postfach 1108, D–8860 Noerdlingen, Germany

Trautenauer Heimatarchiv (Trautenau homeland archives):
Thierschstrasse 11–17/III, Zimmer 303, D–8000 Muenchen 22, Germany

Troppauer Heimatarchiv (Troppau homeland archives):
Postfach 1643, Altes Rathaus, D–8600 Bamberg, Germany

Wagstadter Heimatarchiv (Wagstadt homeland archives):
Mozartstrasse 3, D–8740 Bad Neustadt/Saale, Germany

Waltscher Heimatstube (Waltsch homeland room):
Goethestrasse 12, D–6903 Neckargemuend, Germany

Weidenau-Grosskosse Heimatstube (Weidenau-Grosskosse homeland room):
Helmut Kirchner, Karlplatz A 50, D–8858 Neuburg/Do., Germany

Zuckmantler Heimatstube (Zuckmantl homeland room):
Otto Wolf, Geschnaidte Strasse 3, D–7015 Korntal, Germany

Archiv u. Buecherei der Arbeitsgemeinschaft sudetendeutscher Erzieher (Archives and library of Sudeten-German educators):
Elsbeth Peschka, Rathaus, D–8264 Waldkraiburg, Germany

Seliger Archiv e. V. (Selig archives):
Archivar: Dr. Franz Kunert, Schloss-Strasse 92, D–7000 Stuttgart 1, Germany

Zentralarchiv des deutschen Protestantismus in den boehmischen Laendern (Central archives of German protestantism in Bohemian states):
(at the Institut fuer Reformations- und Kirchengeschichte der boehmischen Laender):
Prof.-Kuehne-Strasse 32a, D–6927 Rappenau, Germany

6.2 *In Austria*

Bibliothek der Heraldisch-Genealogischen Gesellschaft "Adler" (Library of the heraldic-genealogical society "Adler"), Haarhof 4a, A–1010 Vienna, Austria.

Maehrisch-Schlesisches Heimatmuseum (Moravian-Silesian Homeland museum): Schiessstattgasse, Rostochvilla, A–3400 Klosterneuburg, Austria.

Boehmerwald Museum und Ausstellungs- und Schauraum der Erzgebirger (Bohemian Forest museum and exhibition and showroom of Erzgebirgers): Ungargasse 3, A–1030 Vienna, Chancellery: Baeckerstrasse 14, A–1010 Vienna, Austria.

Oesterreichisches Staatsarchiv, Finanz- und Hofkammerarchiv (Austrian state archives, finance and court chamber archives): Johannesgasse 6, A–1010 Vienna, Austria.

Oesterreichisches Staatsarchiv, Kriegsarchiv (Austrian state archives, war archives) Stiftgasse 2, A–1010 Vienna, Austria.

Oesterreichisches Staatsarchiv fuer Verkehrswesen (Austrian state archives for traffic): Aspangstrasse 33, A–1010 Vienna, Austria.

Archiv des evangelischen Oberkirchenrates (Archives of the Protestant supreme council). Severin-Schreiber-Gasse 3, A–1180 Vienna, Austria.

6.3 *In homeland territory*

At the head of the present-day Czech archival system is the archives administration at the Interior Ministry of the Czech Socialist Republic (Archívní Správá MV ČSR, Trída Obráncu Míru 133, ČS–166 21 Praha 6). From this office foreigners must request research permits in writing, which, usually, is granted for the current year. There are no charges for personal research at Czech archives.

Under the jurisdiction of the archives administration in Prague are the following archives:

1. Staní Oblastní Archiv v Plzní (Regional state archives in Plzen), CS–306 28 Plzen, Sledláčkova 44, Czechoslovakia: responsible for the Western Bohemian district.
2. Staní Oblastní Archiv v Litoměřicích (Regional state archives in Litoměřice), CS–412 74 Litomerice, Krajska 1, Czechoslovakia: responsible for the Northern Bohemian district.
3. Staní Oblastní Archiv v Praze (Regional state archives in Prague), CS–120 00 Praha 2, Horská 7, Czechoslovakia: responsible for the Central Bohemian district but not for the Capital City of Prague.
4. Staní Oblastní Archiv v Treboní (Regional state archives in Třeboň), CS–379 11 Třeboň-zámek, Czechoslovakia: responsible for the Southern Bohemian district.
5. Staní Oblastní Archiv v Zámrsku (Regional state archives in Zámrsk), CS–565 43 Zámrsk-zámek, Czechoslovakia: responsible for the Eastern Bohemian district.
6. Staní Oblastní Archiv v Opavě (Regional state archives in Opava), CS–746 00 Opava, Sněmovní 1, Czechoslovakia: responsible for the Northern Moravian district.
7. Staní Oblastní Archiv v Brně (Regional state archives in Brno), CS–600 00 Brno, Zerotínova nám. 3–5, Czechoslovakia: responsible for the Southern Moravian district.
8. Central State Archives Prague (Statní Ustrední Archiv), Karmelitska 2, CS–110 00 Praha 1. – The inventory of these archives does not contain church records.

The Capital City Archives of Prague (Archiv hlavního mesta Prahy, Husova 20, CS–110 00 Praha 1). Vital statistics of Prague are on deposit here.

Since the 1950's all Czech state archives have published synopses of inventories of their materials – in part multi-volume – which also cover vital statistics records. For instance State Archives of the Plzeň (Pilsen) District in 1958 the "prudvodce po archivnich fondech", which on pages 128–173 contains a listing of available church records. This, however, is now outdated and revised editions are being prepared.

The church records from about 1900 to 1945 are on deposit at civil registry offices of the local National Committees. Personal research is impossible here. Written applications for birth, marriage and death certificates from these books have to be made through the diplomatic channels of Czechoslovakia or the foreign ministry of your own country. In foreign countries (for instance: The Czech Embassy, Consular Division, in the capital of your country). The embassy will issue a separate questionaire for each individual request, which has to be completed with dates and Czech-language locality names. Only this way may be completed. With the application a fee of about ten dollars is charged. Fees for each issued certificate are about seven dollars.

Of great importance for research, particularly in the fields of family and homeland historical studies, are the 72 district archives, in Czechoslovakia. They hold usually, old landtitle registers, which in part go back to the 14th century, according to districts — a district roughly corresponds to a European county —. In archival matters these district archives are under the jurisdiction of the regional archives, however in the disciplinary sense, under the jurisdiction of the regional national committee. Foreigners must get a permit to use the archives not only from the central archives administration office in Prague, but also from the regional national committee.

It is also important to mention the Vojenský historický ústav (Military historical institute) in Prague, (CS–130 00 Praha 3, U Památniku 2, Czechoslovakia), which not only holds the military records, but also the military files of all former Czechoslovakian soldiers, including those who served with the Austro-Hungarian army and were still under conscription at the time of the formation of Czechoslovakia in 1918. Upon written application (specifying regiment etc.) the institute will furnish personal information (birth, origin), promotions and service certificates.

A good survey of the Czech archival system, with special emphasis on the regional state archives at Plzeň/Pilsen, is given by the Plzeň State Archives Director Dr. Vladimír Bystricky in an article, which appeared in April 1979 in the family periodical "Der Haubmacher" (Publisher: Hans-Joachim Haeupler, D–8029 Sauerlach/Obb., Germany). In addition we point to Roman Frhr. von Procházka "Moeglichkeiten und Methoden genealogischer und kulturgeschichtlicher Familienforschung in der Tschechoslowakei" (Possibilities and methods of genealogical and cultural-historical family research in Czechoslovakia) in the jubilee volume 1976 of "Sudetendeutsche Familienforschung" (Sudeten-German family research), page 259 ff.

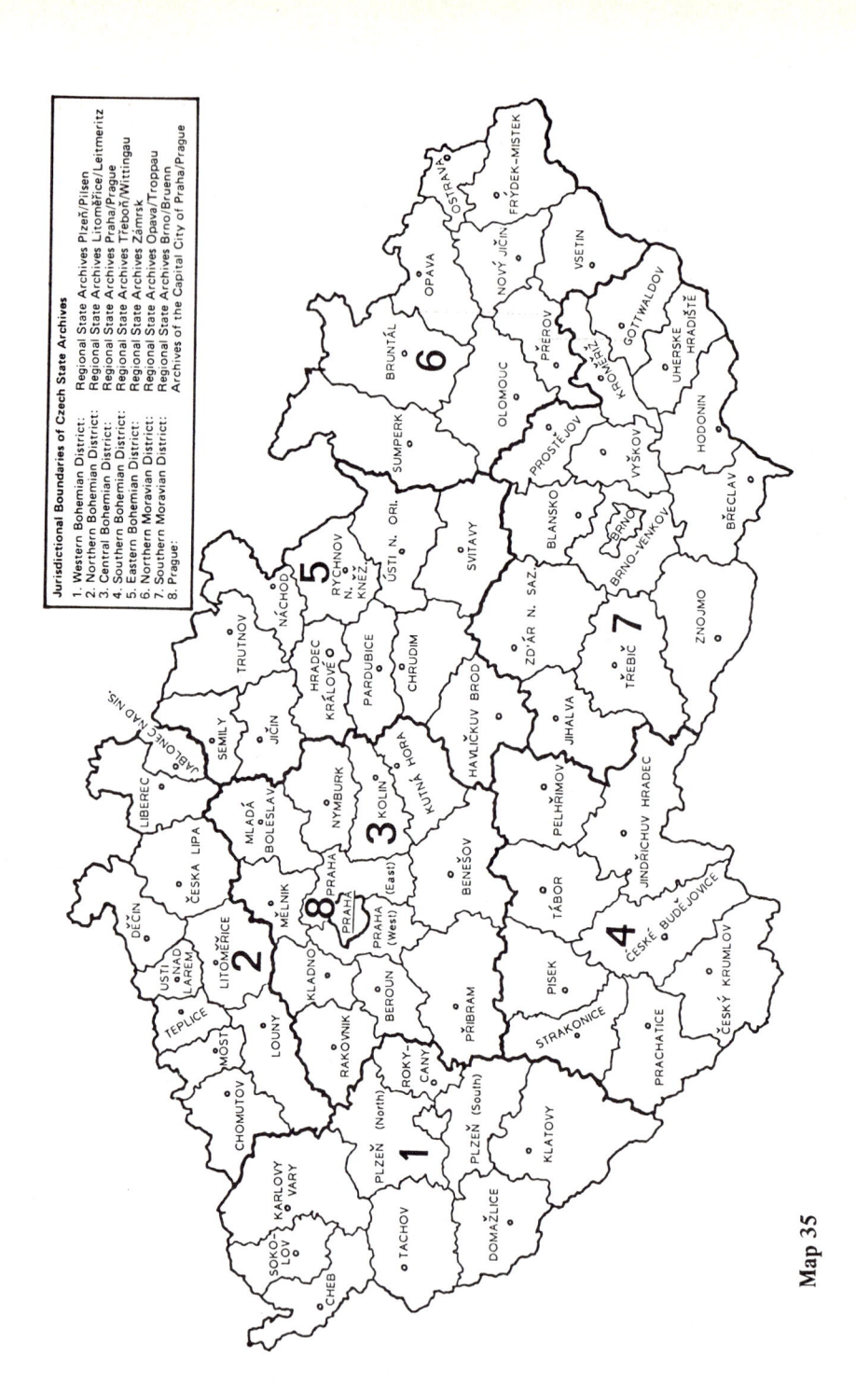

Jurisdictional Boundaries of Czech State Archives

1. Western Bohemian District: Regional State Archives Plzeň/Pilsen
2. Northern Bohemian District: Regional State Archives Litoměřice/Leitmeritz
3. Central Bohemian District: Regional State Archives Praha/Prague
4. Southern Bohemian District: Regional State Archives Třeboň/Wittingau
5. Eastern Bohemian District: Regional State Archives Zámrsk
6. Northern Moravian District: Regional State Archives Opava/Troppau
7. Southern Moravian District: Regional State Archives Brno/Bruenn
8. Prague: Archives of the Capital City of Praha/Prague

Map 35

7. **Other Research Aids**

7.1 *Hometown/village directory*

Heimatortskartei fuer Sudetendeutsche (Hometown/village directory for Sudeten-Germans) Von-der-Tann-Strasse 9 I, D–8400 Regensburg, Germany, Ph. 0941–53 016.

7.2 *Societies of Sudeten Germans*

    a. Sudetendeutsche Landsmannschaft (Sudeten-German society) e. V. (SL), Federal Office, Postfach 46, Arnulfstrasse 71 V, D–8000 Muenchen 19, Germany, Ph. 089–18 20 55.

    with territorial divisions (state, district, county and local groups).

    Sudetendeutsche Zeitung (Sudeten-German newspaper)
    Publisher: Sudetendeutsche Verlags-GmbH
    Postfach 20 21 23, Paul-Heyse-Strasse 6, D–8000 Muenchen 2, Germany, Ph. 089–5310 42 143.

    b. Sudetendeutsche Landsmannschaft in Oesterreich (Sudeten-German society in Austria) (SLO), Federal business office, Hegelgasse 19/4, A–1010 Vienna, Austria.

    with territorial divisions (state district and local societies)

    Sudetenpost (Sudeten post)
    Postfach 405, A–4010 Linz, Austria.

    c. Homeland divisions
    (partly with their own homeland county societies, see also this Section 8.

    For all homeland regions and counties the Sudetendeutsche Landsmannschaft has elected curators. As these change quite frequently a listing is published yearly by Verlagshaus Sudetenland GmbH in Taschenbuch fuer die Amtstraeger der Sudetendeutschen Landsmannschaft (Pocket book for executive members of the Sudeten-German society), Arnulfstrasse 71, D–8000 Muenchen 19, Germany.

7.3 *Homeland information centers*

for Regierungsbezirk (Administrative district) Aussig
at Landesausgleichsamt Bayern, Leonrodstrasse 56, D–8000 Muenchen 19, Germany

for Regierungsbezirk Eger
at Landesausgleichsamt Hessen, Luisenstrasse 13, D–6200 Wiesbaden, Germany

for Regierungsbezirk Troppau
at Landesausgleichsamt Baden-Wuerttemberg, Postfach 1284, D–7000 Stuttgart 1, Germany

Bohemia and Moravia (Southern Bohemia and Southern Moravia, formerly Protectorate Bohemia and Moravia)
at Landesausgleichsmat Bayern, Leonrodstrasse 56, D–8000 Muenchen 19, Germany.

7.4 *Historical societies*

    1. Collegium Carolinum e. V., Forschungsstelle fuer boehmische Laender (Research center for Bohemian states)
    Office: Thierschstrasse 11–17/IV, D–8000 Muenchen 22, Germany

    Publications:

    Bohemia, Jahrbuch des Collegium Carolinum (Yearbook of the Collegium Carolinum)

Biographisches Lexikon zur Geschichte der Boehmischen Laender (Biographical dictionary for the history of Bohemian states)

   numerous other publications.

2. Historische Kommission der Sudetenlaender e. V. (Historical commission of Sudeten districts), Head office: Heidelberg
   Secretarial office: Thierschstrasse 17/IV, D–8000 Muenchen, Germany.

3. Gesellschaft zur Foerderung ostmitteleuropaeischen Schrifttums e. V. (Society for the advancement of East-Central European literature)
   Rueckertstrasse 6, D–6200 Wiesbaden, Germany

   Cultural quarterly "Sudetenland".

4. Adalbert-Stifter Verein e. V. (Adalbert-Stifter society)
   Office: Thierschplatz 4/I, D–8000 Muenchen 22, Germany.

5. Archiv fuer Sudetendeutsche Volkskunde (Archives for Sudeten-German ethnic studies)
   Roonstrasse 31, D–6300 Giessen, Germany

7.5 Church institutions

1. Gemeinschaft evangelischer Sudetendeutscher (Circle of Protestant Sudeten-Germans)
   Boltensternstrasse 1, D–4000 Duesseldorf, Germany

   Periodical: Glaube und Heimat (Faith and homeland)

2. Johannes-Mathesius-Gesellschaft (Johannes-Mathesius-society)
   Prof.-Kuehne-Strasse 32a, D–6927 Bad Rappenau, Germany

   Publications: Yearbook "Erbe und Auftrag der Reformation in den boehmischen Laendern" (Heritage and commission of the Reformation in the Bohemian states).

   "Mathesiana", quarterly of culture and current events

   Biographisches Handbuch zur boehmischen Reformationsgeschichte (Biographical handbook of Bohemian Reformation history)

8. Other Hints

8.1 Genealogical work groups

See 2.1 above.

8.2 Cultural institutions

a. in the Federal Republic of Germany

   Heimatverband der Boehmerwaelder – Deutscher Boehmerwaldbund – (Homeland union of Boehmerwalders – German Bohemian Forest Union –)
   Office: Schloss-Strasse 92, D–7000 Stuttgart, Germany

   Deutscher Boehmerwaldbund e. V. (German Bohemian Forest Union)
   Office: Deisenhofer Strasse 49, D–8000 Muenchen 90, Germany

   Hilfsverein Aussig e. V. (Relief society Aussig)
   Liebherrstrasse 4, D–8000 Muenchen 22, Germany

Bund der Eghalanda Gmoi e. V. (Union of Eghalanda Gmoi)
Federal office: Egerland-Kulturhaus, D–8590 Marktredwitz, Germany, with state associations, work groups and Eghalanda Gmoi.

Bund der Niederlaender e. V. (Union of Niederlaenders)
Warnsdorf, Rumburg, Schluckenau
Chairman: Paul Vogel, Frauenalber Strasse 35, D–7500 Karlsruhe 51, Germany

Maehrisch-Schlesischer Sudetengebirgsverein e. V. (Moravian-Silesian Sudeten mountain club)
Postfach 82, D–7312 Kirchheim unter Teck, Germany

Riesengebirgler Heimatkreis Trautenau e. V. (Giant mountaineers' homeland county Trautenau society)
Office: Wuerzburg (foster city), Neubaustrasse 12, D–8700 Wuerzburg, Germany
Chairman: Dr. Josef Klug, Moorenbrenner Strasse 270, D–8500 Nuernberg, Germany

Vereinigung der Teplitz-Schoenauer e. V. (Society of Teplitz-Schoenauers)
Chairman: Josef Richter, Gerlachstrasse 29, D–6230 Frankfurt/Main-Hoechst, Germany

Heimatkundlicher Verein fuer Suedboehmen e. V. (Homeland studies society for Southern Bohemia)
Chairman: Alois Harasko, Deisenhofer Strasse 49/II, D–8000 Muenchen 90, Germany

Rothmuehler Heimatkundeverein e. V. (Local historical society for Rothmuehle)
D–6229 Hallgarten/Rheingau

Volkskundlicher Arbeitskreis fuer den mittleren Boehmerwald „Kuenische Freibauern" (Ethnic study group for the Central Bohemian Forest)
Office: Bahnhofstrasse 7a, D–8371 Bayer. Eisenstein, Germany

Schoenhengster Heimatbund e. V. (Homeland union of Schoenhengst)
Office: Postfach 1180, Noerdliche Ringstrasse 33, D–7320 Goeppingen, Germany

b. *in Austria*

Oesterreicher Heimatbund Beskidenland (Austrian homeland union for Beskidenland)
Agnesstrasse 72, A–3400 Klosterneuburg, Austria

Landesverband der Eghalanda Gmoin in Oesterreich (State association of Eghalanda in Austria)
Chairman: Dr. Alfred Zerlik, Fadinger Strasse 4, A–4020 Linz, Austria

Dachverband der Suedmaehrer (General association of Southern Moravians)
Chairman: Pf. Prof. Dr. Josef Koch, Pfarramt, A–2224 Niedersulz, Austria

"Thaya", Bund der Suedmaehrer in Oesterreich ("Thaya", Union of Southern Moravians in Austria), Federal house: Zollergasse 16/I, A–1070 Vienna, Austria
Business manager: Rudolf Moedritzer, Klitschgasse 16, A–1130 Vienna, Austria

5. SOUTHEASTERN EUROPE

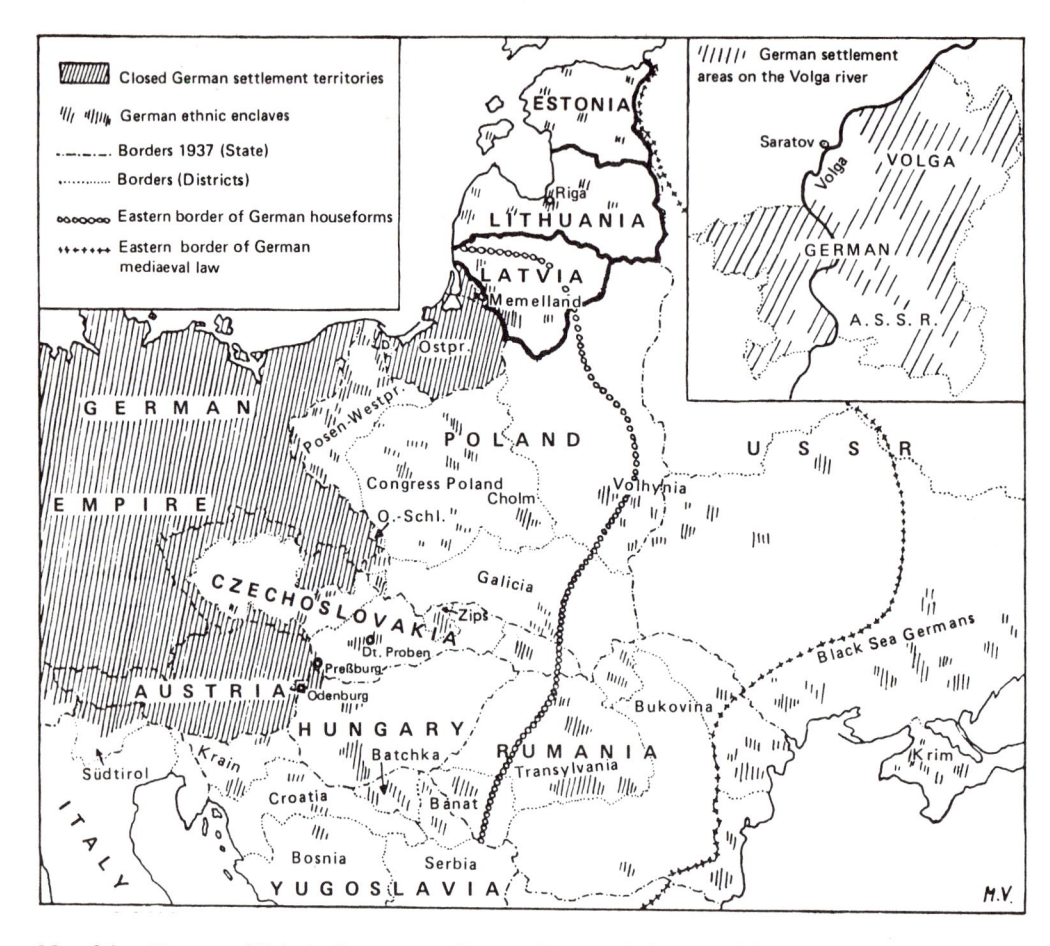

Map 36 Extent of Ethnic Germans in Eastern Europe before World War II

The territorial term "Southeastern Europe" is not always consistently used in social studies. In historical works the complete area of historical Hungary, i. e. including Slovakia, is used, although modern Southeastern Europe generally includes only Hungary, Rumania, Yugoslavia, Albania, Bulgaria, Greece and the European portion of Turkey. The Carpatho-Germans are usually called Southeast Germans.

Part I.

1. Research Areas

Bukovina (Buchenland) on the eastern slopes of the Carpathian Mountains, in northeastern Rumania between the Dnestr and Bistrita Aurie (Goldene Bistritz) Rivers. Center: Cernovcy (Czernowitz).

Dobrogea (Dobrudscha) between the Black Sea and the bend of the mouth of the Danube River.

The Carpathian states (Slovakia and the Carpatho-Ukraine)
The Hauerland (Slovakia), Center: Nitrianske Pravno (Deutsch-Proben).
Spiš (Zips) (Slovakia), Center: Kežmarok (Kaesmark).
Bratislava region (Pressburger Land) and Schuett enclave (Schuettinsel) Center: Bratislava (Pressburg), (Slovakia).
Ethnic enclave Mukačevo (Munkatsch), Center Mukačevo (Munkatsch), (Carpatho-Ukraine).
Ethnic enclave Theresienthal (Carpatho-Ukraine), Center: Deutsch Mokra.

Western Hungary between Neusiedler Lake and Mura and Danube Rivers in the districts of Gyoer (Raab), Mosonmagyaróvár (Wieselburg), Sopron (Oedenburg), Vasvár (Eisenburg), Center: Koeszeg (Guens) Szombathely (Steinamanger) and the bordering Austrian Burgenland.

Slovenia (Yugoslavia) with Untersteiermark. Center: Maribor/Drava (Marburg/Drau), Southern Kaernten, Prekmurje (Uebermurgebiet) and Krajnska (Krain), Center: Ljubljana (Laibach) and ethnic enclave Kocevje (Gottschee).

Transylvania, Carpathian region in Rumania. Center: Sibiu (Hermannstadt) and Brosov (Kronstadt).

Bessarabia between the Prut and Dnestr Rivers in Rumania. Center: Tarutino.

2. Genealogical Institutions

2.1 *Present institutions*

Forschungsstelle Suedosteuropa der AGoFF (Research center Southeastern Europe of AGoFF)
Director: Bundesbahndirektor a. D. Dr. Ing. Hans Bartsch, Appartement 3, Am Roemerbrunnen 2, D–7812 Bad Krozingen, Germany, Ph. 07633–25 60.

In charge of all inquiries including those research groups not listed otherwise.

In co-operation with Suedostdeutsche Historische Kommission (Southeastern German historical commission), Guellstrasse 7, D–8000 Muenchen 2, Germany.

Periodical: Suedostdeutsche Vierteljahrblaetter (Southeastern German quarterly leaves), commissioned by Suedostdeutsches Kulturwerk, Guellstrasse 7, D–8000 Muenchen 2, Germany.

Research groups:

a. *Research group of Buchenland (Bukovina)*

in co-operation with
- aa) Raimund-Friedrich-Kaindl-Gesellschaft (Raimund-Friedrich-Kaindl-Society), Stuttgart, Germany; President: Prof. Dr. Herbert Mayer Raingaerten 19, D–7065 Winterbach, Germany

    Periodical: Der Suedost-Deutsche (The Southeastern-German).

- bb) Forschungsstelle Galizien der AGoFF (Research center Galicia of AGoFF), Director: Ernst Hexel, Im Gries 20, D–5300 Bonn 2, Germany.

b. *Research group Dobrudscha (Dobrogea)*

c. *Research group Karpatendeutsche (Germans from the Carpathian Mountains)* from Slovakia and the Carpatho-Ukraine.

In co-operation with Karpatendeutsches Kulturwerk, Kaiserstrasse 223, D–7500 Karlsruhe, Germany; Director: Gymnasial Professor a. D. Erich Sirchich, Dammerstockstrasse 11, D–7500 Karlsruhe 1, Germany; Deputy: Rechtsassessor Anton von Koenczoel, Schwarzwald-Strasse 31, D–7801 Reute/Freiburg, Germany, Ph. 076–41 67 12 (knows Hungarian language).

Periodical: Die Karpatenpost (The Carpathian Post), monthly publication of Karpatendeutsche Landsmannschaft Slowakei (Society of the Carpathian Germans from Slovakia), Stuttgart, Germany.

Karpatenjahrbuch (Carpathian yearbook), published by Arbeitsgemeinschaft der Karpatendeutschen aus der Slowakei (Group of Germans from the Carpathian Mountains in Slovakia).

d. *Research group Westungarn/Burgenland (Western Hungary/Burgenland)*

Heinz Somogyvár, Bei der Rolandmuehle 9, D–2000 Hamburg 50, Germany, Ph. 040–880 46 74.

e. *Research group Slovenien (Slovenia)*

Ethnic enclave Gottschee (Kočevje).

f. *Research group Siebenbuergen (Transylvania)*

In co-operation with Genealogische Sektion des Arbeitskreises fuer Siebenbuergische Landeskunde (Genealogical section of the work group for Transylvanian studies), Schloss Horneck, D–6953 Gundelsheim/Neckar, Germany.
Periodical: Korrespondenzblatt (Newsletter).

g. *Research group Bessarabien (Bessarabia)*

not yet assigned, for information see 7.4 page 140.

4. **Gazetteers**

J. Jekelfalassy: Ortslexikon der Laender der Ungarischen Krone, 5th ed., Budapest 1893.

Mayerhofer: Ortslexikon von Oesterreich-Ungarn, Wien 1896.

Spezial-Ortsrepertorium von Krain, Wien 1894.

5. **Bibliographies and Literature**

5.1 *Published after 1945:*

for 2.1.a
Rudolf Wagner, Die Bukowina und ihre Deutschen, Eckartschriften (Bukovina and her Germans, Eckart writings), pamphlet 69, Vienna 1979.

for 2.1.b
Hans Petri, Geschichte der deutschen Siedlungen in der Dobrudscha (History of German settlements in Dobrogea), Suedostdeutsches Kulturwerk, Muenchen 1956.

for 2.1.c
Adalbert Hudak, Die Karpatendeutschen, Eckartschriften (Eckart writings of Germans from the Carpathian Mountains), pamphlet 55, Vienna 1955.

for 2.1.e
Hans Gerstner, Das Deutschtum in Krain (Ethnic Germans in Krajnska) excluding Gottschee region, Eckartschriften, pamphlet 71, Vienna 1979.

for 2.1.f
Dr. Andreas Mathiae, Siebenbuergen (Transylvania), Deutscher Buchverlag, Itzehoe 1967.

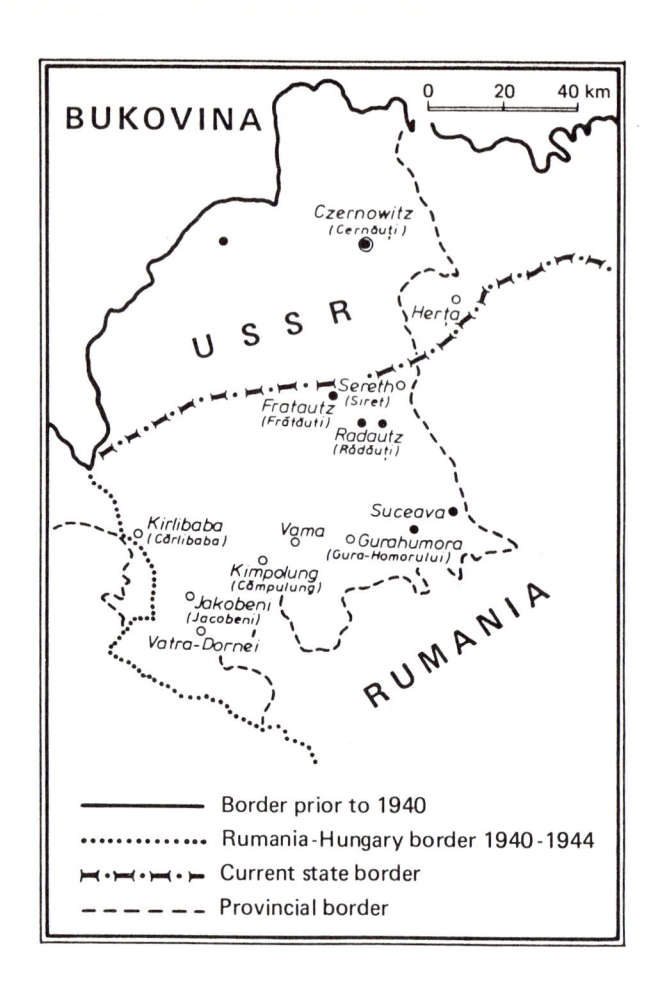

Map 37

Legend:
- Border prior to 1940
- Rumania-Hungary border 1940-1944
- Current state border
- Provincial border

The princes of Moldavia brought Bukovina (German: "Buchenland"), the territory on the eastern slopes of the Forest-Carpathian Mountains and the source regions of the Prut and Siret Rivers, under their rule at the end of the 14th century. In 1768 Russian troops occupied the principality, which was under the supreme rule of the Ottoman Empire. Russia allowed the occupation by Habsburg troups in 1774 and the Ottoman Empire had to cede the territory to Austria in 1775. After 1782 many German speaking settlers were brought from inner Austria to the region as farmers and miners. At the same time a strong migration began from Rumania and the Ukraine. In particular over the period of 1830 to 1850 the government planned the settlement of German farmers. In 1850 Bukovina received the status of a crownland and opted for inclusion into Rumania in 1918. In 1940 the USSR occupied Northern Bukovina, which was regained by Rumania in 1941, and finally ceded to the USSR in 1947. Today Northern Bukovina belongs to the Ukrainian SSR of the Soviet Union and Southern Bukovina to Rumania.

Germany concluded treaties with the Soviet Union and Rumania in September and November 1940, respectively, on the re-settlement of the German population. By the end of 1940 97 500 inhabitants left Bukovina.

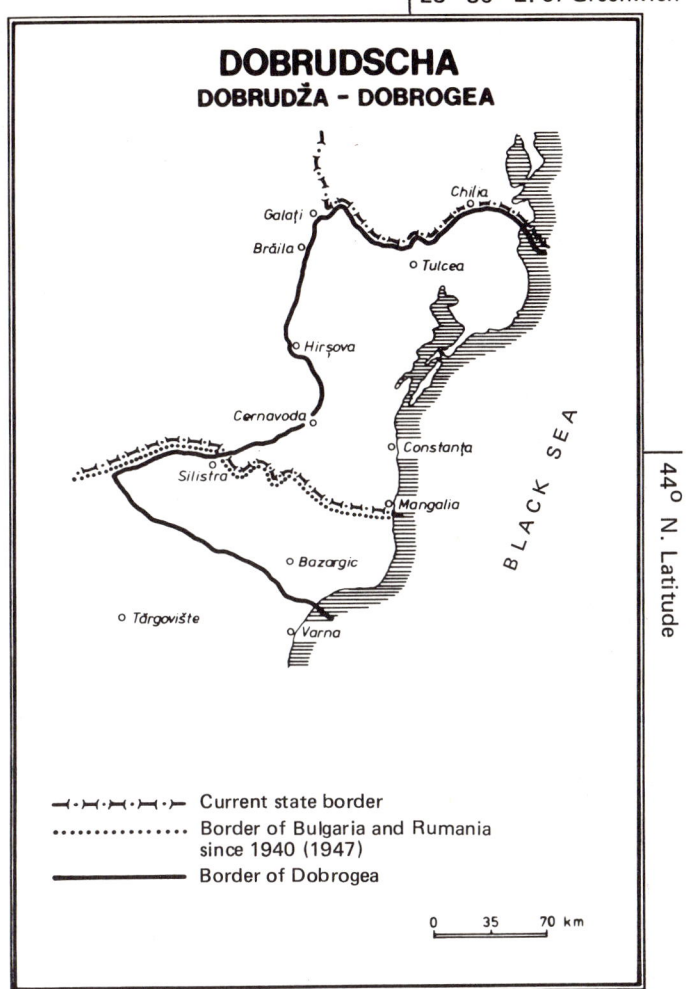

Map 38

Dobrudscha, (Rumanian: Dobrogea, Bulgarian: Dobrudza), is the territory between the Lower Danube and the Black Sea. Added to Wallachia in 1388, Dobrogea came under the rule of the Ottoman Empire. At the Berlin Congress in 1878 Rumania received the northern portion, and newly formed Bulgaria received the southern portion (called Cadrilater). This portion also went to Rumania after the 2nd Balcanic War in 1913, and reverted to Bulgaria after the peace treaties of Bucarest until the Peace of Neuilly in 1919 secured the possession. In the Treaty of Craiova on September 7, 1940 Rumania had to cede Southern Dobrogea to Bulgaria again. This ruling was confirmed between Rumania and Bulgaria in 1947. Jurisdiction, in particular that of Southern Dobrogea, has not been unchallenged recently.

German population groups, which had settled there since the end of the 19th century, were resettled by treaty between Rumania and Germany on September 5, 1940, and about 15 000 people have left Dobrogea.

Map 39

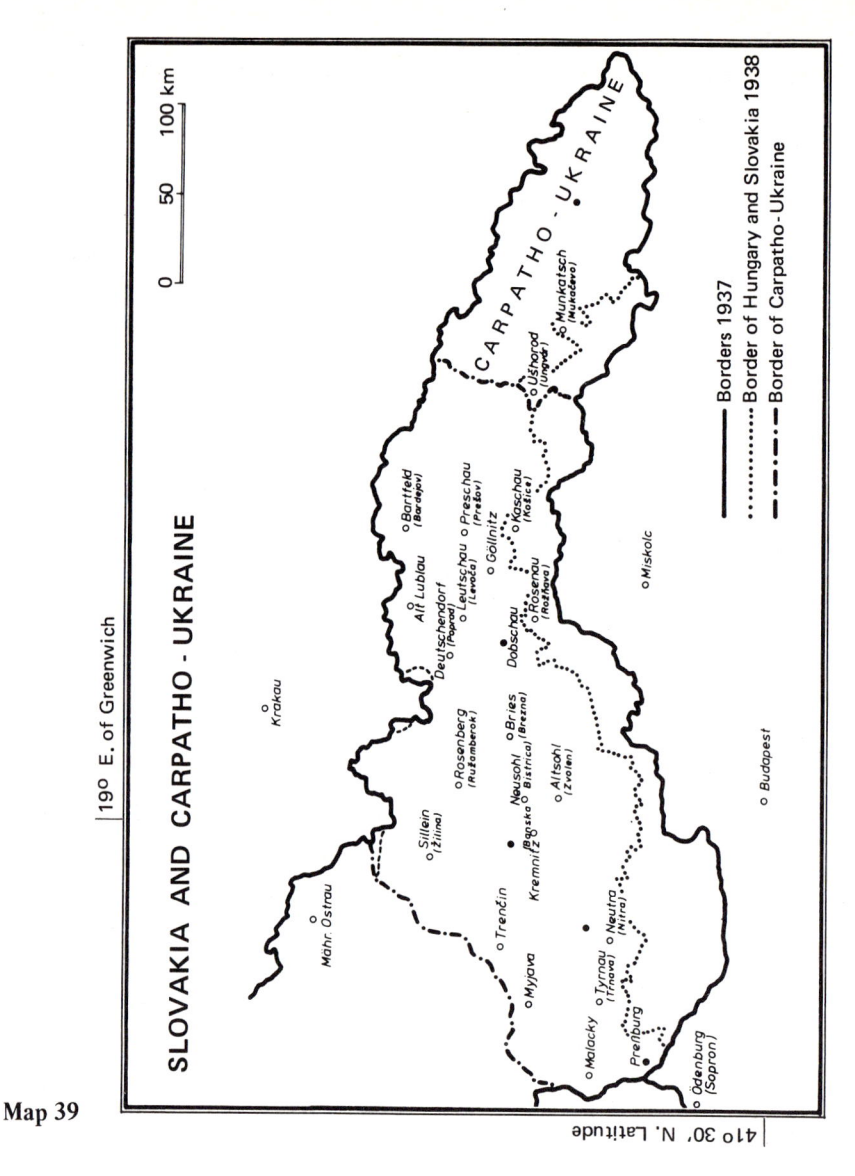

SLOVAKIA AND CARPATHO-UKRAINE

Prior to 1918 Slovakia was a part of the Kingdom of Hungary ("Upper Hungary") and along with the Bohemian states of the Habsburg Monarchy became a part of Czechoslovakia in 1918. In 1938 she received an autonomous status and had her own identity between 1939 and 1945 when Czechoslovakia was re-established. After the Vienna Umpire's Decision of November 2, 1938 the ČSR had to relinquish a wide border area holding a large Hungarian population, and in March 1939 the Carpatho-Ukraine (also: Carpatho-Russia) to Hungary. After her re-establishment in 1945 she had to renounce these territories to the Soviet Union.

The German ethnic group, the Carpatho-Germans, lived mainly in the Pressburg (Bratislava) region, the Hauerland, the Upper and Lower Zips (Spiš), the Deutsch-Probener (Nitrianske Pravno) and many smaller language enclaves.

130

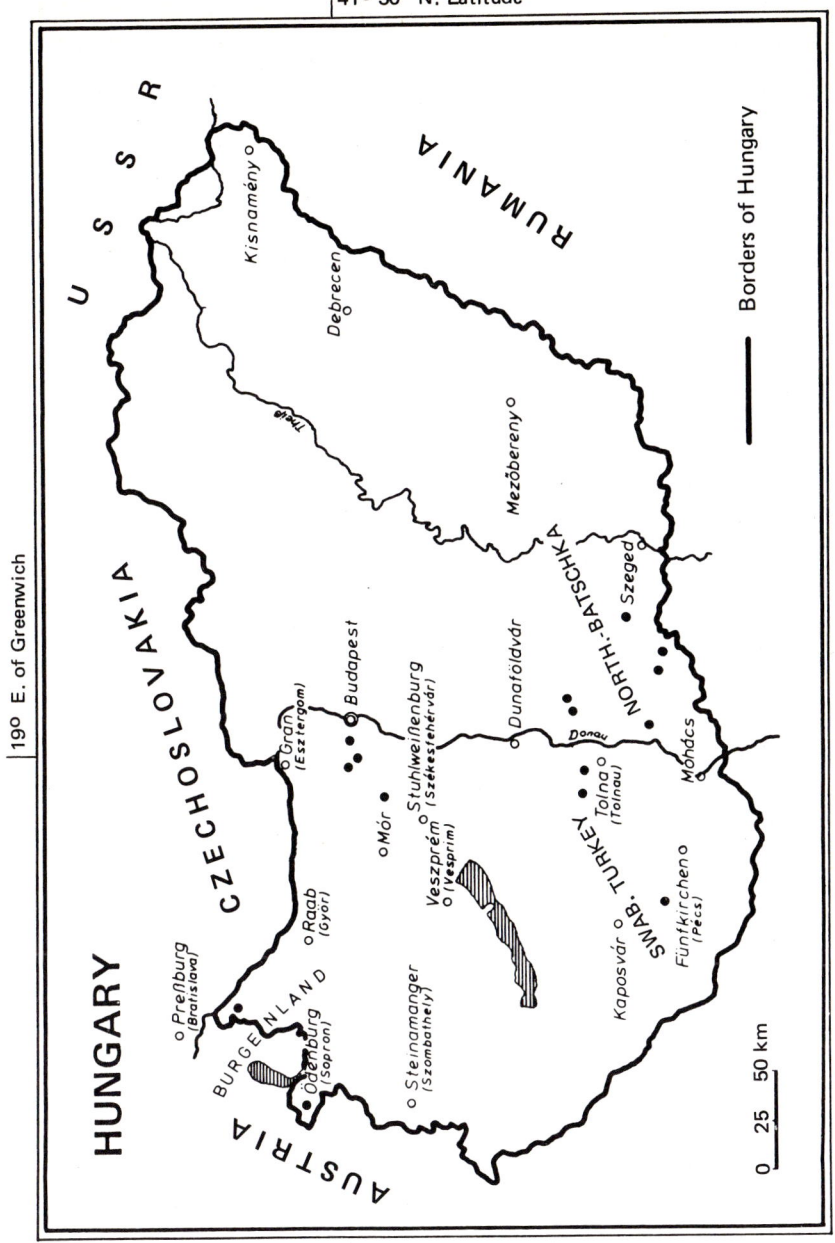

Map 40

Here only territories with German or German speaking populations within the borders of former and present Hungary are dealt with: including Eastern Burgenland and German settlements in Western and Southern Hungary and "Schwaebisch Tuerkei".

GOTTSCHEE   KOČEVJE

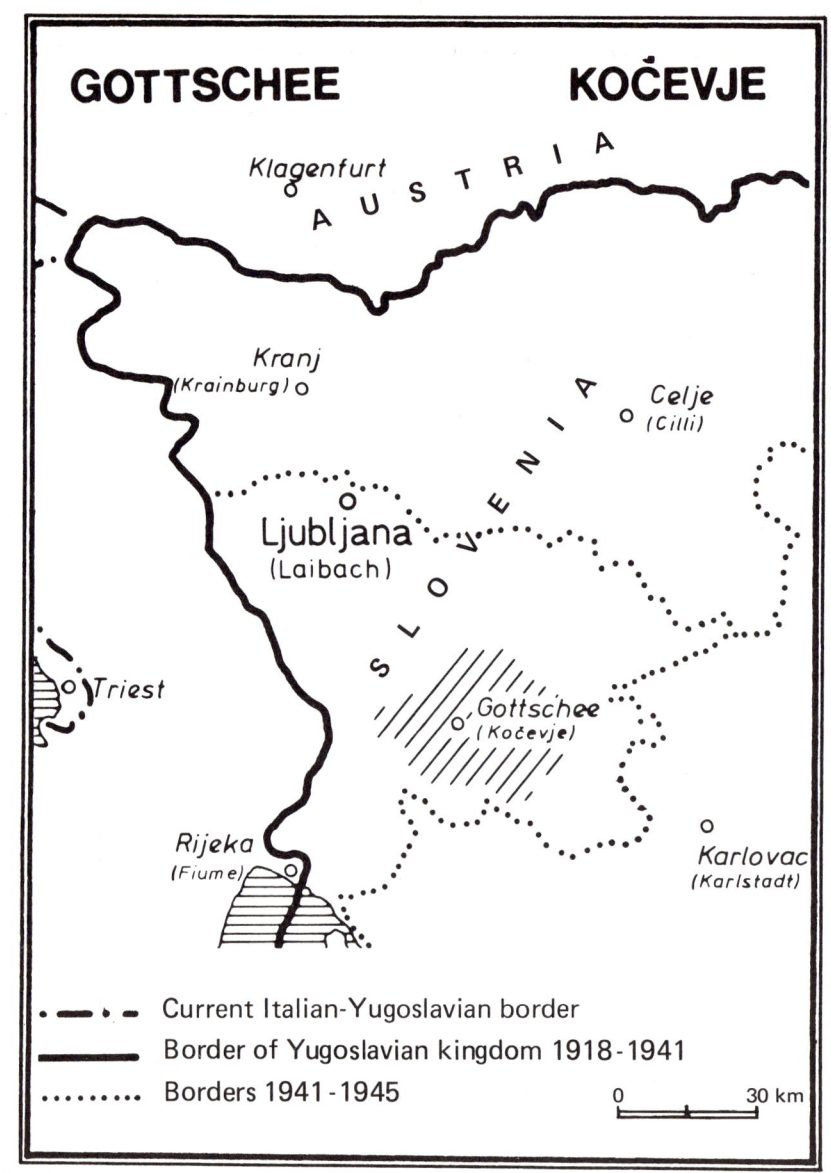

- — · — Current Italian-Yugoslavian border
- ——— Border of Yugoslavian kingdom 1918-1941
- ········ Borders 1941-1945

Map 41

Slovenia

Of the German speaking population, which lived in Slovenia prior to World War II, only the Gottscheers from the Mideaval settlement of Gottschee have been mentioned in homeland books. In contrast the German speaking stratum of city societies in Ljubljana (German: Laibach), Kranj (German: Krainburg) or Maribor (German: Marburg on Drau) formed more of a socially closed ethnic group with its own tradition.

The Gottschee Germans were re-settled after the occupation of Slovenia during World War II.

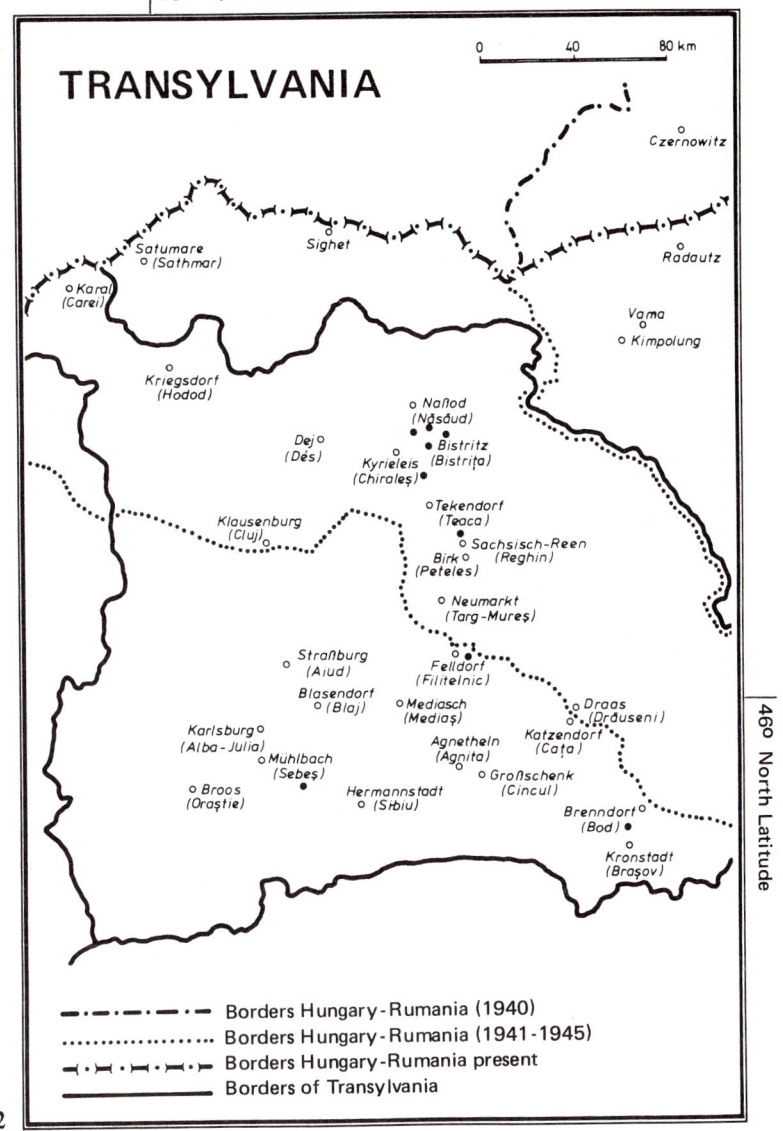

Map 42

Transylvania (Rum.: Transilvania, Germ.: Siebenbuergen, Hung.: Erdély) is one of political-historical and ethnic-nationals most complicated areas in Southeastern Europe, including the "Siebenbuergen Sachsen" (Transylvania Saxons) who formed their own "nation" by rights given to them in the "Andreanum" of 1224, which lasted to the second half of the 19th century. Prior to 1876 the Saxons did not have any special nobility privileges within their autonomous territory, "Koenigsboden" (Crownland). Transylvania was a grand principality under the House of Habsburg as "side-land" of the Hungarian Crown from 1688 to 1867. After the settlement of 1868 she remained an intregal part of Hungary and fell to Rumania in 1918 where she still is. The Vienna Umpire's Decision of 1941 gave Northern Transylvania to Hungary, in 1945 the former border was re-established.

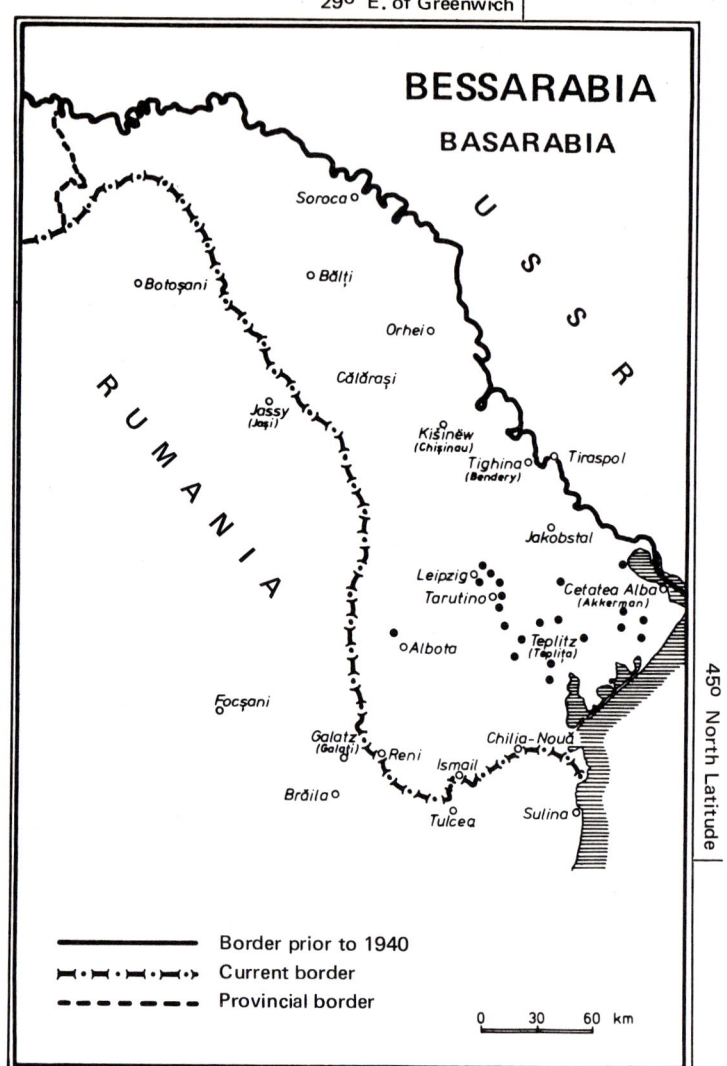

Map 43

BESSARABIA
BASARABIA

- ——— Border prior to 1940
- ⊢•⊢•⊢•⊢ Current border
- - - - - Provincial border

Since the Middle Ages Russia, the princes of Moldavia and Wallachia and the Ottoman Empire competed over Bessarabia, the territory between the Dnestr, Danube and Prut Rivers and the Black Sea. The Russian Czar received the territory in 1812 and, particularly between 1814 and 1842, tried to consolidate the possession through the settlement of Germans. As a result of the Crimean War the Principality of Moldavia received the territory, but had to relinquish it to Russia at the Congress of Berlin in 1878. After the October Revolution and the collapse of the czarist empire in 1918, Rumania annexed the whole territory until it was occupied by the USSR in 1940. In 1941 Rumania and German troops re-conquered the region, but lost it to the Red Army again in 1944. At the Peace of Paris in 1947, Rumania had to confirm the possession. Presently the major portion of Bessarabia with the capital of Kišinëv is part of the Moldavian SSR, the north and southeast of the Ukrainian SSR.

PART II. DANUBE-SWABIAN SETTLEMENTS

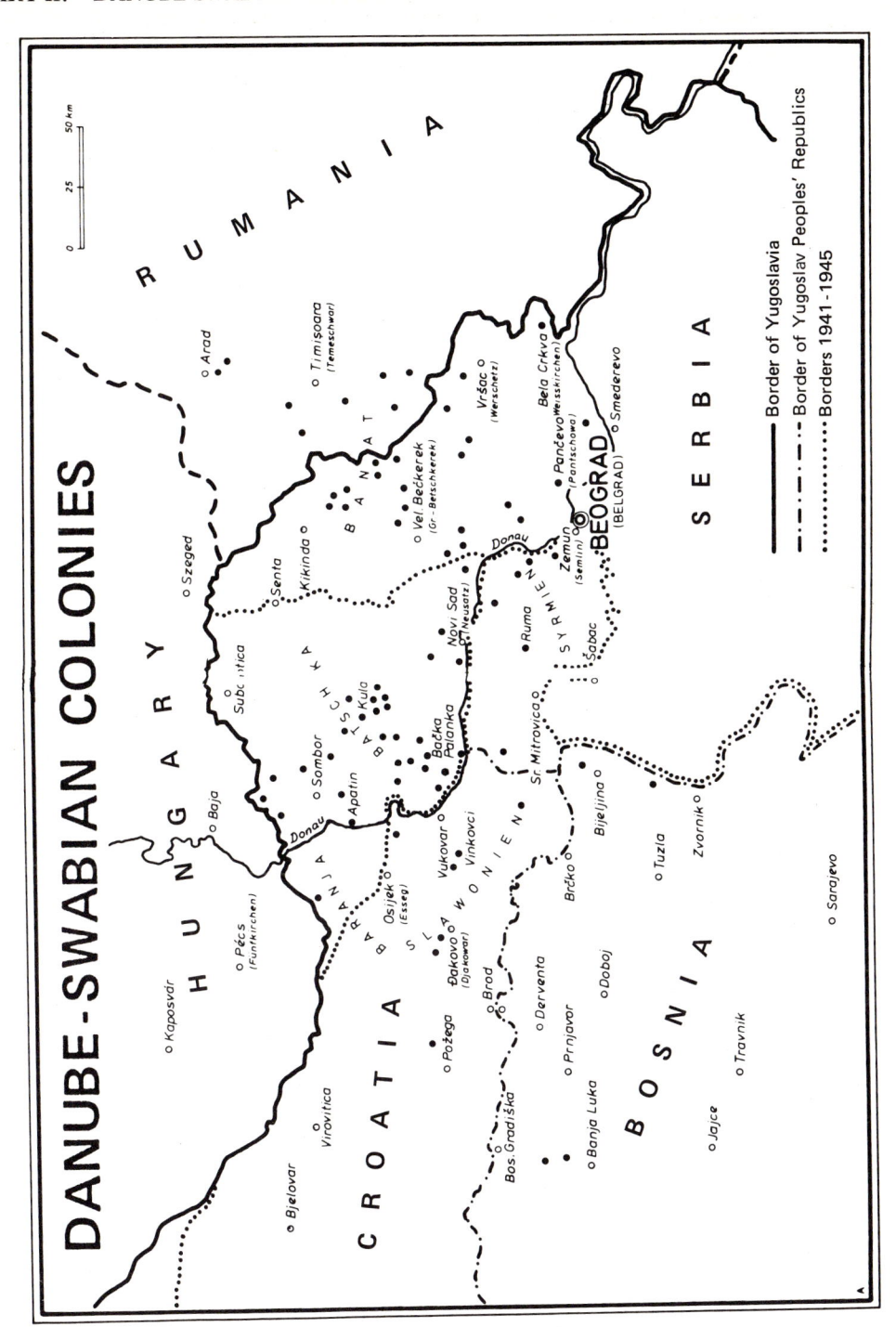

Map 44

The name "Donauschwaben" (Danube-Swabians) designating the modern day German settlers of Rumania, Yugoslavia and Hungary was coined as recently as 1922. It has gained acceptance as the all-inclusive group name for Germans from Banat, Bácska (Batschka), Croatia (Kroatien), Slovania, (Slawonien), and Srem (Syrmien), Swabian Turkey (Schwaebisch Tuerkei) – see Hungary –, the Hungarian Central Highlands – see Hungary –, as well as the Satu Mare region (Sathmar).

1. **Research Areas**

    a. *Southwestern Hungarian Central Highlands*

    between Lake Balaton (Plattensee), Raba River and Elbow of the Danube River.

    b. *Schwaebische Tuerkei (Swabian Turkey)*

    between Lake Balaton, Danube and Drava Rivers, Center: Pécs (Fuenfkirchen).

    c. *Slavonia*

    between Sava and Drava Rivers (Yugoslavia). Center: Osijek (Esseg).

    d. *Srem*

    between Sava and Danube Rivers.

    e. *Bácska (Batschka)*

    between Danube and Tisza Rivers in the southern part of the Hungarian Basin (Yugoslavia and Hungary). Center: Novi Sad (Neusatz) and Baja.

    f. *Banat*

    between Tisza and Danube Rivers and the Carpathian Mountains (Rumania, Yugoslavia, Hungary). Center: Timişoara (Temeschburg).

    h. *Satu Mare (Sathmar)*

    in the northeastern border region of Rumania. Center: Nagykároly (Gross-Karol).

2. **Genealogical Institutions**

2.1 *Presently existing institutions*

   a. **Forschungsstelle Donauschwaben der AGoFF** (Research center Danube-Swabians of AGoFF.
   Dr. Helmut Flacker, Tunibergstrasse 12, D–7801 Ehrenkirchen 4.

   b. **Arbeitskreis donauschwaebischer Familienforscher** (AdFF) (Working circle of Danube-Swabian family researchers).

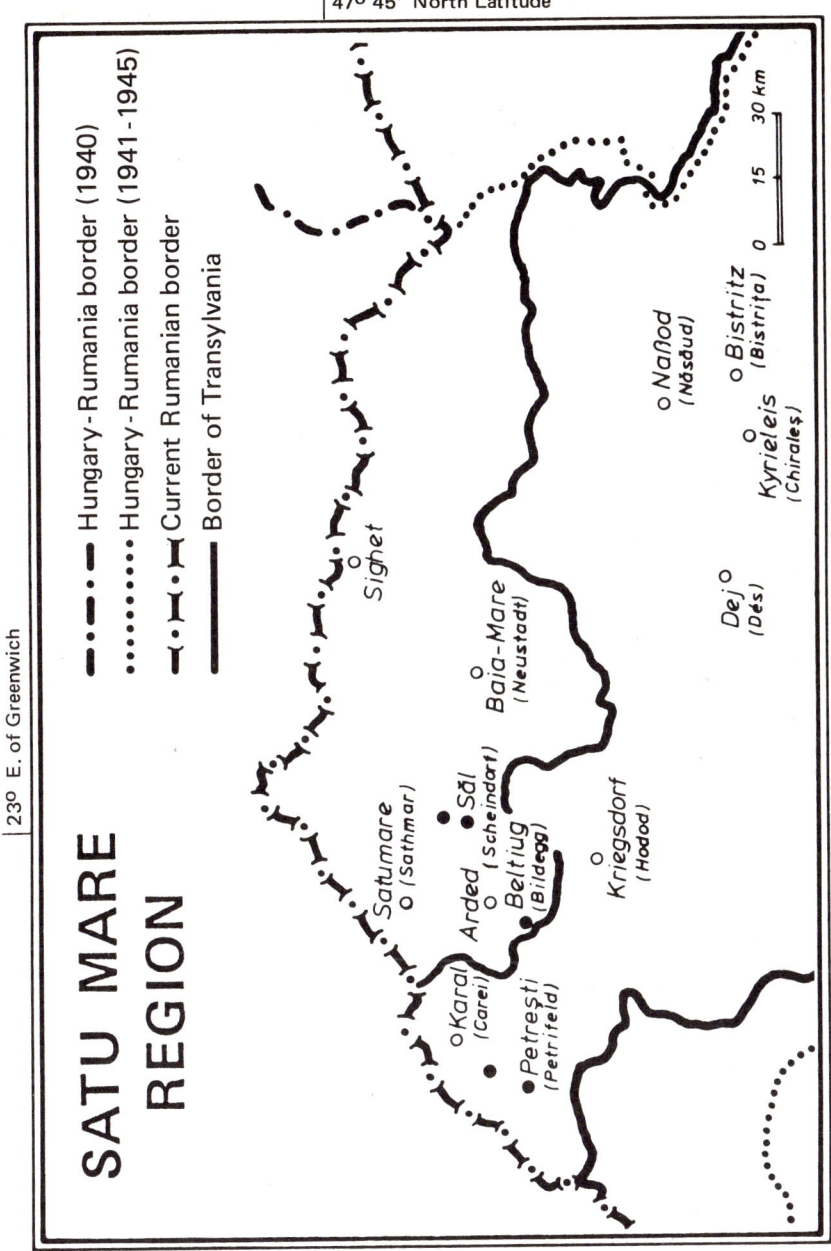

Into the Satu Mare region (Germ: Sathmar) around the cities of Satu Mare and Carei (Germ: Karol) an independent group immigrated from "Swabia" between 1712 and 1815.

Research helpers are for

1. **Bácska (Batschka)**:
   Paul Scherer, Elbinger Str. 3 A, D–7500 Karlsruhe 1, Germany
   Wilhelm Kungl, Karlsbader Str. 35, D–6944 Hemsbach, Germany

2. **Banat**:
   Dr. Helmut Zwirner, Poststrasse 3, D–6650 Homburg/Saar, Germany
   Josef Schiefer, Brufertstrasse 21a, D–7550 Rastatt, Germany
   Hans Sonnleitner, Schaedlerweg 2, D–8000 Muenchen 81, Germany
   Anton Kraemer, Frankenstrasse 18, D–6507 Ingelheim, Germany

3. **Slavonia (Slawonien)**
   Stefan Stader, Rostocker Strasse 5, D–6750 Kaiserslautern, Germany

4. **Srem (Syrmien)**
   Walter Nehlich, Eichelberg 19, D–5169 Heimbach 1, Germany

5. **Swabian Turkey (Schwaebische Tuerkei)**
   Dr. Guenter Junkers, Bergische Landstrasse 210, D–5090 Leverkusen 1, Germany
   Mathias Volk, Ahornweg 32, D–7500 Karlsruhe 31, Germany
   Johann Mueller, Gerockstrasse 83, D–7120 Bissingen, Germany

c. *Periodical:*

Donauschwaebische familienkundliche Forschungsblaetter, Mitteilungen des AKdFF (Danube-Swabian genealogical research leaflets, bulletins of the AKdFF).

3. Documents of Vital Statistics

3.1 *Church records*

a. Die Banater Kirchenbuecher (Church books of Banat). An inventory of filmed church books is at the Bibliothek des Instituts fuer Auslandsbeziehungen as of 1979. Edited and compiled by: Josef Schmidt, Charlottenplatz 17, D–7000 Stuttgart 1, Germany.

b. Inventory of the Hungarian State Archives, Volume 72.
Microfilm copies of ecclesiastical vital statistics to October 1, 1895. Inventory catalogue compiled by Margit Judak, Budapest, 1977.

4. Gazetteers

I. Regenyi, A. Scherer, Donauschwaebisches Ortsnamenbuch (Danube-Swabian gazetteer), published by: AKdFF, Darmstadt, Germany 1980.

Brigl, Ortslexikon fuer die Koenigreiche Kroatien und Slawonien, Agram 1888.

5. Bibliographies and Literature

Suedosteuropa-Bibliographie (Southeastern European bibliography), Munich 1956ff.
A. Scherer, Donauschwaebische Bibliographie (Danube-Swabian bibliography), Part I 1935–1955, Munich 1966, Part II 1955–1965, Munich 1974 (Publications of Suedostdeutsches Kulturwerk. Series B 18.30).

Buecherei des deutschen Ostens, Herne. Catalog. Herne 1973, pages 644–690.

Haus des deutschen Ostens, Duesseldorf. Library. Sonderkatalog Donauschwaebischer Literatur (Special catalogue of Danube-Swabian Literature), (editor: Guenter Junkers). Duesseldorf 1977.

6. Archives and Libraries with Source Material on Homeland Regions

6.1 *in the Federal republic of Germany*

Buecherei des deutschen Osten (Library of the German East)
Berliner Platz 1, D–4690 Herne, Germany.

Bibliothek Stiftung Haus des deutschen Ostens, (Library of the Foundation House of the German East)
Bismarckstrasse 90, D–4000 Duesseldorf, Germany.
Special catalogue of Danube-Swabian literature, edited by: Dr. Guenter Junkers, 1977.

Haus der Donauschwaben (Danube-Swabian House)
Postfach 180, Goldmuehlestrasse 30, D–7032 Sindelfingen, Germany.

Siebenbuergische Buecherei (Transylvanian Library),
Schloss Horneck, D–6953 Gundelsheim, Germany.

Suedostdeutsches Kulturwerk, Bibliothek (Southeast German Cultural Foundation, Library)
Guellstrasse 7, D–8000 Muenchen 2, Germany.

6.2 *in Austria*

See Section "A" 6.4.

6.3 *in Hungary*

Magyar Országos Levéltár, H–1250 Budapest I, Bécsi kapu-tér 4, Hungary.

Parts I and II

7. Other Research Aids

7.1 *Hometown/village directories*

a. Heimatortskartei Suedosteuropa-Ostumsiedler, Abteilung Deutsche aus Ungarn, Rumaenien, Jugoslawien, Slowakei und Ruthenien (Hometown/village directory of Southeastern European eastern re-settlers, department of Germans from Hungary, Rumania, Yugoslavia, Slovakia and Ruthenia)
Rosenbergstrasse 50, D–7000 Stuttgart, Germany, Ph. 0711–61 87 52.

b. Heimatortskartei Suedosteuropa-Ostumsiedler, Abteilung Deutsche aus Russland, Bessarabien, Bulgarien und Dobrudscha (Hometown/village directory of Southeastern-European eastern re-settlers, department of Germans from Russia, Bessarabia, Bulgaria and Dobrogea)
Adress as 7.1.a, Ph. 0711–62 03 11.

7.2 *Local Societies*

a. Landsmannschaft der Banater Schwaben aus Rumaenien in Deutschland e. V. (Society of Banat Swabians from Rumania in Germany)
Sendlinger Strasse 55, D–8000 Muenchen 2, Germany.

- b. Landsmannschaft der Buchenlanddeutschen e. V. (Society of Germans from Bukovina)
  Artilleriestrasse 20, D–8000 Muenchen 19, Germany.
- c. Landsmannschaft der Donauschwaben aus Jugoslawien – Bundesverband e. V. – (Society of Danube-Swabians from Yugoslavia – Federal Federation –)
  Charlottenplatz 17 II, D–7000 Stuttgart, Germany.
- d. Karpatendeutsche Landsmannschaft Slowakei (Carpathian-German society from Slovakia)
  Breslauer Strasse 32, D–7014 Kornwestheim, Germany.
- e. Landsmannschaft der Siebenbuerger Sachsen in Deutschland e. V. (Society of Transylvanian Saxons in Germany)
  Sendlinger Strasse 48, D–8000 Muenchen 2, Germany.
- f. Landsmannschaft der Deutschen aus Ungarn – Bundesverband – (Society of Germans from Hungary – Federal Federation –)
  Himmelreichstrasse 4, D–8000 Muenchen 2, Germany.
- g. Landsmannschaft der Bessarabiendeutschen (Society of Germans from Bessarabia)
  Florianstrasse 17, D–7000 Stuttgart 13, Germany.
- h. Landsmannschaft der Dobrudscha- und Bulgariendeutschen (Society of Germans from Dobrogea and Bulgaria)
  Hasenbergstrasse 35, D–7016 Gerlingen, Germany.

7.3 *Homeland information centers*

- a. Rumania – at the Landesausgleichsamt Bayern
  Leonrodstrasse 56, D–8000 Muenchen 19, Germany.
- b. Hungary, Slovakia including the Carpatho-Ukraine, Yugoslavia, Bulgaria, Bessarabia and Dobrogea at Landesausgleichsamt Baden-Wuerttemberg
  Schloss-Strasse 92, D–7000 Stuttgart, Germany.

7.4 *Historical Associations*

- a. Suedostdeutsche Historische Kommission (Southeastern-German historical commission)
  Guellstrasse 7, D–8000 Muenchen 2, Germany.
- b. Suedostdeutsches Kulturwerk (Southeastern-German cultural work)
  address as 7.4.a.
- c. Heimatmuseum der Deutschen aus Bessarabian (Homeland museum of Germans from Bessarabia), Director: Rektor a. D. Christian Fliess
  Lindachstrasse 37, D–7130 Muehlacker, Germany, Ph. 070–41 66 14

  with "Roemer-Kartei" pertaining to origins of re-settlers from Bessarabia and genealogical indexes.

7.5 *Church institutions*

- a. Hilfskomitee der Siebenbuerger Sachsen und evang. Banater Schwaben (Relief society of Transylvanian Saxons and Protestant Banat Swabians)
  Himmelreichstrasse 4, D–8000 Muenchen 22, Germany.
- b. Hilfskomitee der evang. Deutschen aus Ungarn (Relief society of Protestant Germans from Hungary), address as 7.5.a.

c. Hilfskomitee der evang.-luth. Slowakeideutschen (Relief society of Protestant-Lutheran Germans from Slovakia)
Schwabstrasse 2, D–7000 Stuttgart, Germany.

d. Hilfskomitee der evang. Landeskirche von Jugoslawien (Relief society of the Protestant church of Yugoslavia)
Teutonenstrasse 59, D–5300 Bonn 2, Germany.

e. Hilfskomitee fuer die evang. Umsiedler aus der Bukowina (Relief society for Protestant re-settlers from Bukovina)
Artilleriestrasse 20, D–8000 Muenchen 19, Germany.

f. Hilfskomitee der evang.-luth. Kirche aus Bessarabien (Relief society of the Protestant-Lutheran church of Bessarabia)
Koenigswoerther Strasse 2, D–3000 Hannover, Germany.

g. Hilfskomitee fuer die evang. Kirche aus der Dobrudscha (Relief society for the Protestant church from Dobrogea)
Zabergaeustrasse 53, D–7000 Stuttgart-Zuffenhausen, Germany.

h. Ungarndeutsche, Abteilung der Caritas-Fluechtlingshilfe (Germans from Hungary, department of Caritas refugee help)
Rosenbergstrasse 50, D–7000 Stuttgart 1, Germany.

7.6 Fosterships

Hometown/county/area or ethnic group	Fosters *)
Homeland area Bessarabia	
Ethnic group from Bessarabia	Stuttgart, city (BaWue)
Lichtenthal, parish	Kirchberg-Murr, parish (BaWue)
Seimeny, parish	Ludwigsburg, city (BaWue)
Homeland area Carpathian Mountains	
Ethnic Germans from the Carpathian Mountains	Karlsruhe, city (BaWue)
Krickerhau, parish	Voerde, Ndrh., parish (NW)
Homeland area Hungary	
Bacsalmas/Batschka (Bacska)	Backnang, city (BaWue)
Oedenburg/Western Hungary, city	Bad Wimpfen, city (BaWue)
Homeland area Transylvania	
Society of Transylvanian Saxons in Germany	Nordrhein-Westfalen (NW), state
Homeland area Yugoslavia	
Apatin/Danube (Batschka)	Ulm, city (Bay)
Batschka-Palatinate expellees from Josephinean settlements	Landau, county (RhPf)
Rudolfsgnad, parish	Leutenbach/Waiblingen, parish (BaWue)

Homeland area Bukovina

Society of Germans from Bukovina	Swabia, administrative distr. (Bay)

Homeland area Dobrudscha (Dobrogea)

Society of Germans from Dobrogea	Heilbronn, city (BaWue)

Homeland area Danube-Swabian

Southeastern Germans from Hungary, Yugoslavia, the Banat-Swabians from Rumania	Baden-Wuerttemberg, state (BaWue)
Danube-German Society in Rheinland-Pfalz	Rheinland-Pfalz (RhPf), state

Initials in brackets represent West German States in which the foster towns are located. For details see appendix.

8. **Research Opportunities in Southeastern Europe**

Hungary:

The State Archives in Budapest hold film copies of all available church books to 1895, however only books prior to 1867 may be used. Copies will be supplied after church permission has been granted.

Rumania:

Enquiries to Protestant church offices have not been answered. Ministers expect problems. The Protestant State office replies negatively only. Researches at the county archives of Arad were turned away. Enquiries at the state archives in Bucarest have been answered negatively.

Yugoslavia:

Enquiries at the Supreme Protestant Church Directorate have been left unanswered. See OFK vol. 9 Nr. 2 for other Yugoslavian information.

Appendix

Arbeitsgemeinschaft ostdeutscher Familienforscher e. V.
(Working group of East German Family Researchers)

Objectives and Organisation

The **Arbeitsgemeinschaft ostdeutscher Familienforscher (AGoFF)** had already been active for a decade when it gave itself a constitution and was registered as a society at the district court at Herne, Westphalia, Germany in 1958. It is a union of more than 800 non-professional family researchers, who search for their ancestors, who lived in the former Prussian Provinces of Pomerania, Brandenburg (East), Posen, West Prussia, East Prussia and Silesia, which lie east of the Oder-Neisse-Line within present Poland, and in the Sudeten-German regions and in German settlements in Eastern and Southeastern Europe.

Individual research territories overlap because ancestors only rarely remained in fixed area and migrated for professional and other reasons. Married newcomers came, and new ties with other regions were established. For in-depth research

Research Centers
(Forschungsstellen)

were organized which are in charge of a province or a designated region (Baltic States, Danube-Swabia, Galicia, Central Poland/Volhynia, Brandenburg (East), East Prussia, Pomerania, Posen, Silesia, Sudeten Region, Russia, Southeastern Europe, West Prussia-Danzig). Apart from collecting genealogical data, all news and documents on how and where research can continue, are collected. Manuscripts, maps, pictures and books of their designated region and index research results are given to them on loan. They improve research opportunities for our members through informed guidance: **commissioned searches cannot be accepted, however.**

Top Ancestor Index
(Spitzenahnenkartei)

Here all "first appearing" ancestors in East German territories are indexed in duplicate, one card staying with the collecting office, the second going to the appropriate research center. Through the Top Ancestor Index valuable contacts have already been established. Forms for preparation of an index are supplied to our members free of charge.

Our own literature (books and periodicals), which pertains to several of the above mentioned settlements as well as that of general genealogical value, is collected by us at the

Society Library

It is on permanent loan at Bibliothek der Stiftung "Haus des deutschen Ostens" (Library of the Foundation "The House of the German East"), located at Bismarckstrasse 90, 4000 Duesseldorf, Germany where members directly or through the inter-library loan service of German libraries may borrow them. The complete inventory of the above library consists of more than 35.000 catalogued volumes.

We are in close contact with

Buecherei des deutschen Ostens (BddO), Berliner Platz 11, D—4690 Herne, Germany
(Library of the German East in Herne, Germany).

It contains presently more than 36 000 volumes, with early prints and contemporary literature covering almost all aspects of the German East. Books may be loaned in Germany and abroad through the inter-library loan service. A reading and working room has available some 100 East German newspapers and periodicals. The BddO inventory is listed in a printed catalogue which may be purchased.

The quarterly

"Ostdeutsche Familienkunde" (OFK)
(Eastern German Genealogy),

published since 1953, collects and publishes research results. Here appear larger articles and sources on Eastern German genealogy.

Preserving Research Results

How do our members preserve the fruits of their research from loss or destruction? Experience has taught us that this is achieved best through publishing. Large series publications, as published by Verlag Degener & Co, in Neustadt/Aisch, Germany and C. A. Starke, Limburg/Lahn, Germany, are best for this purpose. This type of publication is prefered over private printing, because numerous customers — among them libraries of the whole world — subscribe to them regularly, so that the preservation of research results is assured even in the event of desaster.

However, if the preserved material or the newly researched results is small or the cost to the customer for the work is high and of limited value, then printing is often less worthwhile. To preserve such "small material", we have started our periodical

"Archiv ostdeutscher Familienforscher" (AOFF)
(Archives of Eastern German Family Researchers)

since 1952. Up to 1979 7 volumes have been completed with 3 017 pages, their contents made accessible through a name and locality index. In 1980 volume 8 has begun.

AGoFF-Wegweiser
(AGoFF-Guides)

for research of ancestors from East German and Sudeten-German territories as well as from German settlements in Eastern and Southeastern Europe.

These **Guides** list civil status and church books for these regions, places are named which deal with personal and genealogical research in these areas and evaluate the material. Listed are hometown/village directories and societies which have information of present and former places of expellees. It is important to know which West German cities are fosters of East German cities and counties. In foster cities exist service offices, directories of inhabitants, homeland rooms, museums and archives from which valuable hints may be obtained. Also homeland bulletins are published by numerous counties and cities which contain valuable articles for homeland studies and numerous family news items. The "Guides" are available in both, English and German, from Verlag Degener & Co., Inh. Gerhard Gessner, D—8530 Neustadt/Aisch, Germany.

A comprehensive

Membership List

with additional listings of research interests of each member is available in print and is continuously up-dated on the back cover of AOFF.

We not only advise our members in their research work but also in setting up and suitably presenting the results such as family history, ancestor, lineage or decendant charts. We give suggestions about printing and illustrating. We help to avoid mistakes, losses and blunders. We can make suggestions on how the old homeland can be made as live in the eyes of future generations, so that the destiny of the family receives a timely and local setting and background.

About our work, its further development and much more information we communicate with our members through the

Arbeitsberichte
(Working Reports)

which are published several times a year.

Finally the day will come for all of us when we have to part with all the collected material. If we have no interested heir, there is the danger that our work scatters, decays, or ends upon the dumps. To prevent a loss we advise our members in setting up a

genealogical testament.

You may deed the genealogical estate to one of our research centers permanently or until an interested heir has grown up, or, by special agreement, leave it to the Johann-Gottfried-Herder-Institut as a loan or legacy. At all these places we have the possibility to view, index and evaluate the legacy, if necessary redirect it, so that it is still useful when the researcher has gone.

If you read this, and think that **we** may be useful to you, please come to us, also if you think that **you** can help our society with your advice and work or your reserach results.

Finally let us summarize: Our member receive yearly four issues of "Ostdeutsche Familienkunde" and five or more issues of "Archiv ostdeutscher Familienforscher" and several issues of "Arbeitsbericht" for the annual dues presently set at 40.00 DM (or full equivalent).

Arbeitsgemeinschaft ostdeutscher Familienforscher e.V.
Sitz Herne
Konten der Arbeitsgemeinschaft ostdeutscher Familienforscher e. V.
Richardstraße 48 A, 4000 Düsseldorf
Girokonto 1804 4883 bei der Stadt-Sparkasse Düsseldorf (BLZ 300 501 10)
Postscheckkonto Essen 1 184 73–435
Jahresbeitrag DM 40,–

Organisation

Executive Council (Paragraph 9 of By-Laws)

Chairman:
> Detlef Kuehn
> Fuhrweg 29, D–5300 Bonn-Holzlar, Germany, Ph. 0228–48 28 04

Deputy-Chairman:
> Dr. Heribert Haendel
> Argelanderstrasse 50, D–5300 Bonn 1, Germany, Ph. 0228–21 59 22

Secretary:
> Aribert von Knoblauch
> Buergermeister-Schmidt-Strasse 49, D–5093 Burscheid, Germany, Ph. 0217–46 04 34

Treasurer:
> Helmut Topp
> Richardstrasse 48 A, D–4000 Duesseldorf 1, Germany, Ph. 0211–21 73 81

Deputy-Secretary:
> Frau Heike Brachwitz
> Sperlingstrasse 11a, D–4236 Hamminkeln 4, Germany, Ph. 02857–36 90

Deputy-Treasurer:
> Dr. Franz Waldmann
> Spreewaldweg 36, D–4401 Senden, Germany

Additional Member:
> Adolf Fischer
> Juttastrasse 20, D–8500 Nuernberg, Germany, Ph. 0911–40 00 65

Greater Executive Council (Paragraph 10 of By-Laws)

Promotion, Public Relations:
> Bernhard Rutow
> Lerchenweg 3, D–7404 Ofterdingen, Germany

Editors:
Ostdeutsche Familienkunde
> Dr. phil. Roland Seeberg-Elverfeldt
> Nietzschestrasse 25, D–5300 Bonn 2, Germany, Ph. 0228–32 17 80

Archiv Ostdeutscher Familienforscher
> Hans P. Jansen
> Fasanenweg 21, D–6057 Dietzenbach, Germany, Ph. 06074–2 57 32

Library:
>   Mrs. Barbara Hofmann
>   Director of the Bibliothek der Stiftung "Haus des deutschen Ostens"
>   Bismarckstrasse 90, D–4000 Duesseldorf, Germany, Ph. 0211–35 95 81
>   Business Hours: see Section I, 2.1

Top Ancestor Index:
>   Miss Ruth Hoevel
>   Steinweg 15, D–3550 Marburg/Lahn, Germany

Church Records Information Center:
>   Mrs. Heike Brachwitz
>   Sperlingstrasse 11a, D–4236 Hamminkeln 4, Germany, Ph. 02857-3690

Publications Distribution Center:
>   Herbert Sylvester
>   Nachtigallenweg 14, D–5000 Koeln 50, Germany

Research Centers of the Arbeitsgemeinschaft ostdeutscher Familienforscher

Baltic States:
>   Winno von Loewenstern
>   Parkstrasse 45, D–5060 Bergisch-Gladbach 1, Germany, Ph. 0220–46 41 21

Brandenburg (East):
>   Dipl.-Ing. Alfred Bley
>   Im Langgewann 65, D–6940 Weinheim-Lue., Ph. 06201–5 36 44

Central Poland-Volhynia:
>   Rudolf Peiker
>   Ostpreussenring 138, D–2400 Luebeck 14, Germany, Ph. 0451–30 25 40

East Prussia:
>   Information pertaining to East Prussia is supplied by our sister society Verein fuer Familienforschung in Ost- und Westpreussen e. V., Sitz Hamburg.
>   Address: Dr. Wolf Konietzko
>   Eichstrasse 6, D–2200 Elmshorn, Germany, Ph. 2101–16 18 65

Galicia:
>   Ernst Hexel
>   Im Gries 20, D–5300 Bonn 2, Germany, Ph. 02221–34 55 20

Danube-Swabia:
>   Dr. Helmut Flacker,
>   Tunisbergstrasse 12, D–6801 Ehrenkirchen 4, Germany

Pomerania:
>   Dr. Max Bruhn
>   Ollsener Strasse 24, D–2116 Hanstedt-Nordheide, Germany, Ph. 04184–73 55

Posen:
>   Otto Firchau
>   Nachtigallenweg 6, D–4902 Bad Salzuflen, Germany, Ph. 05222–1 36 61
>   He is also director of Abteilung Familienforschung fuer die Provinz Posen und das Deutschtum in Polen (Department of genealogy for the province of Posen and ethnic Germans in Poland) of the Forschungsstelle Ostmitteleuropa im Lande Nordrhein-Westfalen (Research center East-Central Europe in the state of North-Rhine-Westphalia)

Germans from Russia:
> Dr. Paul Edel, Bischof-Fischer-Strasse 114, D–7080 Aalen 1, Germany, Ph. 07361–6 14 85

Silesia:
> Neidhard von Stein
> Suedweg 137, D–3064 Bad Eilsen, Germany, Ph. 05722–83 81 and 8 43 49

Sudeten Region and Sudeten-German Genealogical Archives:
> Adolf Fischer
> Juttastrasse 20, D–8500 Nuernberg, Germany, Ph. 0911–4 09 65

Information pertaining to Sudeten-German Genealogical Archives:
> Frau Lore Schretzenmayr
> Erikaweg 58, D–8400 Regensburg, Germany, Ph. 0941–2 18 14

Southeastern Europe:
> Dr. Ing. Hans Bartsch
> Appartement 2, Am Roemerbrunnen, D–7812 Bad Krozingen, Germany

West Prussia-Danzig:
> Walter Kapahnke, An der Hellrüsche 24, D–4902 Bad Salzuflen, Germany, Ph. 05222–6 18 66.

Initials used after foster towns:

Bay	= Bayern — Bavaria
BaWue	= Baden-Wuerttemberg
Hess	= Hessen — Hesse
NS	= Niedersachsen — Lower Saxony
NW	= Nordrhein-Westfalen — North Rhine Westphalia
RhPf	= Rheinland-Pfalz — Rhineland-Palatinate
S	= Saarland
SH	= Schleswig-Holstein

Glossary

Exulant	= Religious exile, this term is used in connection with such religious exiles as the Huguenots of France of the 16th and 17th centuries and the Salzburgers after 1732.
Gemeinde	= church, Parish, hamlet, municipality
Heimatstube	= Clubroom (homeland room) of expellees generally containing reading material and other paraphernalia pertaining to a specific group and home country.
Kreis	= County, an administrative district within a Regierungsbezirk, headed by a Landrat.
Landsmannschaft	= Society of Germans or society of expellees from territories east of the Oder-Neisse-Line, grouped in territorial jurisdictions.
Regierungsbezirk (Reg.-Bez.)	= Administrative district within a province. This term has been used before, during and after the Third Reich. It contains a number of Kreise.
Reichsgau or Gau	= Administrative district. This term was used for various German areas between 1933 and 1945 only, little province.
Stadt	= Town, city.
Stadtkreis	= Town or city and its immediate surrounding territory which may include villages.
Wojewodztwo	= Polish administrative district generally containing several powiats (counties).

Map Index

	1.	German Empire, 1945 Partition	10
	2.	Origin of Ethnic German Expellees from Eastern and Southeastern Europe	28
	3.	Germany and the former German Settlement Regions in Central Europe	29
	4.	Former German Territories east of the Oder-Neisse-Line	33
	5.	East Prussia	35
+	6.	East Prussia, Counties (= Kreise)	36
	7.	East Prussia, Territorial Changes 1914–1945	43
	8.	West Prussia	44
+	9.	West Prussia and Danzig (Gdansk), Counties (= Kreise)	45
	10.	Free City of Danzig (Gdansk)	50
	11.	West Prussia, Territorial Changes 1914–1945	50
	12.	Pomerania	51
+	13.	Pomerania, Counties (= Kreise)	52
	14.	Brandenburg (East)	58
+	15.	Brandenburg (East), Counties (= Kreise)	59
	16.	Brandenburg, Partition 1945	60
	17.	"Grenzmark"-Posen (Poznan)-West Prussia, Dissolved 1938	60
+	18.	Silesia, Lower and Upper Silesia (= Nieder- und Oberschlesien)	66
	19.	Lower Silesia (= Niederschlesien)	67
	20.	Upper Silesia, Territorial Changes 1914–1945	73
	21.	Upper Silesia (= Oberschlesien)	74
	22.	Province of Posen (Poznan)	75
+	23.	Posen (Poznan) Region, Counties (= Kreise)	76
	24.	German Settlement Areas in Eastern Europe	82
⊕	25.	Poland	83
	26.	Galicia	87
	27.	Poland, Administrative Divisions 1975	92
⊕	28.	Baltic States	94
⊕	29.	Russia/Soviet Union	99
	30.	German Settlement Areas in Southern Russia	100
	31.	Black Sea Germans	101
	32.	German Settlement Region on the Volga River	101
	33.	"Sudetenland", Bohemia, Moravia, Austro-Silesia	103
+	34.	Bohemia, Moravia, Silesia, Counties (= Kreise)	105
	35.	Czech State Archives, Jurisdictional Districts	120
	36.	Eastern Europe, Extent of Ethnic Germans	124
⊕	37.	Bukovina	128
⊕	38.	Dobrudźa	129
⊕	39.	Slovakia and Carpatho-Ukraine	130
⊕	40.	Hungary	131
⊕	41.	"Gottschee" (Kocevje)	132
⊕	42.	Transylvania (= Siebenbürgen)	133
⊕	43.	Bessarabia	134
⊕	44.	Danube-Swabian Settlement Areas in Yugoslavia and Rumania	135
⊕	45.	Satu Mare Region	137

+ = Maps from the work: Kessler, Wolfgang: Ost- und suedostdeutsche Heimatbuecher und Ortsmonographien nach 1945 (Eastern and Southeastern chronicles and Locality Monographs after 1945) a bibliography to the historical study of the territory of expellees. Stiftung Ostdeutscher Kulturrat OKR, 1979 K. G. Saur Verlag, Muenchen, Artist: Jozo Dzambo, Bochum.

⊕ = Comment to maps 6, 9, 13, 15, 18, 23, 34:

        ▭ Shaded areas: A Chronicle is available for these counties   ○ locality, city/town.

        • Locality with a Chronicle.

1. Family name (surname) index

Axtheim 64

Bachmann 89
Baeck 78
Baer 46
Bahlow 54
Bartsch 125
Bendel 116
Berger 56
Beske 64
Birke 106
Blaschka 108
Bley 60
Brachwitz 15
Braun 115
Brehmer 57
Bruhn 53, 57
Buerger 113
Burkon 107

Cornberg, von 77
Croy 106

Diehlmann 37
Dimpfel 25
Dolleschel 107
Dreiseitel 113

Edel 100
Eichler 115, 116
Eilmes 78
Engel 114
Erlbeck 106
Ernst 40

Farnsteiner 37
Feldmann 96
Firchau 77
Fischer 104, 106, 112
Flacker 136
Fließ 140
Floegel 113
Friederichs 26
Friedrichs 70
Friedrichsen 96
Froetschl 106

Gabbert 79
Gause 40
Gerlach 91
Gerstner 127
Gesierich 107
Geßner 25
Gießel-Dienel 107
Giradin 12
Glenzdorf 26
Goertz 12, 14, 46
Goldbeck 46

Grigoleit 89
Grund 79

Hackenberg 115
Haeupler 119
Handke 64
Harasko 113, 123
Heigl 115
Heike 85
Heinz 107
Heling 37
Hellmessen 106
Hemmerle 112
Henning 78
Hexel 88, 89, 125
Heydenreich 12
von Hirchheydt 97, 98
Hornschuch 109
Hubatscheck 116
Hudak 127
Huettl 106

Jakobson 46
Jaeger-Sunstenau 112
Jaki 91
Jaksch 115
Janetzke 12
Judak 116
Junker 116
Junkers 138, 139

Kaiser 106
Kallbrunner 89
Kapahnke 46
Kaps 14
Kessler 17
Kind 54
Kirchner 117
Kirstein 78
Klaubert 106, 114
von Kleist 98
Klueber 13
Klug 123
Klytta 13
Kneifel 85
Koch 123
Koehler 57, 116
Koenig 16
Kohlbaum 113
Konietzko 37
Kossmann 85
Kowalis 70
Kraemer 138
Kraus 115
Krause 16
Kriegelstein 105, 106
Kriemer 106, 107
Kroemer 115
Krug 16
von Krusenstjern 96
Kube 115
Kuehn 11

Kuehnel 113
Kuenzel 114
Kuhn 113
Kuhnert 117
Kungel 138

Lassahn 55
Lattermann 77, 85, 89
Learned 13
Lebeda 110
Lehmann 62
Lerche 106, 107
Lewanski 85
Lodgman von Auen 113
von Loewenstern 95
Lueck 77
Luming 79

Maenner 112
Makasy 106
Marschner 107
Mathiae 127
Matzel 79
Maxin 37
Mayer 126
Meissner 114
Melles 107
Merten 37
Messow 16
Meyer 40, 64
Moedritzer 123
Mueller 15, 16, 89, 138
Mueller-Sternberg 17

Nehlich 38
Niekammer 54, 61
Nigratschka 116
Nolde 12

Ohlhoff 79
Olesch 62

von Pantzer 96
Pany 116
Paul 56
Peiker 84, 88, 89
Penner 12
Peschka 117
Petri 127
Petrizilka 108
Pine 13
Pischel 113
Pohl 115
Polzer 114
von Prochazka 109, 119
Proksch 114

Rainhold 111
Randt 69, 110
Rauch, von 97
Reckziegel 107
Reichmann 116

Reiprich 105, 106
Reise 25
Rhode 81, 91
Ribbe 25
Richter 114, 116, 123
Roedling 116
Roessler 107
Roessner 107, 108
Rose 39

von Sass 96
Schaller 111
Scherer 138
Schiefer 138
Schlesinger 62
Schlott 40
Schluetter 114
Schmidt 62, 86, 137
Schmiegel 79
Schneider 89, 113, 114
Scholz 115
Schretzenmayr 104, 106
Schuetz 79
Schumacher 40
Schwartz 61
Schwarz 112
Schwoy 111
Seebohm 113
Seyfert 47, 54
Sirchich 126
Smeser 15
Sommer 111
Somogyvár 126
Sonnleitner 138
Spohr 25
Sprinzl 113
Spruth 54, 55
Stader 138
Starke 25, 26
von Stein 68
von Streitberg 115
Streubel 114
Strzala 116
Stumpp 101
Sturm 110
Swientek 69, 111
Sykora 106

Tham 107
Thanheiser 115
Thomson 96
Traeger 106

Uebelacker 106
Unger 98

Vogel 123
Volk 138
Volkmann 77
Vollack 17

Wagner 127
Wald 39
Wamser 108
Weber 107, 108
Wehner 40, 54, 70
Wehrmann 53
Weiß 96
Welding 96
Wermke 40, 47
Wesselovsky 114
Wichmann 37
Wieland 107
Woerster 16
Wolf 117
Wolny 111
Wondrack 115
Wurzberger 114
Wuschek 112

Zenker 115
Zerlik 123
Zettl 113
Ziegler 55
Zwirner 138

2. Index geographical

a) countries, landscapes, provinces, districts, regions, states

Administrative district:
Regierungsbezirk:
    Allenstein = Olsztin 30, 31, 36, 41, 81
    Aussig 30, 121
    Breslau 14, 30, 67, 71
    Bromberg = Bydgoszcz 30, 48, 77
    Danzig = Dansk 31, 48
    Eger 30, 122
    Frankfurt/Oder 30, 58, 59, 64
    Gumbinnen 30, 31, 36, 40, 41, 42
    Hohensalza 31
    Kattowitz 30, 31, 67, 72
    Koenigsberg Pr. 30, 36, 39, 40, 41, 42
    Koeslin = Koszalin 30, 56
    Liegnitz 30, 67, 71
    Litzmannstadt 31
    Marienwerder = Kwidzyn 30, 36, 44, 46, 47, 48
    Oppeln 30, 31, 67, 72
    Posen 31
    Schneidemühl = Pila 30, 53, 56
    Stettin = Szczecin 30, 56
    Troppau 30, 121
    Westpreußen (West Prussia) 30, 36, 45
    Zichenau 31, 35
Reichsgau:
    Danzig-Westpreussen – Dansk-West Prussia 30, 31, 35, 45, 75
    Niederdonau (Lower Danube) 30
    Oberdonau (Upper Danube) 30
    Sudetenland 104
    Wartheland 31, 75, 76, 84
Adriatic Coast Region 32
Albania 124
Alsace-Lorraine 16
Altburgund 81
Altmark 58
Anhalt 11
Austria 19
Austria-Silesia 7, 11, 19, 68, 108
Bácska 7, 82, 135, 138
Baden-Württemberg 142
Baltic States 7, 31, 82
Baltikum 31, 95, 97
Baltische Staaten 31
Banat 7, 82, 134, 138
Banschaft Belgrad 32
Batschka 135, 138
Belgrad area 32
Beskidenland 123
Bessarabia 7, 22, 82, 101, 125, 126, 134, 139, 141
Bessarabien 32, 101, 126, 139, 140
Bezirk
    Bialystock 31, 84
    Polesien 31
    Polenje 31
    Wolhynien 31
Boehmen 30
Boehmen-Maehren 30
Bohemia 7, 11, 30, 103, 105
Bohemia-Moravia 19, 104, 121
Bohemian Forest 107
Border territory Poznanz-West Prussia 9, 47, 52, 75
Brandenburg (East) 7, 58, 59
Brandenburg (Ost) 59
Bratislava region 125
Bromberg region 78
Bromberger Land 78
Buchenland 125, 128
Bukovina 7, 32, 82, 125, 127, 128, 140
Bukowina 32, 127, 128
Bulgaria 32, 101, 124, 129, 139, 140
Bulgarien 32, 101, 139
Burgenland 82, 126

Carpathian Mountains 141
Carpatho-Ukraine 7, 39, 125, 126
Courland 95
Crimea (ASSR) 31
Croatia 137
Central Bohemia 108
Central Germany 11
Central Hungary 32
Central Poland 7, 82, 84, 85, 93
Czechoslovakia 9, 10, 19, 28, 29, 30, 67, 104, 111, 130

Danzig = Dansk 7, 9, 11, 31, 34, 44, 46
Distrikte (districts)
  Galicia 31, 84, 87, 88, 89, 90
  Galizien 31, 87, 88, 89, 90
  Krakau 31
  Lublin 31
  Radom 31
  Warschau 31
Dobrogea 7, 32, 82, 101, 125, 126, 129, 139, 140, 141, 142
Dobrutscha 32, 82, 101, 125, 126, 129, 139, 140, 141, 142
Donaubanschaft 32
Don- und Wolgagebiet 31
Draubanschaft 32
Drinabanschaft 32

East Central Europe 20
East Prussia 9, 14, 19, 30, 34, 35, 37, 38, 39, 40, 41, 42
Eastern Galicia 87, 88
Eastern Poland 93
Eastern Pomerania 52
Eastern South Hungary 32
Eastern Upper Silesia 20
Eastern Volhynia 31
Ermland 37, 39
Estland 31
Estonia 7, 11, 31, 82, 94, 95, 96, 97

Galicia 7, 82, 84, 87, 88, 89, 90
Generalgouvernement 31
Gottschee 125, 126
Great Poland 92
Große Walachei 32
Gyoer 125

Hauerland 82, 125, 130
Hinterpommern 52
Hultschin region 9
Hultschiner Laendchen 107
Hungary 11, 32, 82, 124, 130, 131, 135, 139, 140, 141

Jugoslawien 32, 140

Karpato-Ukraine 30
Kleine Walachei 32
Kocevje 125, 126
Komitat
  Eisenburg 125
  Oedenburg 125
  Raab 125
  Wieselburg 125
Krain 125
Krajnska 125
Krim 31
Kroatien 136
Kuestenbanschaft 32
Kuhlaendchen 107

Latoia 7, 11, 28, 29, 31, 82, 94, 95, 96, 97
Lettland 31
Litauen 31, 35
Lithuania 7, 11, 28, 29, 31, 82, 94, 95, 96, 97
Livonia 95
Lower Lusatia 59, 62
Lower Silesia 7, 11, 19, 30, 66, 67, 71, 72
Lusatia 59

Maehren 30
Masovia 37
Masuren 37
Mecklenburg 11, 52
Memelgebiet 31
Memel region 7, 11, 31, 36, 41, 42
Memelland 19, 41
Miltary Government 31
Mittelungarn 32
Moldau 32
Moldava 32
Morava region 32
Moravia 7, 11, 30, 103, 105, 107
Morawabanschaft 32
Mosonmagyaróvár 125

Netze River district 76
Neumark 58, 59, 60, 61, 62, 65
New Mark 58
Niederlausitz 61
Niederschlesien 30, 71, 72
Nördliches Siebenbürgen 32
Nordböhmisches Niederland 107
Nordkaukasus 31
Nordrhein-Westfalen 72, 141
Northern Bohemia 106
Northern Caucasus 31, 100
Northern Livonia 95
Northern Moravia 107
Northern Poland 92
Northern Transylvania 32

Oberschlesien 7, 11
Oberungarn 32
oestliches Südungarn 32
Old Mark 58
Ostoberschlesien 31
Ostpreußen 30, 34, 35, 37, 38, 39, 40, 41, 42
Ost Wolhynien 31

Poland 6, 7, 9, 11, 22, 23, 24, 28, 29, 31, 77, 82, 83
Polen 31
Pomerania 7, 9, 11, 51
Pomerania-West 53
Prekmurje 125
Pressburger Land 125
Province (Provinz)
  Brandenburg 7, 9, 11, 30, 61
  Grenzmark Posen-Westpreussen = Border territory 47, 52, 75, 77
  Kurland = Courland 95
  Lettgallen 95
  Niederschlesien = Lower Silesia 7, 11, 14, 30, 66, 67, 68, 69, 70, 71, 72
  Oberschlesien = Upper Silesia 7, 11, 14, 30, 36, 66, 67, 68, 69, 70, 71, 72
  Ostpreussen = East Prussia 7, 9, 11, 14, 30, 40, 45, 84
  Polish Livonia 95
  Pommern = Pomerania 7, 9, 11, 52, 53
  Posen = Poznan 7, 9, 75, 76, 11
  Sachsen = Saxony 11
  Schlesien = Silesia 67
  Semgallen 95
  Südlivland = South Livonia 95
  Westpreußen = West Prussia 7, 9, 11, 14, 39, 44, 46, 47
Protektorat Böhmen und Maehren 30, 111
Protectorate Bohemia and Moravia 30, 104, 111, 121

Republic of Czechoslovakia 108, 109, 111
Rheinland-Pfalz (state) 142
Rumania 11, 32, 82, 124, 125, 128, 129, 133, 134, 139, 142
Russland = Russia 7, 82, 99
Ruthenien = Ruthenia 139

Sachsen = Saxony 11
Sathmar = Satu Mare 7, 136, 137
Savebanschaft = Save region 32

Schlesien = Silesia 7, 9, 19, 25, 26, 66, 67, 68, 69, 70, 71, 72
Schönhengstgau 107
Schuettinsel 125
Schwaebische Tuerkei = Swabian Turkey 7, 82, 131, 138
Schweden = Sweden 56
Siebenbürgen = Transylvania 126
Slawonien = Slawonia 7, 82, 138
Slowakei = Slovakia 7, 30, 82, 124, 125, 130, 139
Slowenien = Slovania oder Slovenia 125, 126, 132
Soldauer Laendchen = Soldau region 9, 41
Sopron 125
South Livonia 95
Sowjetunion (UdSSR) = Soviet Union or Russia (USSR) 7, 11, 31, 99, 101, 130
Spis 82, 125, 130
Suedböhmen = Southern Bohemia 108, 121, 123
Suedkaukasus = Southern Caucasus 31, 100
Suedliches Siebenbürgen = Southern Transylvania 32
Suedmaehren = Southern Moravia 108, 121, 123
Suedosteuropa = Southeaststern Europe 7, 100, 124, 125
Suedpolen = Southern Poland 92
Sudetendeutsche Gebiete = Sudeten-German territories 7, 9, 11, 30, 103, 104
Sudetenland 9, 104
Sudeten regions 103
Syrmien = Srem 7, 82, 136, 138

Thueringen = Thuringia 11
Transylvania 7, 82, 125, 126, 133, 141
Tschechoslowakei = Czechoslovakia 30
Tschechoslowakische Reupublik 108, 109

Uebermurgebiet = Premurje 125
UdSSR 31
Ukraine 31
Ungarn = Hungary 11, 32, 82, 124, 130, 131, 135, 139, 140, 141
Untersteiermark 125
Upper Hungary 32, 130

Upper Lusatia 67, 68
Upper Silesia 7, 11, 19, 66, 67, 74

Vallachia 32
Vardar 125
Vasvár 125
Volga German Republic 31
Volhynia 7, 82, 84, 85, 86, 99
Vorpommern = Pomerania-West 11, 53
Vrbas region 32

Wallachina 129, 134
Wardarbanschaft = Vrbas region 32
Warmia 37, 39
Wartheland 77, 78, 81, 84, 85, 91
Weissrußland = White Rusia 31
Weissruthenien = White Ruthenia 31
Werbassbanschaft = Vardar 32
Westboehmen = Western Bohemia 106
Westgalizien = Western Galicia 87, 88
Westpolen = Western Poland 92
Westpreussen = West Prussia 19, 25, 35, 37, 39, 40, 41, 44, 45, 46
Westrumaenien = Western Rumania 32
Westungarn = Western Hungary 32, 125, 126, 131
Westliches Südungarn = Western South-Hungary 32
Wolgadeutsche Republik 31
Wolhynien 85, 86

Yugoslavia 11, 28, 29, 32, 82, 124, 139, 140

Zetabanschaft = Zeta regions 32
Zips = Spis 82, 125, 130

b) counties, districts

Angerapp 42
Arad 142
Arnswalde 52, 53, 58

Bartenstein 42
Bendsburg 67, 72
Beuthen-Tarnowitz 67, 72
Bielitz-Biala 72, 113
Blachstedt 67, 72
Bromberg 75, 76

Cammin 57
Crossen 63
Czarnikau 76

Danzig 14, 48
Darkehmen 42
Demmin 57
Deutsch Krone 44, 52
Dramburg 53, 58

Ebenrode 42
Elchniederung 42

Filehne 76
Flatow 44, 52
Forst 59, 63
Frankfurt/Oder 59, 63
Fraustadt 71, 75
Friedeberg 52, 53, 58

Gerdauen 42
Gleiwitz 72
Goldap 42
Greifenberg 57
Groß Wartenberg 67
Guben 59, 63
Guhrau 67
Gumbinnen 31, 42

Heiligenbeil 42
Heilsberg 41
Heydekrug 42
Hindenburg 67, 72
Hohensalza 76

Ilkenau 67, 72
Insterburg 42

Kattowitz 67, 68
Koenigsberg NM 59, 63
Koenigsberg Pr 41, 42
Koenigshütte 67
Kolmar 76
Krenau 67, 72

Labiau 42
Landau 141
Landsberg (Warthe) 59, 61, 63
Lebus 59, 63
Lublinitz 67

Memel 42
Meseritz 63, 75
Militsch-Trachtenberg 67

Namslau 67
Naugard 57
Netzekreis 44, 52
Neumarkt 58
Neustettin 53
New Mark 58
Nowy Targ 90

Old Mark 58
Oststernberg 59, 63

Pillkallen 42
Pless 67
Preussisch Eylau 42

Ratibor 67
Regenwalde 57
Rybnik 67

Samland 42
Sathmar 136
Saybusch 72
Schloßberg 42
Schubin 76, 79
Schwerin 59, 63, 75
Soldin 59, 63
Sorau 59, 63
Sosnowitz 72
Stallupoenen 42

Tarnow 90
Tarnowitz 67
Teschen 72
Tetschen 117
Tilsit-Ragnit 42
Tost-Gleiwitz 67, 72

Warthenau 67, 72
Wehlau 42
Weststernberg 59, 63
Wirsitz 75, 76, 79

Zittau 71
Zoppot 48
Zuellichau-Schwiebus 59, 63

c) *Individual Localities Cities, Villages*

Aachen 17
Aalen 100, 148
Allenstein 92
Amberg 101
Anweiler 37
Apatin/Donau 141
Arnau 114
Arnsberg 97, 98
Arnswalde 58
Asch 106, 114
Atzenhausen 98
Augsburg 63, 116
Aussig 106, 108, 114, 122

Backnang 141
Bad Eilsen 68, 148
Bad Hersfeld 116
Bad Krozingen 125, 148
Bad Muender 26

Bad Muenstereifel 41, 49
Bad Neustadt 117
Bad Rappenau 117, 122
Bad Rothenfelde 79
Bad Salzuflen 46, 77, 147, 148
Bad Sooden-Allendorf 116
Bad Wimpfen 141
Baern 106, 114
Bamberg 71, 117
Bandrow 88
Basel 12
Bayerisch Eisenstein 123
Bedzin 72
Beienrode 42
Bendsburg 67, 72
Bensheim 114
Bergen 79
Bergisch Gladbach 95, 147
Berlin Ost 13
Berlin West 13, 14, 17, 18, 21, 47, 54, 55, 57, 62, 63, 78, 79, 64, 141
Beuthen 67, 68, 72
Biala Podlaska 93
Bialosliwie 80
Bialystok 93
Bielefeld 64, 91
Bielitz 72, 108
Bielitz Biala 93
Bielsko-Biala 93
Bilin 106
Bischberg 114
Bischofteinitz 106, 114
Bissingen 138
Blachstedt 67, 72
Block 93
Bochnia 90
Boeblingen 116
Boehmisch Leipa 116
Bonn 11, 14, 17, 22, 39, 40, 47, 51, 61, 69, 88, 107, 126, 141, 146, 147
Bonn-Bad Godesberg 15, 88, 107, 111, 126, 141
Boppard 18
Boston 20
Bratislava 125
Braunau 106, 114
Braunschweig 63, 64
Bremen 21
Breslau 14, 25, 69, 70, 92
Brieg 27, 71
Brno 118
Bromberg 76, 77, 78, 79, 81, 92
Brosov 125
Bruch-Ladung-Wiesa 114
Brünn 109, 111, 114, 118
Brüx 106, 114
Buchau 114
Budapest 139

Budweis 109
Bueckeburg 12
Bukarest 142
Bunzlau 68
Burg 97
Burgstetten 106
Burscheid 146
Bydgoszcz 80

Camberg 115
Cernovcy 125
Chelm 93
Chicago 24
Chodau 114
Chrzanow 72
Crossen 59
Czarnikau 76
Czernowitz 125
Czestochowa 93

Danzig 9, 14, 19, 37, 45, 46, 47, 50, 92
Darmstadt 70
Dauba 107, 115
Deutsch Gabel 107, 115
Deutsch Mokra 125
Deutsch Proben 125
Dietzenbach 146
Dinkelsbuehl 116
Dorpat 97
Dortmund 21, 63
Dramburg 58
Duesseldorf 11, 19, 21, 65, 78, 86, 106, 122, 139, 146, 147
Durmersheim 108
Dusslingen 114
Dux 107, 114

Eger 10
Ehrenkirchen 136, 147
Eichenbruck 79
Eisenburg 125
Elbing 92
Elblag 92
Elbogen 106, 114
Erfurt 16
Ergolding 107
Erkenschwick 114
Erlangen 115, 146
Exin 79

Falkenau 106
Filehne 76
Forchheim 114
Forst 59
Frankenforst 95
Frankfurt/Main 13, 14, 15, 106, 117, 123
Frankfurt/Main-Hoechst 123
Frankfurt/Oder 27, 59
Freiburg 17, 20
Freiwaldau 107, 114

155

Freudenthal 107, 114
Friedberg 106
Friedeberg 58, 68
Friedland 107, 114
Furth i. W. 114
Fulda 115
Fulnek 114

Gablonz 107, 114
Garden City 13
Geislingen 113
Gerlingen 140
Giebau 114
Giessen 122
Gnietno-Katedra 80
Goeppingen 113, 123
Goettingen 12, 25, 26, 38, 109
Graslitz 106
Greeley 100
Greifswald 53
Groebenzell 106
Grosshansdorf 98
Gross Karol 136, 137
Grudziatz 25
Gruenberg 63, 71, 92
Grulich 107
Guben 59
Guens 125
Guenzburg 117
Gumbinnen 40
Gundelsheim 126, 139

Haida 115
Halle i. Westf. 16
Hallgarten 123
Hambuehren 64
Hamburg 13, 41, 56, 81, 126
Hamminkeln 15, 146
Hannover 20, 64, 78, 81, 87, 91, 97, 98, 139, 141
Hanstedt-Nordheide 53, 147
Heidelberg 115
Heidenheim 115
Heilbronn 141
Heimbach 138
Hemau 106
Hemmingen 78
Hemsbach 138
Herford 64
Hermannstadt 125
Hermstal 79
Herne 9, 40, 47, 55, 62, 68, 70, 96, 101, 113, 139
Herrnhut 12
Hilden 106
Hindenburg 67
Hirschberg 92
Hirschenhof 95
Hoerlkofen 116
Hohenelbe 107
Hohensalza 76
Hohenstadt 107

Holzgelingen 106
Homburg/Saar 138
Huenfeld 115
Huenfelden 116
Hutthurm 113

Iglau 108, 114
Illertissen 114
Ingelheim 138
Ingolstadt 116
Insterburg 42

Jaegerndorf 107
Jaslo 90
Jauernig 115

Kaaden 106, 114
Kaesmark 125
Kaiserslautern 13, 138
Kalisch 92
Kaltenbach 114
Karlsbad 106, 114
Karlsruhe 123, 138, 141,
Kassel 11, 20, 38, 102, 197
Kattowitz 67, 68, 71, 92
Kaufbeuren 115
Keynia 80
Kezmarok 125
Kiel 20
Kiel-Kronshagen 97
Kielce 93
Kirchberg 106, 141
Kirchheim/Teck 115, 123
Klosterneuburg 117, 123
Koblenz 14, 17, 37, 70, 91
Koeln 17, 147
Koenigsberg NM 59, 64
Koenigsberg Pr. 40, 41
Koenigsbrunn 116
Koenigshuette 67
Koenigswinter 71
Koeslin 52, 92
Komotau 106, 115
Konin 92
Komotau 106, 115
Korntal 117
Kornwestheim 140
Krainburg 132
Krakau 23
Kraków 90, 93
Krenau 67, 72
Krickerhau 141
Kronstadt 125
Krosno 93

Laatzen 57
Laibach 125
Landau 41
Landsberg 60, 61, 63, 64, 65, 92
Landskron 107
Langoens 114

Lebus 59
Leer 40
Leipa 115
Leipzig 14, 16, 18, 39, 40, 41, 47, 61, 80, 89
Leitmeritz 109, 115, 118
Lemberg 89
Leningrad 100
Leslau 92
Leutenbach 141
Leverkusen 85, 138
Lichtenstadt 116
Lichtenthal 141
Liebenau 116
Liegnitz 68, 92
Linz 26, 121, 123
Lippstadt 114
Lissa 92
Litomerice 118
Ljubljana 125
Lodsch 93
Lodz 93
Logan 70
Lomzá 93
Lorsch 115
Lublin 88, 93
Lublinitz 67
Luditz 106, 116
Ludwigsburg 113, 141
Luebeck 44, 48, 49, 55, 56, 72, 81, 84, 88, 147
Lueneburg 21, 79, 80, 96, 97

Maehrisch Neustadt 116
Maehrisch Ostrau 108
Maehrisch Schoenberg 107, 116
Maehrisch Trübau 107
Magdeburg 16
Mainz 72, 81, 86, 91
Makowa 88
Malchen 37
Mannheim 108
Marburg/Drau 125, 132
Marburg/Lahn 12, 14, 16, 18, 20, 38, 56, 85, 89, 96, 97, 147
Margonin 78
Maribor 125
Marienbad 106, 116
Marienwerder 27
Marktoberdorf 113
Marktredwitz 112, 113, 123
Marnheim 12
Memel 39
Memmen Gerberg 115
Memmingen 115
Merseburg 18, 41
Meseritz 59
Mies 106, 116
Miltenberg 114
Moenchengladbach 85

Mrocza 80
Mueden 78
Muehlacker 140
Muenchen 14, 20, 22, 89, 96, 104, 106, 107, 109, 111, 112, 117, 121, 122, 123, 125, 138, 139, 140, 141
Muenster 20, 38, 39, 42, 47, 48
Muenstereifel 41, 149
Munkatsch 125

Nagykaroly 136
Naklo 80
Neckargemuend 117
Neubistritz 108
Neuburg/Donau 116, 117
Neudek 106, 116
Neu Esting 107
Neugablonz 115
Neu Sandez 93
Neusatz 136
Neustadt 12, 13, 15, 25, 26, 54, 70, 96
Neutitschein 107
Niederebersdorf 116
Niedersulz 123
Niemes 116
Nitrianske Pravno 125
Nikolajew 100
Nikolsburg 108
Noerdlingen 117
Nowy Sacz 93
Nuernberg 61, 62, 64, 107, 108, 109, 112, 114, 123, 146, 147

Obornik 79
Ochsenfurt 114
Odessa 100
Odrau 116
Oedenburg 125, 141
Oer-Erkenschwick 114
Ofterdingen 146
Olching 107
Olkusz 72
Olmuetz 110
Opava 118
Oppeln 68, 71, 92
Osijek 136
Ostrolenka 93

Pappenheim 114
Passau 71
Pecs 136
Percholdsdorf 108
Pforzheim 115
Piotrkow-Trybunalski 93
Plan 116
Pless 67
Plzen 118
Plzni 118

Podersam 106
Posen 77, 79, 80, 85, 89, 92
Potsdam 18, 27
Prag 109, 110, 111
Prague 109, 111, 118, 119
Praha 48
Pressburg 125, 130
Pressnitz 106
Przemysl 90, 93
Pyritz 53

Radom 93
Rappenau 117
Rastatt 116, 138
Ratibor 67, 68, 70
Regensburg 14, 104, 106, 110, 121, 148
Rehau 114
Reichenbach 68
Reichenberg 107, 108, 116
Reiskirchen 116
Remagen 15
Reute 126
Reval 95
Rheinbach 115
Riga 96
Roehrnbach 115
Roemerstadt 107, 116
Rotenburg 79
Rudolfsgnad 141
Rumburg 107, 123
Rybnik 67
Rypin 84
Rzeszów 90, 93

Saaz 106
Salt Lake City 14, 23
St. Joachimsthal 106
St. Petersburg 99
Sauerlach 119
Saybusch 72
Schivelbein 58
Schlackenwerth 116
Schluckenau 107, 116, 123
Schneidemuehl 92
Schondorf 106
Schorndorf 109
Schwabach 86
Schubin 76
Scottdale 85
Seevetal 37
Seimeny 141
Selb-Eckersreuth 106, 114
Sibin 146
Sickte 12
Siedlce 93
Sieradz 93
Sindelfingen 138
Sipiory 80
Skierniwice 93
Soest 56
Soldin 59

Sonthofen 72
Sopron 125
Sosnowitz 72
Speyer 21
Springe 98
Stade 17
Stanislau 88
Steinamanger 125
Steinschoenau 115
Sternberg 107, 117
Stettin 40, 54, 92
Stockholm 56
Stolp 92
Stuttgart 20, 21, 63, 70, 91, 101, 102, 107, 113, 117, 121, 138, 139, 140, 141
Suwalki 92
Szombathlej 125

Tachau 106, 117
Tarnobrzeg 90. 93
Tarnow 90, 93
Tarnowitz 67, 73
Tarutino 125
Temeschburg 136
Tepl 106
Teplitz-Schoenau 107, 117, 123
Teschen 72
Tetschen-Bodenbach 107, 117
Thorn 48, 92
Tilsit 42
Timisoara 136
Tirschenreuth 116
Tost 67, 71
Trautenau 107, 117, 123
Treboň 118
Troppau 107, 117
Tutzing 116

Uelzen 56
Ulm 141
Usseln 107

Vaihingen 115
Vasar 125
Vienna 19, 38, 90, 108, 109, 111, 117, 118, 121, 123
Vierkirchen 85
Viernheim 113
Vislhofen 107
Voerde 141

Wagstadt 107, 117
Waldenburg 92
Waldkraiburg 113, 117
Waldsassen 114
Waltsch 117
Warendorf 78
Warnsdorf 101
Warsaw 22, 84, 88, 89
Warszawa 23, 24, 35, 80, 93
Warthenau 67, 72

Washington 13
Waynesboro 12
Weiden 117
Weidenau 117
Weiershof 12, 14
Weinheim 60, 147
Weinstadt 107
Weissenburg 115
Weissenhorn 116
Wendisch Evern 79
Wendlingen 113, 116
Wesel 79
Wien 19, 69, 90, 103, 108, 111, 115, 123
Wiesbaden 97, 121, 122
Wieselburg 125
Wimpfen Bad 141
Winterbach 126
Winterkasten 107
Wirsitz 76
Wischau 108
Wongrowitz 79
Wrocław 69, 71
Wuerzburg 40, 72, 96, 123
Wuppertal 15
Zámrsk 118
Zamosc 93
Zawiercie 72
Zeitlarn 107
Zichenau 93
Zirndorf 116
Zittau 71
Znaim 108
Zuckmantel 117
Zwittau 107

Outstanding works, all in German language, from the speciality publishing house DEGENER & CO.:

PERIODICALS, ALMANACS:

GENEALOGIE - German periodical for family research, founded in 1952, 32 annual sets so far, 12 numbers a year.

MITTELDEUTSCHE FAMILIENKUNDE - The periodical for the territories Saxony, Thuringia, Anhalt, Brandenburg, Mecklenburg and Berlin; founded in 1960, 4 numbers a year.

NORDDEUTSCHE FAMILIENKUNDE - The periodical for the territories Lower Saxony, Schleswig-Holstein, Hamburg, Bremen, Oldenburg and East Frisia; founded in 1952, 4 numbers a year.

OSTDEUTSCHE FAMILIENKUNDE - The periodical for the formerly German Eastern territories Silesia, Pomerania, East and West Prussia, as well as for the areas formerly settled by German ethnic groups in the Baltic countries, Poland, Russia, Bohemia, Moravia and Southeast Europe; founded in 1953, 4 numbers a year.

GENEALOGISCHES JAHRBUCH

Every year an extensive volume containing the most important findings of research. - Pedigrees of great Germans. Every volume from 120 to 200 pages. Founded in 1961.

VERLAG DEGENER & CO., INH. GERHARD GESSNER
D-8530 NEUSTADT/AISCH, (West-Germany)
P. O. Box 1340

SERIAL WORKS:

DEUTSCHES FAMILIENARCHIV

Findings of genealogical research in ancestral and genealogical trees, chronicles and picture documents from the property of many German families. Until now 87 volumes in large octavo. More volumes in preparation. Have your own family history printed too.

DEUTSCHE WAPPENROLLE

The coat of arms of German bourgeois families published in 41 volumes so far. More volumes at regular intervals. Have your own coat of arms entered and published too. A deed will then be issued by the editor of the DEUTSCHE WAPPENROLLE.

GENEALOGISCHES HANDBUCH DES BAYERISCHEN ADELS

The pedigrees of the Bavarian families of nobility with genealogy, descriptions of coat of arms and personal data. 15 volumes so far.

IMPORTANT SEPERATE WORKS:

FAMILIENGESCHICHTLICHE BIBLIOGRAPHIE

This work (8 extensive volumes so far) lists the titles of all genealogical works published in books or periodicals of genealogical literature in the German language since 1897. An unique work.

TASCHENBUCH FÜR FAMILIENGESCHICHTSFORSCHUNG

The economy-priced reference book pertaining to all questions of genealogy. 9 editions already. Practically no research work is possible without this handbook.

VERLAG DEGENER & CO., INH. GERHARD GESSNER
D-8530 NEUSTADT/AISCH, (West-Germany)
P. O. Box 1340